Faith, Health and Prosperity

'Brilliant. Careful. Charitable. Comprehensive. Humble. Sensitive. Biblical. Uncompromising. Pastoral. Well-researched ...The ramifications of the movement for our faith are immense. The report proves once again that it matters what you believe. Here is a great resource and guide. Read it with care.'

Rev Dr Derek Tidball,
Principal, London Bible College

'Although there are profound theological and historical questions pertaining to the prosperity message and movement, ultimately these issues must be addressed on biblical grounds. The report brings considerable exegetical skills to bear on the debate, and makes what I believe to be a seminal contribution. This is a book for heart and head. I recommend this work with enthusiasm.'

Daniel McConnell,
Author of The Promise of Health and Wealth

Faith, Health and Prosperity

A Report on 'Word of Faith' and 'Positive Confession' Theologies by ACUTE (the Evangelical Alliance Commission on Unity and Truth among Evangelicals)

Edited by
Andrew Perriman

First Published in 2003 by Paternoster Press

09 08 07 06 05 04 03   7 6 5 4 3 2 1
Paternoster Press is an imprint of Authentic Media,
PO Box 300, Carlisle, Cumbria, CA3 0QS, UK
and PO Box 1047, Waynesboro, GA 30830-2047
www.paternoster-publishing.com

The NRSV is used unless otherwise stated

British Library Cataloguing in Publication Data

A catalogue record for this book is available from
the British Library

ISBN 1-84227-188-1

Cover design by FourNineZero
Printed in Great Britain by
Cox and Wyman, Reading

Contents

Foreword

Issues of faith, health and prosperity have a resonance for me which is autobiographical as well as theological. In May 1960, when I was eight, my mother left my father in Kingston, Jamaica and flew with me and two of my sisters to settle in Kentish Town, North London. As well as the considerable culture shock we all experienced, life in a single parent, inner city, first-wave immigrant family was financially tough. I was provided with free school meals and uniform, while at times my mother did three different menial jobs simply to keep things afloat. Through it all, however, we were supported, encouraged and inspired by the fellowship of our local Pentecostal church. Despite various teenage doubts and struggles, this New Testament Church of God remained my second home, and eventually I went on to become a pastor within the same denomination.

My own brand of Pentecostalism has never formally aligned itself with the 'Word of Faith' movement on which this report is largely focused, and I myself share the concerns expressed here about the errors and excesses of that movement. At the same time, however, I welcome the balanced and carefully contextualised approach taken by ACUTE. While eschewing the Word of Faith package as such, many Christians with backgrounds like mine would nonetheless testify to the validity of trusting God for his practical, material provision, as well as for less tangible blessings. Many, too, would question the familiar assumption that economic poverty is, in and of itself, a Christian virtue.

Aided in no small measure by Andrew Perriman's skilled editorship, I am pleased to say that our theological commission has taken due account of the many nuances, gradations and qualifications which must attend any serious treatment of the inter-relationships between faith, health and prosperity. Too often, evangelical work in this area has reduced either to broadsides against extreme 'name it and claim it' heresies, or to defensive apologetics penned by Word of Faith practitioners themselves. By contrast, in the following pages ACUTE has once again produced a thorough, scholarly, irenic text on a divisive and contentious matter - one which will significantly advance the debate on 'health and wealth', 'prosperity teaching', 'positive confession' and a host of related questions. I welcome it, and commend it as a first-rate resource not only to the evangelical community, but to the Christian Church as a whole.

Rev Joel Edwards
General Director, Evangelical Alliance (UK)

A Note on the Background and Production of the Report

The following report is the fruit of a lengthy process of research, reflection and discussion conducted by, and under the auspices of, the Evangelical Alliance Commission on Unity and Truth among Evangelicals (ACUTE). ACUTE was formed in December 1993 to work for consensus on theological issues that test evangelical unity, and to provide, on behalf of evangelicals, a co-ordinated theological response to matters of wider public debate. Under the leadership of its first Co-ordinator, Rev. Dave Cave, ACUTE defined a number of issues which might merit serious investigation along these lines, and which might benefit from the production of detailed written reports. Among topics earmarked for such attention in ACUTE's first few meetings were evangelical identity, the National Lottery, homosexuality, the debate about hell, the Toronto Blessing, and so-called 'prosperity', 'faith' or 'health and wealth' teaching. Papers on the first two of these appeared in 1996, after which Dave Cave moved on and was succeeded by Rev. Dr David Hilborn. Under Dr Hilborn's direction, ACUTE has published the following reports and studies in collaboration with Paternoster Press: Faith, Hope and Homosexuality (1998), The Nature of Hell (2000), 'Toronto' in Perspective (2001), Evangelicalism and the Orthodox Church (2001), One Body in Christ: The History and Significance of the Evangelical Alliance (2001) and God and the Generations: Youth, Age and the Church Today (2002). As this list confirms, most of the priorities set in the early days of ACUTE have now been addressed, while certain additional topics have also been covered. That this particular report has taken somewhat longer to complete than the others is down to two main factors.

First, the identification of prosperity teaching as a cause for concern was prompted to a significant extent by debate within the Alliance on the exegetical and fundraising methods deployed by the evangelist Morris Cerullo and his international organisation, Morris Cerullo World Evangelism (MCWE). MCWE's European branch had offices and staff in the UK, and in this connection was affiliated to the Evangelical Alliance. Doubts were first aired about Mr Cerullo's theology of, and approach to, financial giving by certain Alliance Council members during the early 1990s, but by 1995 more formal consultation was initiated between representatives of the Council and MCWE. The relevant teaching and fundraising methods at issue in Mr Cerullo's ministry are discussed in the body of this report, but at heart criticism focused on the direct link he appeared to make between the level of donors' contributions to his own particular ministry and the extent of God's blessing upon those donors' lives. Not only were Alliance Council members and senior staff alarmed at the suggestion of so automatic an equation between material offering and divine favour; they were more specifically perturbed that Mr Cerullo seemed to be claiming for himself and MCWE a special anointing in respect of the mediation and administration of such favour. Bilateral discussion continued into 1996, when the possible resignation of MCWE from the Alliance was mooted on several occasions. Each time this matter was raised with Mr Cerullo and his representatives, however, they declined to withdraw MCWE from membership. Eventually, the full Alliance Council, meeting at High Leigh in September 1996, addressed the problem as a matter of urgency. As they did so, they were supplied with a dossier and theological commentary on the issue compiled by Dave Cave. After considerable discussion, the Council voted 49-0, with 1 abstention, to request formally that MCWE resign from membership.

This MCWE did shortly afterwards. The report presented here is intended as a broad-ranging examination of prosperity teaching in its many different aspects and degrees, and is certainly not preoccupied with offering a retrospective justification for the Council's actions vis à vis Mr Cerullo and MCWE. Indeed, while this difficult episode did undoubtedly act to some extent as a catalyst for what follows, the period which has elapsed between the 1996 Council vote and the publication of this book should be taken as evidence of the fact that ACUTE has been keen to address the 'prosperity' debate in general terms on a number of fronts, rather than as an immediate, knee-jerk reaction to the Cerullo affair alone.

The second reason for the long gestation of this report is linked to the first. As the depth and detail of the study confirms, so-called 'prosperity' or 'health and wealth' teaching is far from monolithic; in fact, the subject is not only controversial and sensitive, but theologically, sociologically and historically complex. As such, ACUTE has been determined to approach it in a considered, scholarly fashion. From the outset, we have sought to avoid the polemic so often generated by both proponents and antagonists of the 'faith movement', preferring to track down and work with an extensive range of primary sources, and to subject them to close biblical, theological, and cultural scrutiny. The result, we believe, is a text which will advance the debate on Christian attitudes to faith, health and prosperity in an important way.

After identifying the 'prosperity gospel' as a theme for study in 1994, ACUTE appointed a special working group to look further into it. Chaired first by Dave Cave and then by David Hilborn, the group comprised the following:

Rev Roger Abbott (British Evangelical Council)
Rev Hugh Osgood (Pastor, Cornerstone Christian Church, Bromley, Kent)
Dr Keith Warrington (Lecturer in New Testament, Regent College, Nantwich)
Dr David Allen (Lecturer in Church History, Mattersey Hall, Doncaster)

Mrs Pauline Summerton (Associate Chaplain, Whittington Hospital, London)

Members of the group produced preliminary papers on biblical, theological, historical and ethical aspects of faith, health and prosperity, and these papers were discussed at various meetings of the group held between 1995 and early 1998. Having completed this initial work, the group recognised that considerably more research and reflection would be needed before it could produce the kind of report which the topic had come to demand. While resolving to make provision for such further work to be done, the group decided that in the interim, it would be helpful to convene a wider consultation on the prosperity gospel, in order to take soundings on more recent developments within the faith movement, and to confirm those areas on which further study would be required. This consultation duly took place at the London offices of the Evangelical Alliance on 2nd June 1998. Attended by 54 key evangelical leaders and teachers, the meeting was moderated by Bishop Joe Aldred, Director of the Centre for Black and White Christian Partnership at the Selly Oak Colleges in Birmingham. Six speakers gave papers, some of which were relatively sympathetic to the faith movement, and others relatively critical. Rev. Douglas Williams, a Pentecostal pastor from Walthamstow, spoke on 'The Origins and Development of Prosperity Teaching'. Dr Peter Gammons, Founder and Leader of The Cathedral of Faith in Orlando, Florida, addressed 'Prosperity Teaching and the Bible'. Andrew Brandon, author of the critical 1987 study *Health and Wealth* (Kingsway), examined 'Prosperity Teaching and Hermeneutics'. Rev. Colin Dye, Pastor of Kensington Temple, London, presented a paper entitled 'Prosperity Teaching and Pastoral Practice'. Dr Vinay Samuel from the Oxford Centre for Mission Studies spoke on 'Prosperity Teaching and the Poor', and Rev. Hugh Osgood of the ACUTE working group concluded the day with a study on 'Prosperity Teaching and Evangelical Unity'.

Although the styles and approaches of these papers were deemed too diverse to be published together commercially in one volume, when combined with the original working group papers, and with written responses from those who attended the consultation, they formed a significant corpus of material – a corpus which ACUTE decided should function as the basis for a full, thoroughly researched and edited report. By mid-2000, it had become clear that David Hilborn's work on existing ACUTE and Evangelical Alliance projects would necessitate the delegation of this editorial task to someone else, and it was decided to appoint Dr Andrew Perriman to carry it out. The ACUTE Steering Group had been impressed by Dr Perriman's study Speaking of Women: Interpreting Paul (Apollos, 1998), and over the next 18 months joined with the original working group members to offer peer review of the various drafts which he produced. ACUTE owes an immense debt to Dr Perriman for the considerable extra work he has done in addition to that already contained in the corpus, for the elegant way in which he has written up and structured the report, and for his graciousness when faced with so much feedback from so many! Where the finished text draws directly on a paper from the 1998 consultation, this is duly referenced. Otherwise, for all Dr Perriman's invaluable editorial work, the end-product is very much owned by ACUTE as a whole, and should be seen as defining its collective mind on the issue at hand. Indeed, the desire of the Steering Group to check, amend and supplement the report as thoroughly as possible is another reason why it has been so long in the making.

In addition to Dr Perriman, the working group, ACUTE Steering Group members and those involved in the consultation, thanks are also due to Paul Gifford of the School of African and Oriental Studies for encouragement and comment, to Carolyn Skinner and Julia Murphy for consistently efficient secretarial support, and to Peter Little and all at Paternoster Press for their publishing advice and professional expertise. As well as once again providing the Foreword for an ACUTE report, the Alliance's General Director, Rev Joel Edwards, has enthusiastically backed this project from inception to completion; everyone involved is very grateful to him.

January 2003

Introduction

The church has always been in two minds about the spiritual value of material wealth. In its public statements, if not always in practice, it has usually taken a position on the obvious moral high ground, repudiating excessive wealth in favour of a modest, and preferably sacrificial, lifestyle. Sometimes the bias towards poverty has taken extreme forms, both as a matter of personal piety and with regard to social action and political alignment. But the gospel has also, undeniably, been a force for self-betterment and financial responsibility and in that respect has often proved to be a catalyst for social progress and the creation of wealth. In certain contexts, the church has adapted very well to the expectations and needs of a ruling elite or prosperous bourgeoisie. As there have been extreme acts of self-denial, there have also been conspicuous displays of affluence and the power that accompanies it. This has been especially true in the United States since the end of World War Two.

It is probably fair to say, however, that mainstream evangelicalism in the West today prefers to view material prosperity not as a predictor of divine favour or disfavour but as a spiritually neutral commodity. The phrase 'neither poverty nor riches' (cf. Prov. 30:8) encapsulates the position very well. The evangelical conscience, with its traditional distrust of worldliness on the one hand, and its historical commitment to social justice on the other, is bound to be uneasy with the possession and pursuit of great wealth. But extravagant acts of renunciation are also likely to be viewed with suspicion – partly because we tend to distrust the motivation behind such recklessness, but also because, with our financial obligations and our standards of living to maintain, we regard this as a distinctly unattractive and precarious model of discipleship. We respond to the story of the rich young ruler who was told to sell his possessions and give to the poor with a nervous, 'Yes, but….' Although such 'saints' as Francis of Assisi and Mother Teresa are often held up by evangelicals as supreme examples of Christlikeness and their lives ransacked for sermon illustrations, they are rarely emulated.

Attitudes towards physical health have been rather less ambivalent. Generally speaking, in keeping with the spirit of the age, we regard health as a desirable thing and sickness as an evil to be avoided at all costs – sometimes quite literally. But there is still ambivalence: the desire for good health is potentially held in check by the thought that God may prefer to use bodily suffering for our sanctification or for his glory. We remember that Paul prayed in vain to be relieved of his thorn in the flesh (2 Cor. 12:7).

Between the mortification of the flesh and the narcissistic cult of the body, between self-indulgence and self-denial, between the covetous pursuit and the monastic repudiation of wealth, the evangelical church in the West has aspired to walk an ideal middle path of right living, responsible stewardship, and moderation in all things. What counts before God is not the state of the body but the state of the soul, not how much we have but how we use it. On the face of it this is a very reasonable and biblical position to take. We acknowledge with thanksgiving that God is the source of all good things and that he satisfies the material needs of his children. We safeguard the priority of spiritual commitments. We remain an integral part of the modern economy without having to feel that we have become totally indifferent to the plight of the world's poor. We give proper recognition to the fact that the planet cannot sustain a culture of rampant consumerism, and that we must learn to be good managers of God's creation.

The middle path, however, is not without its dangers: in a sense, it is neither here nor there. Two problems in particular are worth mentioning. One is that our determined moderation may restrict the diversity and scope of Christian life and witness: we become uncomfortable with the more extreme lifestyles, we find it difficult to relate to those who live them, we withdraw from the risk of controversy to a more congenial middle ground. The other is that we may lose sight of the radical nature of Christian discipleship: the middle path all too easily merges into the broad highway of the modern Western lifestyle.

Challenges to the ethos of moderation have usually come from the political and theological left. The church in the West is reproached for having prostrated itself before the monstrous idol of Capitalism, for having insulated itself from the unpleasantness of life, for having neglected its calling to love and serve the poor. The so-called 'prosperity gospel', on the other hand, attacks the spiritual mediocrity of the middle ground from the opposite direction, arguing not only that the material blessings of health and wealth are good and godly things but that they are the inalienable right of every believer – ours through the confession of faith and obedience to the word of God. The ethos of poverty exemplified by St Francis and Mother Theresa is not simply ignored; it is roundly condemned.[1] Sickness and poverty are the work of Satan and should not be regarded as a means of attaining sanctification. On the contrary, John Avanzini argues, such an assumption is debilitating: 'Another tradition that's kicked the financial legs out from under many a child of God is the belief that there is something godly about being poor.'[2] The believer has been given the power to overcome any hindrance whether to her own well-being or to the advancement of the kingdom of God.

Kenneth Copeland, probably the most influential of the current generation of prosperity teachers, likes to tell the story of the poor man who saved up to buy a ticket to sail to America. Having only enough money left to buy bread and cheese to eat on the ship, he watched with envy as the other passengers dined in splendour. When the ship arrived in New York, he learned to his dismay that the meals he had watched others enjoying were included in the price of the ticket. 'So many

Christian people,' Copeland argues, 'are living on bread and cheese when God's best is theirs all the time.'[3] They are ignorant of what is included in the ticket. As his wife Gloria has put it, a large number of Christians are 'going to realize too late that they were cheated and swindled out of their earthly inheritance by religious tradition'.[4] F.K.C. Price comments in the same vein: 'Unfortunately, there are many Christians who wear poverty and lack of material prosperity as a badge of holiness. They consider their lack of this world's goods as a criterion for spirituality, when, in fact, the Bible does not support this hypothesis at all.'[5]

It is this 'challenge' both to the theology and to the spirituality of mainstream evangelicalism that this report attempts to assess. The phenomenon under consideration is a movement that arose in the United States after the Second World War. It goes under various names: 'Word of Faith', 'Positive Confession', the 'message of the Prevailing Word', the 'prosperity gospel', the 'health and wealth gospel', or in more derogatory fashion, the 'name it and claim it' or 'blab it and grab it' gospel. The movement has resisted developing a denominational identity. It has structured itself instead, for the most part, in an *ad hoc* fashion around a number of independent ministry organizations and their high profile eponymous leaders (and often their wives): Kenneth Hagin Ministries, Kenneth Copeland Ministries, Charles Capps Ministries, John Avanzini Ministries, and others.

In this report we will principally use the term 'Word of Faith' to designate the distinctive set of practices and beliefs associated with these organizations and the 'Faith' churches that have been influenced by them. The term 'prosperity teaching' will provide a useful alternative: it is the link between faith and material prosperity that especially distinguishes the modern 'faith' movement from earlier manifestations, and it is this link also which has been most controversial. The argument about faith, however, and the expectation of health and wealth permeate the wider church in various guises and at different levels, without necessarily exhibiting a direct dependence on the Word of Faith movement.

Some explanation also needs to be given regarding the sense in which the term 'evangelical' is used in this report. Historically, it designates a mostly Protestant movement within the larger Church, characterized, according to the well-known definition put forward by David Bebbington, by its high view of Scripture, its emphasis on the cross of Christ and justification by faith through grace, its commitment to personal conversion and discipleship, and its social activism.[6] It must be stressed that these characteristics are *distinctive for* evangelicalism rather than *definitive of* it. Indeed, we shall see that in many cases it is much more importantly represented as an orthodox, mainline Christian coalition – one that is broad enough to have more recently embraced Pentecostal and Charismatic expressions of the faith, while at the same time aligning with other orthodox Christian traditions on a range of doctrinal, ethical and political issues.[7] In order to account for the standpoint of this report, however, the definition can be made both more concrete and more general. On the one hand, we aim to speak especially for the Evangelical Alliance in the United Kingdom – a constituency dominated by Protestants, Pentecostals and Charismatics, but open in principle to all individuals who can sign its Basis of Faith and agree with its defining Practical Resolutions. On the other, we have sought to present a non-partisan, intelligent and faithful interpretation of Scripture and to uphold the priorities which Jesus Himself established for the church. Having said that, of course, we need to recognize that while we have endeavoured to address the subject with fairness and objectivity, we do not escape the limitations of our particular perspective and competence, and that not all who may properly call themselves evangelicals will agree either with the detailed arguments or the overall thrust of the report.

PART ONE

The history and teaching of the Word of Faith movement

1

The Word of Faith movement

There are no comprehensive accounts of the development and spread of the modern Word of Faith movement. The main sources available to us are the writings of Word of Faith teachers, which are inclined to be informal, anecdotal, and more often than not self-promoting, and the limited historical and biographical material provided by the critics, which frequently has been assembled for the purpose of discrediting the movement. The survey presented in this chapter, therefore, should not be regarded as exhaustive: it is intended merely to give an impression of the nature and scope of the Word of Faith phenomenon as it emerged and spread in the second half of the twentieth century. The historical background to this development will be examined in chapter 5.

The founding fathers

Kenneth Hagin

The Word of Faith movement draws its identity and momentum from the personalities of its leaders. The man who is generally recognized as the 'daddy' of the movement is Kenneth Hagin. In keeping with his position Hagin has his own 'nativity' stories, complete with an 'annunciation' to his mother which, he claims, was revealed to him later in life by Jesus: 'I appeared to your mother before you were born and told her to fear not; the child would be born and would bear witness concerning my Second Coming.'[1]

Despite the auspicious start, Hagin had an unhappy and unhealthy childhood.[2] He was born in McKinney, Texas, in 1917 with a heart defect that condemned him to constant ill-health. Matters at home were made worse by the desertion of his father when he was six and his mother's subsequent nervous breakdown. At the age of fifteen his heart condition worsened, leaving him bedridden with intermittent paralysis and delirium. According to his own account, two spiritual experiences during this period of illness transformed his life and set the agenda for his ministry. First, Hagin claims that during the first night of his illness he 'died' three times, on each occasion descending to the threshold of hell, only to be summoned back by a voice from heaven – an ordeal which persuaded him to give his life to Christ. Secondly, he received a revelation regarding Jesus' assurance to his disciples in Mark 11:23-24 that a person who does not doubt in his heart will be able to command 'this mountain' to throw itself into the sea and 'it will be done for him'.

Convinced by this revelation that God would do for him whatever he asked, Hagin began to pray with single-minded determination to be healed – to negligible effect. Six months later the real point of Jesus' words dawned on him:

> In this moment, I saw exactly what that verse in Mark 11:24 meant. Until then I was going to wait till I was actually healed. I was looking at my body and testing my heartbeat to see if I had been healed. But I saw that the verse says that you have to believe *when* you pray. The *having* comes after the *believing*. I had been reversing it. I was trying to *have* first and then *believe* second.... "I see it. I see it!" I said with joy. "I see what I've got to do, Lord. I've got to believe that my heart is well while I'm still lying here on this bed, and while my heart is not beating right. I've got to believe that my paralysis is gone while I'm still lying here helpless, flat on my back."[3]

Hagin understood that it was not enough simply to *ask* for healing, or even to believe that, having asked, he *would* be healed. What he needed to do was believe that he was *from that moment* healed, whatever the actual condition of his body might be. So, as he tells the story, he forced himself from bed and groped his way around the room. It took some time, and the symptoms would occasionally return, but eventually Hagin *believed* himself back to health. He finished his schooling and then set out as a 'Baptist boy preacher' to proclaim the good news of divine healing to the world.

Having received the 'baptism of the Holy Spirit' in 1937, Hagin began to lose favour with the Baptists: 'I received the left foot of fellowship from among the Baptists,' he jokes, 'and came over among the Pentecostals.'[4] From 1939 to 1949 he ministered as an Assemblies of God pastor and found himself drawn into the circle of independent healing evangelists that emerged after the war. During this period he came to sense increasingly that his calling was not to emulate the ministries of the great platform performers, such as William Branham and Oral Roberts, but to be a teacher and a prophet for the healing revival.[5] The anointing to the teaching ministry came out of the blue in 1943 when, as he puts it, the teaching gift 'just clicked down on the inside of me like a coin drops inside a pay phone'.[6] The anointing to prophethood came nine years later.[7] In 1966 Hagin moved to Tulsa, Oklahoma, where he began broadcasting his 'Faith Seminar of the Air' and in 1974 founded the $20 million Rhema Bible Training Centre, which now claims an average annual enrolment of 1,800 students and offshoots around the world. Rhema Bible Church has a membership of about 8,000. It was at Hagin's church that Randy Clark, a key figure in the emergence of the so-called 'Toronto Blessing' in the mid-1990s, received his 'anointing' through Rodney Howard-Browne – a circumstance which for some critics is already enough to discredit this controversial renewal movement.[8]

Kenneth and Gloria Copeland

Hagin's ministry has been taken over by his son, Kenneth Hagin Jr., but the real successor to his 'You Can Have What

You Say' theology is Kenneth Copeland.[9] While studying at Oral Roberts University (and working as a co-pilot on Roberts' crusade flights), Copeland was given a set of Hagin's teaching tapes by Hagin's brother-in-law, Buddy Harrison. It was an act of qualified generosity since Harrison expected the money to be paid later, but it proved foundational for Copeland's own ministry.[10]

The Kenneth Copeland Evangelistic Association was formed in 1968 in Fort Worth, Texas. Publication of a newsletter, *The Believer's Voice of Victory*, began in 1973. Radio programmes followed in 1975, the first television programme went on the air in 1979, and a communion service was broadcast by satellite to 20 countries in 1982. Copeland claimed that the Lord had instructed him to put forth the Word 'on every available voice'. According to the organization, the *Believer's Voice of Victory* television programme is currently broadcast on more than 500 stations around the world. In addition to the usual output of these mega-ministries Copeland has recorded a number of Gospel albums (securing Grammy nominations) and starred in 'faith-building adventure films' in such roles as the cowboy Wichita Slim. Kenneth Copeland Ministries (KCM) now has offices in the UK, South Africa, Australia, Canada and the Ukraine. An international prison ministry reportedly reaches an average of 60,000 new inmates a year. Copeland is today probably the best known and most influential figure in the Word of Faith movement, though not everyone is comfortable with his aggressive Texan style. His wife Gloria was named 'Christian Woman of the Year' in 1994 – an award, made by the Oklahoma Church of God Ladies Ministries Board, that has also been bestowed upon Ruth Graham, Beverly LaHaye, Shirley Dobson and Marilyn Quayle.

Others

Closely associated with KCM are Jerry Savelle,[11] Jesse Duplantis[12] and the aptly named Creflo A. Dollar Jr. Buddy Harrison has published many of the works of the Faith teachers

(Harrison House) and founded the International Convention of Faith Churches and Ministers (ICFCM) in 1979 as a 'service bureau' for the disparate Faith ministries.[13] Numerous other luminaries have shone, and occasionally burned out, in its firmament: Charles Emmit, Norvel Hayes, John Osteen, Lester Sumrall, F.K.C. Price,[14] Charles Capps,[15] Robert Tilton,[16] John Avanzini,[17] Marilyn Hickey, T.D. Jakes, Jim Bakker, Benny Hinn, and Morris Cerullo. Paul Crouch's Trinity Broadcasting Network has provided a platform for many Word of Faith teachers.[18]

Some of those formerly associated with Word of Faith teaching have since dissociated themselves from the movement and back-pedalled on the more questionable beliefs and practices. Bakker, for example, had a change of heart in prison after his fall from grace and has since claimed that prosperity teaching is seriously misguided and potentially dangerous.[19] Benny Hinn has reportedly attributed much of the controversy provoked by his book *Good Morning Holy Spirit* to his lack of formal Bible training. Revisions were made to the book after Hinn met with representatives from the Christian Research Institute in 1990.[20] But he has continued to generate controversy. In their book *The Confusing World of Benny Hinn* (1995), G.R. Fisher and M.K. Goedelman catalogued a wide range of errors and failings, accusing him of mishandling Scripture, lying about his family background, professing to have received special revelations in support of his heretical views, making unsubstantiated claims for healing miracles, and pronouncing curses on his critics.[21]

A global phenomenon

Word of Faith teaching has had a big impact in the developing world through the print and broadcasting media and the large scale crusades of evangelists such as T.L. Osborn, who claimed in the early 1970s that more than 400 churches a year were being established world-wide through his ministry.[22] Lester Sumrall, described by Brouwer, Gifford and Rose as 'jingoistic, more aggressive, and positively anti-intellectual' in comparison to Kenneth Hagin,[23] developed a ministry in Guatamala, Liberia and the Philippines from the 1950s. The impact in Africa, in particular, has been enormous. Jerry Savelle established the Overcoming Faith Center Churches in Kakamega, Kenya, along with a Medical Centre, and Bible Training Centre, and has ministry headquarters in Nairobi and offices in Johannesburg and Tanzania.[24] Copeland was a prominent speaker at the 'Fire Conference' held in Zimbabwe in 1986.[25] Reinhard Bonnke's massive crusades in Africa have closely linked salvation with the expectation of miraculous healing, but Bonnke has also been associated with the prosperity gospel – if only in the minds of Africa's destitute who flock to his rallies in their millions.[26]

Although there is some debate over the importance of the American evangelists for the emergence of prosperity teaching in Africa,[27] it is clear that the movement is now thoroughly indigenized and has produced a number of its own highly effective advocates, including Benson Idahosa in Nigeria, Nicholas Duncan-Williams and Mensa Otabil in Ghana, and Nevers Mumba in Zambia. Nigeria has proved especially fertile ground for prosperity teaching, and Nigerian leaders have subsequently had a major influence on black Pentecostal churches in the UK. Given the growth of Christianity in Africa and the corresponding decline in the West, the success of prosperity teaching there could have quite significant repercussions. Paul Gifford, Reader in African Christianity at the School of Oriental and African Studies of the University of London, has noticed the trend and points out that if 'the Gospel of Prosperity continues to be a fairly standard part of the African evangelical revival, it will eventually be a significant element in world Christianity'.[28]

Ray McCauley, who had studied under Kenneth Hagin in Tulsa, founded Rhema Bible Church in Johannesburg, South Africa, in 1979.[29] In its early years Rhema was closely associated with the apartheid régime, but in 1990 McCauley admitted that the church had been 'party to an inhuman political ideology'.[30] The church now claims a membership of more than 30,000, two-thirds of whom are black, and according to its website has 'a multi-faceted social outreach that embraces two hospices, caring for HIV-AIDS patients and the poorest of the poor, three orphanages, a street children project and numerous other programmes and feeding schemes that provides [sic] thousands of meals each week'.[31] The church achieved notoriety in 1999 when Hansie Cronje, South Africa's cricket captain and a prominent member of the church, admitted taking money from bookmakers. It was easy for critics to conclude that Rhema's gospel of prosperity and success was responsible for nurturing Cronje's greed.

Gifford argues that there are cultural reasons for the success of prosperity teaching among black Africans. Apart from the obvious attraction that the promise of wealth has for the poor, he points out that Africa lacks the Western Church's tradition of asceticism: 'Africa's new Christians do not come to Kenneth Hagin or the Copelands or McCauley from a tradition influenced by the Desert Fathers, monasticism or St Francis of Assisi.'[32] Traditional religion is meant to ensure fertility, abundance and longevity: Gifford quotes Crowther's comment that the Yoruba religious search was for 'peace, health, children and money'.[33] Wealth and success, therefore, are quite naturally seen as signs of supernatural blessing, whether from God or from the ancestors; a person of substance and status is expected to be generous. At the same time, the high esteem in which pastors are held has allowed them to exploit their congregations with relative impunity. Gifford also points to a more mundane reason for the popularity of prosperity teaching: Hagin, Copeland, and others have been quick to supply free books and tapes to churches and seminaries that cannot afford to buy their own teaching materials.

In Brazil prosperity theology has been rampant during the last decade following years of political and economic chaos. The Universal Church of God's Kingdom, led by Edir Macedo, now claims three million members in Brazil and another three million worldwide. It owns the third largest television network in the country in addition to radio stations, newspapers, and a bank. Although the church has been severely criticized by evangelicals in Brazil for the inordinate pressure put on members to give and its tendency to equate poverty with sinfulness, it has also gained quite widespread commendation for its humanitarian work in the slums of Rio de Janeiro and Sao Paulo, and for the socio-economic and racial diversity of its congregations.[34]

Brouwer, Gifford and Rose draw attention to the influence of prosperity teaching in neo-Pentecostal churches in Guatamala and of American missionary organizations such as Agua Viva, which was founded in 1979 by Jim Zirkle, a graduate of Rhema Bible School. They note that Agua Viva missionaries were flying two planes given to them by Kenneth Copeland Ministries.[35]

In other parts of the world a number of prominent leaders are associated with Word of Faith teaching. Brian Houston, Pastor of Australia's fastest growing church, Hills Christian Life Centre, is a close friend of McCauley and has written a book entitled *You Need More Money*. The enormously successful Korean pastor David Yonggi Cho, who popularized the 'King's Kid' label, has acquired an ambiguous reputation among evangelicals globally. While many have been impressed by the growth of his Yoido Full Gospel Church, with its well-organized cell-group structure and emphasis on prayer, he has also been accused of promoting spiritual techniques that are more occult than biblical, and many have been alarmed by the church's preoccupation with material prosperity. Cho's gospel has been described as a Christianized version of Nichiren Shoshu Buddhism.[36] In the early eighties Ulf Ekman studied at Rhema Bible Training Center in Tulsa and on returning to Sweden established the Livets Ord ('Word of Life') church and Bible School in Uppsala. Livets Ord regards itself as the divinely appointed centre for faith teaching in Europe, though the strong element of nationalism and Christian Zionism in its programme locates it outside the mainstream of the Word of Faith movement.[37] The Oslo Kristne Senter in Norway, founded on Faith principles by Åge Åleskjær, is now the largest congregation in the country. In more recent years Stanley Sjöberg and Hans Braterud have also been influential in promoting Word of Faith ideas in Scandinavia.[38] In 1997 KCM began targeting the Pacific Islands in the belief that the islands of the world would be 'among the last places in the earth where a great outpouring of God's Glory would manifest before Jesus' return'.[39]

Prosperity teaching in the UK context

British evangelical culture has traditionally been unreceptive towards prosperity teaching and the blandishments of its proponents. Buddy Harrison influenced Bryn Jones Covenant Ministries in the 1980s. KCM has organized conventions and has had the support of the Full Gospel Business Men's Fellowship.[40] A handful of churches have been influenced by McCauley's Rhema Bible Church. Paul Scanlon in Bradford has had close links with McCauley and Brian Houston. He has also brought in speakers such as Jesse Duplantis and the Copelands for events at his Abundant Life Centre; and a weekly television programme called 'A Voice to the Nations' is broadcast in Europe, South Africa and Australia. Smail, Walker and Wright find 'strong echoes' of faith teaching in 'some of the so-called new churches and from evangelists as diverse as Colin Urquhart and Don Double'.[41]

A few ministries have sought to emulate the success and flamboyance of the American organizations. Peter Gammons claims to have ministered to more than 100 million people in 70 countries as a healing evangelist during 30 years of ministry. In 1999 he founded Cathedral of Faith in Orlando, Florida. The church has plans to build 'America's only Christian City', comprising holiday and retirement homes, schools, a 10,000 seat Cathedral, and 24 hour Prayer Centre.[42] Trevor Newport started Life-Changing Ministries in 1991 having received a 'revelation of prosperity' from God. Since then he and his wife 'have been sowing seeds and standing in faith for many large projects such as cars, a house, successive new church buildings, book publications and even a jet!'[43] 170 churches worldwide are claimed to come under the organization's apostolic covering. Generally speaking, though, Word of

Faith teachings have maintained only a limited existence on the fringe of Pentecostalism and the charismatic movement.

The reasons for the relative lack of success are partly historical and partly cultural. The Word of Faith movement in America draws on powerful spiritual and philosophical currents that reach back to the nineteenth century. British religious sensibilities since the Second World War are the product of an entirely different social narrative. Although British culture has been heavily influenced by American imports, many of the underlying differences remain unchanged, not least with respect to such desiderata as success and wealth.[44] American culture is idealistic and aspirational, intolerant of weakness and failure. British culture, by contrast, tends to be suspicious of idealism, intolerant of the hypocrisy and pretension that so often accompany ambition, wary of the methods of the motivation industry, more focused on how things are than on how they might be, more willing to accept weakness and failure. A predisposition towards irony habitually pricks the bubble of any complacent attempt to think positively. A much stronger sense of individual responsibility for one's circumstances has made Americans more inclined to see personal wealth as a sign of divine approval. Lacking the traditional British embarrassment about money, Americans are more likely to see wealth as something to be invested and exploited. Americans are also more nationalistic than the British and are more likely to recognize themselves in the mirror of Old Testament religion. Obviously these are very sketchy generalizations, but it seems a reasonable assumption that the marginalization of the Word of Faith movement in the UK is largely attributable to cultural factors of this nature.

This should not be taken to mean, however, that the movement can safely be ignored as far as the church in the UK is concerned. Indeed, there have been at least three significant developments in recent years which give a report of this nature a real urgency and relevance.

The first is the controversy that was generated in 1995 when pressure was put on Morris Cerullo to resign from the Evangelical Alliance after his organization's promotional and fund-raising methods came under scrutiny in the national press. A number of specific complaints were upheld by the Advertising Standards Authority. The Alliance expressed concern at the time over the theological content of Cerullo's 'prosperity teaching', the aggressive, self-serving style of his promotional material, and the extravagant claims made for his ministry. The critical issue, however, was the alarm caused by the techniques employed in soliciting financial support for the work of Morris Cerullo World Evangelism, which many regarded as manipulative and dishonest. Cerullo claimed, for example, that 1996 would be a divinely appointed 'Jubilee Year' in celebration of 50 years of his ministry. Supporters were encouraged to send 50p for each year, with the assurance that God would release them from their debts and bestow on them a literal (and very material) hundredfold blessing. This report on the Word of Faith movement originated as a response to some of the theological questions raised by this difficult confrontation.[45]

Secondly, increased access to American televangelism through cable and satellite networks such as the God Channel, God Revival and Inspiration channels has meant that the teachings of Hagin, Copeland, and others are readily available for private consumption, whatever the official position of UK churches might be. These networks also host a small number of homegrown televangelists. This development is consistent with an interesting analysis put forward by Simon Coleman, who argues that 'membership of the community of Faith Christians is described and perceived by adherents in terms of a metaphor that is well adapted to the notion of placelessness: that of spiritual consumption'.[46] Because it has generally not been sanctioned officially by the church, the Word of Faith movement has developed into something of a private religious consumer product, made available to individuals in the form of books, tapes, conferences, and TV programmes.

Thirdly, the rapid growth of African churches in recent years, especially in London, has provided a much more receptive audience for prosperity teaching. No doubt its popularity can be attributed to many of the same cultural and sociological factors as have accounted for the success of the movement in Africa. Kingsway International Christian Centre (KICC) was founded by a Nigerian pastor, Matthew Ashimolowo, in Hackney in East London in 1992 and now has a regular congregation, overwhelmingly black, of more than 7,000. The church has been accused of preaching a gospel of success, using the Bible as a 'manual of empowerment'.[47] The church's website (www.kicc.org.uk) encourages positive confession – the use of words as 'powerful tools' to 'Build your spirit man', 'Paint the picture of your desired future', 'Re-write the negatives spoken into your life', and 'Lift yourself from defeat to victory'. The expectation that God will bless the church, not least through the prosperity and success of its members, is a prominent theme in the services. Although this remains a black Pentecostal phenomenon, KICC can plausibly claim to be the largest church in Europe. It has ambitions to build a 'state-of-the-art' church facility to seat 5,000, to establish 30 satellite congregations around London, and to grow to a membership of 25,000. The emergence of energetic churches such as KICC over the next few years could well give much greater prominence to some form of prosperity teaching in the UK.

Reaction to prosperity teaching

Evangelical reaction to the Word of Faith movement and the argument about prosperity has been for the most part distrustful and censorious. The most aggressive response has come from such defenders of orthodoxy as Hank Hanegraaff, head of the Christian Research Institute (CRI), who has claimed that the movement is 'every bit as cultic as... the Mormons'.[48] While prepared to allow that the views of some Faith teachers are merely 'aberrational', CRI has insisted that the teachings of others (Copeland is named) are 'so opposed to orthodoxy that they can only be regarded as heretical'.[49] Hanegraaff's book *Christianity in Crisis* (1993) is quite unforgiving in its condemnation of the 'deadly errors of the Faith Movement'.[50] Andrew Brandon reached similar conclusions in *Health and Wealth*

(1987), arguing that the most influential Word of Faith teachers 'have a theology which bears all the characteristics of a cult'.[58] In many respects this reaction is simply an extension of the familiar Fundamentalist and conservative-evangelical critique of Pentecostalism and the more outstanding, outspoken, and outrageous healing evangelists, such as A.A. Allen, William Branham and Oral Roberts.[52] This is notably the case with Dave Hunt's *The Seduction of Christianity* (1985), which is strongly dispensationalist and cessationist in its outlook.[53] The attitude of Pentecostalism itself towards the Word of Faith movement has been ambivalent: while at a popular level there has been a natural tolerance, Pentecostal scholarship has sometimes been highly critical both of the teaching and the practice of the movement.[54]

Not all dissenting voices, however, have been so strident. The current debate was sparked off by a book from within the charismatic movement – Charles Farah's *From the Pinnacle of the Temple* (1979). Farah, a professor at Oral Roberts University, had been disturbed by the death of a diabetic boy in California whose parents had refused him insulin, believing that the Lord would heal him. Looking more closely at the teachings of Hagin and others, Farah concluded that much of what passed as faith within the movement – and, indeed, within the charismatic church generally – was in fact presumption.[55] His simple thesis remains apposite, but it is important to note that as a charismatic he endorsed many of the distinctive emphases of Word of Faith teaching. *The Health and Wealth Gospel* (1987) by Bruce Barron, who actually took the trouble to enrol in Hagin's Rhema Correspondence Bible School, has provided a useful resource for people looking for a more sympathetic and constructive appraisal. William DeArteaga's *Quenching the Spirit* (1992) comes nearest to being a coherent defence of Word of Faith teaching, while retaining some critical distance. Most recently Robert Bowman, formerly a researcher and editor for CRI and now president of the Institute for the Development of Evangelical Apologetics (IDEA), has attempted to determine the precise location of the Word of Faith movement on the heresy-orthodoxy scale. His book *The Word-Faith Controversy:*

Understanding the Health and Wealth Gospel (2001), written from a 'noncharismatic but not anticharismatic' perspective,[56] is the product of fifteen years of research and is probably the most balanced and judicious analysis of the movement to date.

Critics have voiced a number of basic concerns. The leading complaint has been that Word of Faith teaching diverges from sound doctrine at certain key points, most notably in its understanding of the atonement and of the function of faith in the Christian life; and that in its defence of these errors it has seriously distorted Scripture.

There has also been quite widespread agreement that although the movement has much in common with Pentecostalism, its true ideological origins are to be found in the metaphysical cults of the nineteenth century, especially Christian Science and New Thought. This argument was presented most forcefully by Daniel McConnell, a student of Farah, in his book *A Different Gospel* (1988) and has since been accepted by opponents of the movement without much question.[57] Word of Faith teaching has also been variously labelled as charismatic humanism and as a form of Christian gnosticism.[58]

The movement has been an unabashed advocate of material prosperity and this has naturally invited the charge that it promotes a lifestyle and ethos fundamentally at odds with the values of the kingdom of God. Analyses of the movement abound with anecdotes about luxury cars and Rolex watches. Sympathies towards prosperity teaching have also been seriously undermined by cultural prejudices and dislike of the flamboyant style of high profile evangelistic ministries in America.

Finally, the success of the movement has depended to a large extent on its claim to hold the key to the *miraculous* provision of 'health and wealth' for its adherents. For various reasons this claim has generally met with scepticism from the wider Christian community. The worst scams and failures are well known.[59] The countless testimonies from ordinary people to the miraculous power of God documented in the magazines and promotional literature are likely to be attributed to error or psychosomatic healing or the work of Satan.

A fair trial

If it should prove necessary to call into question some part, even a significant part, of the teaching and practice of the Word of Faith movement, it is incumbent upon us to do so – as far as possible – in a way which purposefully opens a path towards constructive dialogue and reconciliation. Given the intensity of the controversy and, frankly, the extent to which debate has been marred by misrepresentation, polarization, and invective, there are some basic precautions that need to be taken.

The primary objective must be to evaluate the *teaching* of the Word of Faith movement – the faith ideal, the particular expectation regarding health and prosperity, and the theology that underpins it – rather than to pass judgment on either the practice or the motives of its proponents.[60] The question of moral and pastoral integrity is bound to arise at certain points, and when we come to consider ecumenical relations, we will have to take into account the quality of spiritual life, both individual and corporate, that has been engendered by the teaching. But we should not assume that the teaching is necessarily invalidated by what may appear in certain cases to be its questionable application.

Secondly, in response to criticism the Word of Faith movement has sometimes lashed out at its opponents, occasionally held up its hands in an admission of guilt, but more often has retreated into stubborn dogmatism. What it has not done is mount anything like a serious scholarly defence of its teachings. Some may interpret this as a sign of the indefensibility of the position, but we should at least recognize that we lack the more nuanced and thoughtful reactions to criticism – the fruit of open dialogue – which might have made this particular understanding of the gospel more credible.

Thirdly, while there have been a number of published investigations of Word of Faith teaching, they have been aimed largely at a popular market, and there is a case for saying that even the most moderate of them have not been entirely fair. Opponents have been quick to point out, for example, how

Word of Faith teachers habitually take biblical texts out of context, but they are often guilty of the same elementary error of interpretation when they highlight seemingly heretical pronouncements without taking into account the rhetorical and argumentative framework within which the statement was made.[61] This is not the way to establish the truth – whether we mean by that the formal truth that sets the boundaries of orthodox Christian belief or the personal 'truth' that is the living Word of God.

We will have cause to refer to the 'rhetoric' of the Word of Faith movement at a number of points during this study and it may be helpful to provide an explanation. In the first place, use of the term is not meant to imply, as it often does in popular usage, that Word of Faith discourse is all talk and no substance. 'Rhetoric' denotes the range of linguistic and argumentative means by which a speaker or community seeks to articulate its identity and purpose. Broadly speaking, it encompasses those forms of argumentation that are not covered by the rules of rationalist or scientific discourse. Rhetoric introduces us to the pragmatics of public discourse: it consists of the creative use of language to persuade people of the worth of an ideal or goal or belief. What the use of the term highlights in this case is the fact that the Word of Faith movement employs a style of argumentation or persuasion that differs in important respects from that employed by other movements or groups, and in particular from the sort of religious discourse that we tend to regard as normative. These differences must be taken into account when assessing the statements and claims that are made. The use of the term in this context also reflects the fact that Word of Faith teaching lacks the underpinning of more scholarly forms of discourse. Much of the difficulty with Word of Faith teaching arises because we do not have the more thoughtful and coherent body of scholarly arguments that would normally provide a reference point for the populist rhetoric.

Fourthly, a report such as this is bound to concentrate on what are perceived to be the more deviant aspects of prosperity teaching. The history of the controversy and the current stand-off between the Word of Faith movement and mainstream evangelicalism force us to look closely at those issues which have been a persistent cause of disagreement. However, in the interests of fairness, we must be careful to avoid an unbalanced presentation and assessment of the material. In this regard, it may be noted that the ACUTE Special Consultation on the Prosperity Gospel in June 1998, which gave the initial impetus for this report, sought to bring together pastors and teachers from both sides of the debate and to encourage a candid and constructive dialogue.

A number of scalding critiques of the Word of Faith movement have been published which have not always taken the trouble to identify and affirm those aspects of the teaching that are clearly biblical. The Word of Faith movement overlaps to a considerable extent with mainstream Pentecostalism and much of its teaching would not seem especially unorthodox to charismatically minded evangelicals. Indeed, it must be asked whether the current success of the movement does not owe something to the fact that it has enthusiastically, perhaps over-enthusiastically, embraced certain core elements of Christian truth – the utter trustworthiness of God, the requirement of unwavering faith – that evangelicals have simply not taken seriously enough. Word of Faith teaching is a puzzling mix of the familiar and the unfamiliar, the sublime and the ridiculous. Whatever our final judgment may be, it should not be made on the basis of a narrow focus on the points of doctrinal disagreement.

Finally, many within evangelicalism know the Word of Faith movement only according to the narrow terms of the controversy and as it has been caricatured by its opponents.[62] We cannot assume, however, that the Word of Faith ministries and churches have stood still or remained wholly impervious to criticism. A limited report of this nature cannot take account of all the variations and developments of opinion within the movement, but we can hope to establish as a matter principle for the wider debate the need to evaluate the movement *as it presents itself today*, not as it has been denounced and ridiculed over the last four decades. Judgments have too often been made on the basis of second-hand reports and the opinions of polemicists. The Word of Faith movement must be allowed to speak for itself and some effort made to understand both the practical context in which it speaks and the distinctive rhetoric it uses. The movement cannot be entirely dissociated from its past, but we must allow for the possibility of development and self-correction. There have also been more moderate voices and some more reasoned defences,[63] which may in the long run provide not only a more credible account of the connection between faith and prosperity but also a much more useful basis for discussion.

* * * *

In the next three chapters we will outline the basic teachings of the Word of Faith movement: first, its rather idiosyncratic account of salvation-history, from the creation of the world to the second coming of Christ; secondly, the argument about faith and the means by which it is activated in the life of the believer; and thirdly, the belief that through faith we have access not only to spiritual blessings but also to the much more worldly blessings of health and prosperity. A thorough evaluation of these teachings, principally from a biblical perspective, will be presented in part two of this report.

2

The story of salvation

The basic premise of Word of Faith teaching is very simple. By virtue of Christ's death the believer is entitled not only to salvation and the sanctifying indwelling of the Holy Spirit but also to the material benefits of health and prosperity. These things do not appear automatically in a person's life: they do not turn up by next-day delivery once she has made a commitment to Christ. They need to be claimed by faith and in accordance with the will of God. Often prosperity teaching amounts to little more than a persistent exhortation to do just this.[1] Generally it is linked to the obligation to give, both as a prerequisite for receiving financial blessing and as the natural response to it. In its more advanced manifestations, however, Word of Faith teaching has developed a rather complex theology for the purpose of explaining and defending the central thesis. There are two dimensions to this theology: there is the explanation of the operation of faith, which we will consider in chapter four, and there is the wider salvation-historical narrative, which we will examine here.

Salvation-history according to the Word of Faith movement

Creation and fall

The creation of Adam in the image of God is understood by the Word of Faith movement to comprise a much stronger resemblance between the creator and the creature than would normally be permitted within evangelical orthodoxy. On the one hand, there is a tendency to depict God in graphically anthropomorphic terms, a doctrinal oddity which the Word of Faith movement shares with Mormonism.[2] Kenneth Copeland speaks of God as a 'spirit-being with a body, complete with eyes, and eyelids, ears, nostrils, a mouth, hands and fingers, and feet'.[3] Robert Bowman quotes a taped sermon in which Copeland infers from the statement in Isaiah 40:12 that God 'marked off the heavens with a span' that God is about six feet two inches tall and weighs about 200 pounds.[4] Kenneth Hagin makes the point in slightly more nuanced terms:

> Even though we say that God is a spirit, that doesn't mean He doesn't have a shape or a form in the spiritual realm, because He does.... Even though God is a spirit, we know that He has a face and hands – a form of some kind. He is no less real because He is a spirit than He would be if He had a physical body. Spiritual things are just as real as material things.[5]

On the other hand, Adam has been made more *God-like*. He is understood to have had originally the same nature as God, the 'same class of being',[6] to have been virtually a replication of God in the created world: 'God's reason for creating Adam was His desire to reproduce Himself.... Adam is as much like God as you could get, just the same as Jesus.... Adam, in the Garden of Eden, was God manifested in the flesh.'[7] Hagin calls Adam 'god of this world'.[8]

At creation man was given legal authority over the earth and its material resources for a period of six thousand years, after which the right to rule was to be transferred back to God for a final millennial reign.[9] Adam's act of 'High Treason' against God, however, meant not only that man endured the 'spiritual death' of 'being separated from the life and glory of God',[10] but also that government of the earth and its material resources was handed over to Satan. Whereas before his rebellion man had shared the same nature as God, he now acquired a satanic nature:

> That day in the garden first Eve, then Adam, changed gods. The sin nature of their new god, Satan, took possession of their once righteous spirits. They died spiritually. The very nature of man was changed from one of righteousness or eternal life into one of spiritual death – from the nature of God to the nature of Satan.[11]

Because legal authority had been ceded to man, God was powerless to intervene directly and correct the situation, debarred from his own creation by a technicality of cosmic law.[12] Although for a while mankind preserved some memory of God, transmitted by oral tradition, there could be no direct knowledge of him. Eventually, however, an opportunity for God to begin to remedy the situation presented itself in the person of Abraham. By entering into a covenant with God Abraham provided the legal means for him to regain access to earth.[13] In return, God 'promised to care for Abraham and his descendants in every way – spiritually, physically, financially, socially'.[14] The covenant with Abraham allowed God to speak a Word into the world which would eventually produce Jesus Christ: Mary 'first *received the Word* into her *spirit* (heart) then it was *manifest in her physical body*. THE WORD OF GOD was implanted in her womb, it was the *embryo*, the seed, and it took upon itself flesh, just as the living Word of God placed in your spirit took upon itself new creation – life.'[15] This argument appears to entail the idea that the Word which became flesh was not the pre-existent Son of God but the spoken or confessed Word by which God activated his faith.[16] Outside the covenant with Abraham mankind had no protection from the curse of poverty and disease that was pronounced over Adam in Genesis 3:16-19 and expounded in detail in Deuteronomy 28:15-68.

Without legal authority to act within his creation, God could redeem only through a man. At his incarnation, therefore, Jesus was stripped of all divine attributes. This, in Copeland's view, is the meaning of the self-emptying described in Philippians 2:7. 'Why didn't Jesus openly proclaim Himself as God during His 33 years on earth? For one single reason. He hadn't come to earth as God, He'd come as man.'[17] This man was a 'carbon copy of the one who walked through the Garden of Eden' – man in his unfallen state.[18] In a supposed revelation to Copeland Jesus said, 'They crucified Me for claiming that I was God. But I didn't claim I was God; I just claimed I walked with Him and that He was in Me.'[19] It is then a logical corollary to this christology that the earthly Jesus *functioned* entirely as man, not as God: he had no unique or privileged access to the mind and power of God. Without the anointing of the Holy Spirit that came upon him at his baptism he could perform no miracles; as his disciples would have to learn to do, he relied on faith in the Word of God.[20] Although *in his person* as Son of God Jesus was in a class by himself, *'in ministry*, He is *not* in a class by Himself'.[21] In Copeland's words, 'Jesus ministered on earth as a prophet under the Abrahamic Covenant.'[22] He explains in an article in *Believer's Voice of Victory*:

> Jesus did operate in greater power than we do. But not for the reason most people think. His great anointing was not due to the fact that He is the Son of God. It couldn't have been! For Philippians 2:7 says when Jesus came to earth, He stripped Himself of His divine privileges. He laid aside the rights of deity and ministered as a man.... the reason Jesus was able to operate in unlimited power was because He spoke the words of God.[23]

The atonement

According to the Word of Faith movement's understanding of the atonement Jesus died twice – not only a physical death on the cross but also a spiritual death.[24] The doctrine is sometimes referred to as 'JDS': 'Jesus died spiritually'. The argument is not entirely coherent, but there appear to be two stages to this spiritual death. The first stage was Jesus' transformation from a divine to a satanic creature. Hagin maintains that prior to Gethsemane Jesus' shared Adam's original immortality, but 'when He took upon His spirit nature our sins and our diseases, His body became mortal, and they could kill Him'.[25] The second stage consisted of Christ's sufferings as he endured the full punishment for our sins – not death alone but the full and appalling torments of hell. F.K.C. Price presents the thesis in graphic terms:

> Do you think that the punishment for our sin was to die on a cross? If that were the case, the two thieves could have paid your price. No the punishment was to go into hell itself and to serve time in hell separated from God.... Satan and all the demons of hell thought that they had him bound, and they threw a net over Jesus and they dragged Him down to the very pit of hell itself to serve our sentence.[26]

The argument is, in the first place, theoretical and inferential. Although sickness and sin may manifest themselves physically, they are spiritual in origin – they derive from Adam's spiritual death – and are unaffected by what happens in the body. A purely 'bodily' death, therefore, cannot defeat sin, which is spiritual. So for Christ fully to identify himself with fallen humanity he must go through the process of becoming sin, becoming subject to the rule of Satan. He must endure the same spiritual death that Adam suffered when he was ejected from the garden. Copeland defends his belief that Jesus died spiritually when he took the sin of mankind upon himself:

> I've had ugly books written about me because I said that Jesus died spiritually, but the fact is, I didn't say that – the Bible said it. Jesus became our substitute. If He hadn't died spiritually, then we could never have been made alive spiritually. But He did! ... On the cross, Jesus was separated from the glory of God. He allowed Himself to be made sin for us, and He became obedient to death. He went into the pit of hell and suffered there as though He was the One Who had committed the sin.[27]

The biblical evidence cited in support of the doctrine is somewhat indirect. In the KJV the first part of Isaiah 53:9 reads: 'he made his grave with the wicked, and with the rich in his death'. The Hebrew word for 'death' is plural, and it has been maintained that this messianic prophecy alludes to both a physical and a spiritual death.[28] The analogy between Christ lifted up on the cross and the serpent lifted up by Moses in the wilderness (Jn. 3:14) offers a rather startling argument for the transformation of Christ into something Satanic. Jesus' cry of dereliction from the cross is interpreted as an expression of his spiritual death, of the total separation of Jesus from God: he has become a mere man in torment on the cross. 'And the very inside of God,' Copeland says, 'hanging on that cross, is severed from Him and in that moment of severing, the spirit of Jesus accepting that sin and making it to be sin, He's separated from His God and in that moment He's a mortal man; capable of failure, capable of death.'[29] The statement in 2 Corinthians 5:21 that God 'made him to be sin' is taken to mean that at the time of his death Christ had become, as man had become at the fall, a 'new Satanic creation', as a result of which his spirit was separated from God.[30] Commenting on the statement in 1 Timothy 3:16 that 'God was manifest in the flesh, justified in the Spirit' (KJV), Copeland draws several of these motifs together:

> Now you can't get somebody justified and made righteous in the spirit if it wasn't first unrighteous. The righteousness of God was made to be sin. He [Jesus] accepted the sin nature of Satan in His own spirit and at the moment that He did that He cried, "My God, my God, why hast thou forsaken me?" You don't know what happened at the cross. Why do you think Moses, obeying the instruction of God, hung the serpent up on the pole instead of a lamb? That used to bug me. I said, "Why in the world would you want to put a snake up there – the sign of Satan? Why didn't you put a lamb on that pole." And the Lord said, "Because, it was the sign of Satan that was hanging on the cross." He said, "I accepted in my own spirit spiritual death and the light was turned off."[31]

By means of this spiritual death the legal obligation towards Satan was satisfied, but because Jesus had become a satanic creation, he had to suffer in hell and be 'born again' – just as the believer must be born again – before he could be raised from the dead. Appeal is made to the description of Christ as 'firstborn from the dead' in Colossians 1:18. 'It is important for us to realize,' Copeland says, 'that a born-again man defeated Satan.'[32] Accounts of this event are characteristically lurid and theatrical: 'On that day, God's absolute, utmost goodness invaded the pit of absolute, utmost badness – hell itself – and surged into Jesus' emaciated, sinfilled spirit. The glory of God re-created Him and made Him the firstborn from the dead. All the sin, sickness and demons of hell had to bow their knee and turn Him loose, because they couldn't stand the presence of the glory!'[33]

Having been raised from the dead and having ascended to the right hand of the Father, Jesus is also now on the outside of creation; but he has delegated all his authority on earth to the church – to the extent that he is now powerless to act on earth unless the church exercises the authority that has been given to it. The argument is that as head of the church Christ cannot exercise any authority except through his body.[34] The church, therefore, has recovered the authority over material things that was lost to Satan at the fall: 'Jesus regained for man the God-given authority over the earth that man had transferred to Satan in the Garden of Eden.'[35] The believer has been given the legal right, the 'power of attorney', to make use of the name of Jesus to meet his every need, whether spiritual, physical, or financial.[36] If we exercise that authority, Satan has no choice but to leave us alone, and we will not fail to be blessed.

End-time expectation

The Word of Faith movement shares the conviction, widely held in Pentecostal and Fundamentalist circles, that we are in the final days before the second coming, the rapture of the church and the inauguration of the millennium. With his characteristic flair for evoking the comic melodrama of heaven

Copeland writes: 'I'm telling you, Jesus is coming. He's about to rise off His heavenly throne and return to earth. He may not have stood up yet, but I guarantee you He is out on the edge of His seat!'[37]

The triumphalism that often accompanies heightened apocalytic expectation is given a distinctive 'prosperity' orientation. During the present 'sliver of time' between the 6,000 years of Satan's dominion over the earth and the 1,000 years of Christ's coming reign the church will reap the abundant harvest of 2,000 years of sowing the seed of the gospel. 'It doesn't matter where on this planet you live – there is more glory, more outpouring, more preaching, more Word, more believers, and even more hell on this earth than there has ever been before.'[38] There will also be increased angelic activity. The phenomenon of laughing in the Spirit associated with the 'Toronto Blessing' is interpreted as the laughter of God at the imminent downfall of Satan (cf. Ps. 2:4; 37:13).[39] The church will be triumphant, a 'new breed': 'Jesus is not coming back for a weak, sickly Church that has been defeated and beaten down by Satan. No, praise God, we are going out of here in a blaze of glory.'[40] Advanced technology features prominently in this scenario: 'God has prepared us to handle dangerous levels of prosperity because it's our responsibility to preach the gospel to all the nations so the end can come and Jesus can return. God already has put the technology to do it into our hands. All we need now is the finances.'[41]

Identification with Christ

By assuming our satanic nature in his death Christ fully identified himself with mankind and in that way rescued us from the hegemony that Satan had acquired as a result of Adam's High Treason. We have been redeemed from the 'curse of the law', which is understood to mean the three-fold curse of poverty, sickness and the second death.[42] The task of the believer now is to *identify* herself with Christ in order to actualize the full benefits of redemption and to recover the divine nature that Adam possessed in Eden. 'The basic principle of the Christian life,' Copeland argues, 'is to know that God put our sin, sickness, disease, sorrow, grief, and poverty on Jesus at Calvary. For Him to put any of this on us now would be a miscarriage of justice.'[43]

At the heart of the notion of 'identification' is the idea that the believer has acquired the same nature as Christ, and even, in more extreme formulations, the same nature as God. We have reverted to Adam's unfallen condition – we have become beings in 'God's class'. At one level this argument appears only to affirm the intrinsic value and spiritual capacity of those who belong to Christ, who are also 'called the sons of God' (1 Jn. 3:1 KJV; cf. Heb. 2:10-11): believers are baptized in the same Spirit as Jesus and have received the same anointing to 'put sin, sickness, poverty, broken-heartedness and every other enemy of God under their feet forever'.[44] This was Jesus' promise to the disciples:

> Peter knew why Jesus could do those things. It was because He had the anointing of God on Him. He had burden-removing, yoke-destroying, world-changing, devil-chasing, healing, delivering, explosive, supernatural, universe-creating power of the Holy Spirit flowing through His flesh enabling Him to do what flesh cannot do!
>
> So when Peter heard Jesus say, "You will be baptized with the Holy Ghost and receive power to be my witnesses," he knew what Jesus was talking about. He was saying, "Listen, Peter, the same Anointing that's on Me is about to come on you so that the works I've done, you can do also."[45]

There is considerable impatience with the attitude of self-abasement and the sense of personal worthlessness that Christians often confuse with godliness and humility.

> How dare we, in the guise of religious humility, rob Jesus of the joy and satisfaction He paid for so dearly? How dare we entertain the thought that Jesus' blood just wasn't enough to wash away our unworthiness? ... If we're unworthy, then Jesus didn't get His job done.[46]

> When a person belittles himself, he is actually belittling God's workmanship. He is criticizing something God has made. We should quit looking at ourselves from the natural standpoint, and instead see ourselves as God sees us, as created in Christ Jesus. The Father doesn't see us as anybody else sees us. He sees us in Christ.... Many Christians are defeated because they look at themselves from the natural standpoint. They could be victorious by looking at themselves as God does.[47]

At another level, however, the argument about identification appears in a quite significant way to blur the distinctions between God, Christ and the believer. Hagin has stated, for example: 'Every man who has been born again is an incarnation and Christianity is a miracle. The believer is as much an incarnation as was Jesus of Nazareth.'[48] Such an assertion is possible because, according to Word of Faith teaching, the earthly Jesus was not a unique incarnation of divinity: the indwelling of God in Jesus by the Holy Spirit was no different in kind to the indwelling of God in the believer. It is only a small step from here to the sort of statements that have routinely provoked excited charges of blasphemy:

> Jesus was first divine, and then He was human. So He was in the flesh a divine-human being. I was first human, and so were you, but I was born of God, and so I became a human-divine being!
>
> You don't have a God in you, you are one.
>
> 'You need to realize that you are not a spiritual schizophrenic – half-God and half-Satan – you are all God.'
>
> And you impart humanity into a child that's born of you.... Because you are human, you have imparted the nature of humanity into that born child. God is God. He is a Spirit. And He imparted in you when you were born again – Peter said it just as plain, he said, 'We are partakers of the Divine nature,' that nature is alive eternal in absolute perfection, and that was imparted, injected into your spirit man, and you have that

> imparted into you by God just the same as you imparted into your child the nature of humanity. That child wasn't born a whale. It was born human... Well, now you don't have a human, do you? No, you are one. You don't have a God in you. You are one.
>
> When you say, 'I am a Christian,' you are saying, 'I am *mashiach*' in the Hebrew. I am a little messiah walking on earth, in other words. That is a shocking revelation.... May I say it like this? You are a little god on earth running around.[49]
>
> And when we stand up here, brother, you're not looking at Morris Cerullo; you're looking at God. You're looking at Jesus.[50]

Support for this apparent 'deification' of the believer is found in two main passages: Jesus' allusion in John 10:34-35 to the remarkable statement in Psalm 82:6: 'I say, "You are gods, children of the Most High, all of you..."'; and Peter's argument that through the promises of God believers 'may escape from the corruption that is in the world because of lust, and may become participants of the divine nature' (2 Pet. 1:4). We will examine these texts later.

* * * *

The Word of Faith narrative of redemption climaxes at the point at which complete spiritual success has become a real possibility for anyone who chooses to act in accordance with the word of God: Christ has redeemed us from the sovereignty of Satan, and the authority that Satan formerly held over the material world and its riches has been transferred to us. 'We were not made to be spiritual rugs for Satan to wipe his feet on,' Copeland insists.[51] So there is no excuse for spiritual mediocrity: we should expect to 'operate in a zero failure rate'. How the Word of Faith movement expects this extraordinary potential for spiritual success to be practically realized in the life of the believer is the subject of the next chapter.

3

What you say is what you get

If we are to achieve the level of spiritual and material blessing that is, according to Word of Faith doctrine, ours by right through our identification with Christ, we must somehow overcome the limitations of human nature and connect directly to the power of God. The Word of Faith argument is, on the one hand, that we may transcend the limitations of human understanding by receiving 'revelation knowledge' directly from God; and on the other, that by activating certain spiritual 'laws' that have been built into the universe, the most important being the law of faith, we may gain access to a supernatural power that can dramatically change our material circumstances.

Two types of knowledge

The proponents of Word of Faith teaching take great pains to establish a biblical basis for their distinctive doctrines. In their interpretation of the Scriptures, however, they rely heavily on a thoroughgoing distinction between a natural and a supernatural means of knowing. 'Sense knowledge', they say, comes to us through empirical and rational inquiry, but these methods are unable to tell us anything about God or the spiritual realm. 'Revelation knowledge' comes directly from God, bypassing the senses and the operation of reason.[1] It is embodied principally in the written Word of God, but it is also made available through visions and 'words from the Lord'.

This distinction has had a significant bearing not only on the manner in which Scripture is interpreted and applied, but also on the means by which teaching authority is exercised within the movement. In particular, where Word of Faith teaching diverges significantly from traditional interpretations it is likely to be backed up by some sort of revelatory experience. In many cases this takes the form of a dialogue – sometimes in real time – between the authoritative teacher or prophet and Jesus. A common pattern is for some remarkable truth or insight to be directly revealed by Jesus in a vision, which is at first met with astonishment from the Word of Faith teacher but is then 'proved' to be biblical.[2]

Revelatory experiences come in all shapes and sizes, however, and serve various purposes. In his book *I Believe in Visions* Kenneth Hagin records eight occasions when Jesus appeared to him in order to give direction to his ministry or expound some point of doctrine. Elsewhere he tells how in a vision he caught a woman from his congregation committing adultery:

> One Sunday morning while I was preaching, I suddenly knew in my spirit that it was Saturday night. I was standing on the street in a town that was located a mile away. And I saw a young lady who was a member of my congregation walk down the street. Then I saw a fellow in a car drive up to the curb, sound his horn, and wave at this young lady. She came and got in the car with him. Then they drove out to the country and committed adultery.[3]

The Word of Faith movement teaches that this sort of knowledge is available to all believers: the expectation is that God will clarify the meaning of Scripture, confirm the truth of Word of Faith teaching, and guide people in their daily lives through the rather commonplace experience of revelation. In practice, however, not all visions, and not all visionaries, are equal. The authoritative status of the information given to the 'anointed' prophet or teacher must clearly be defended against criticism or rival claims to revelation. A number of methods are employed for this purpose.

First, men such as Hagin and Kenneth Copeland are recognized as having been ordained and anointed by God for the express purpose of restoring these neglected and misunderstood teachings to the church. They are cast very much in the role of the Old Testament prophet, and wear the mantle of the prophet's authority.[4] This status is validated by the personal charisma of these teachers, by the visible success of their ministries, and by mutual endorsement among Word of Faith teachers.

Secondly, criticism of Word of Faith teaching is frequently countered by a denigration of empirical and rational thought.[5] So, for example, Copeland insists: 'Believers are not to be led by logic. We are not even to be led by *good sense*.... what the world calls good sense is not good at all. It is *bad* sense, corrupted by Satan, the god of this world.'[6] Word of Faith teaching regards the 'reborn' spirit as the dominant and only reliable component in human nature. 'Your body is not you,' Copeland writes. 'Your spirit is you. You are a spirit, and you have a soul, and you live in a body.... That body is not you. That body is where *you* live.'[7] Both the mind, which is part of the soul, and the senses, which belong to the body, must be subordinated to the guidance of the spirit. This sort of argument forestalls anything that might constitute a rational objection to Word of Faith teaching. It also provides a basis for denying the empirical reality of the symptoms of sickness once healing has been claimed. The purpose behind the anti-rationalism, however, is to safeguard faith: 'Common-sense religion,' Copeland warns, 'will tell you not to get your hopes up. God heals some people, but it might not be His will to heal you. That sounds *reasonable*, but it never gets results. You will always be the one that it is not His will to heal.'[8]

Thirdly, as we dig deeper through the substrata of Word of Faith ideology there emerges a more fundamental cosmological dualism – a Manichean drama of absolute good and evil that divides the world between satanic and divine control.[9] One effect of this worldview is a tendency to diminish the middle ground of ordinary human experience. On one side, the normal processes of rational enquiry are assigned to the sphere of Satan, at least in so far as they are perceived to contradict biblical truth and deny the power of faith. On the other, a much larger area of intellectual activity is absorbed into the sphere of revelation knowledge, becoming the prerogative of the authoritative teacher or prophet. In extreme instances the sciences of economics and medicine in particular may be regarded as the work of the devil, whereas a true understanding of the laws of prosperity and healing is believed to come through revelation knowledge.

Finally, those who dare to question or criticize Word of Faith teachers may find themselves publicly rebuked or even anathematized. Hagin relates ('with reluctance') an occasion when a pastor died in the pulpit because 'he didn't accept the message God's Spirit gave me to give him'.[10] In a similar vein, Copeland relates how he once reacted to a minister who strongly opposed the Word of Faith doctrine of Identification by proclaiming: 'That fellow is dead today. Now I said that to warn you. Don't criticize people for preaching [Identification]. If you don't understand it, keep your mouth shut and pray.'[11] At a notorious Denver crusade in 1999 Benny Hinn is reported to have declared: 'I place a curse on every man and woman that will stretch his hand against this anointing. I curse that man who dares to speak a word against this ministry.'[12] This sort of 'spiritual intimidation'[13] is justified by reference to Psalm 105:15 (= 1 Chron. 16:22): 'Do not touch my anointed ones; do my prophets no harm.'

The force of faith

The whole of existence, according to Word of Faith teaching, is governed by two sets of laws: physical laws, which control the material world, and spiritual laws, which determine what goes on in the world of the spirit. Of these the spiritual laws are the more powerful and can influence what happens in the material sphere. Spirit affects matter: 'Since the moment God spoke it into existence, that world has been governed by spiritual forces.'[14] The dominant spiritual law in the life of the believer is the 'law of the Spirit of life', which has superseded the 'law of sin and death' (Rom. 8:2). Other laws govern such things as health and prosperity.[15]

The force that drives these laws is faith – in the first place, the faith of God by which all things were created, but also the faith which believers exercise and by which they acquire for themselves the abundant benefits of redemption. God brought the universe into existence and now sustains it by faith. According to Hebrews 11:1 (KJV) faith is 'the *substance* of things hoped for', from which Copeland draws the conclusion that faith was 'the raw material substance that the Spirit of God used to form the universe'.[16] Similarly, Hagin argues from Hebrews 11:3 ('Through faith we understand that the worlds were framed by the word of God', KJV) that 'God believed that what He said would come to pass.' This is the 'God-kind of faith'.[17]

The same capacity to govern by faith was installed in man at creation: it is 'the creative power of God that He had given to man to use to rule the earth'.[18] Now that we have been restored to the position that Adam originally had, 'the kind of faith that spoke the universe into existence is dealt to our hearts'.[19] It is the power by which we change our circumstances, transform our dreams into reality, and as such it is something which must be wielded, manipulated and utilized. It is said of Copeland that he 'learned to use his faith like a mechanic uses a wrench – by systematically acting on the Word of God and expecting God to bring that Word to pass'.[20]

The degree to which faith is understood as an impersonal and indiscriminate law of the universe is illustrated by the fact that it is found to operate both inside and outside the sphere of the kingdom of God. Hagin is rather candid on this point: 'It used to bother me when I'd see unsaved people getting results. Then it dawned on me what the sinners were doing: they were cooperating with the law of God – the law of faith.'[21]

In the dualistic world of Word of Faith teaching there is inevitably a negative and satanic counterpart to faith, which is fear. If by putting faith into practice we activate prosperity and success, by acting out of fear, entertaining fearful thoughts in our minds, speaking fearfully, expressing doubts, we are bound to produce failure in our lives. Copeland puts the case: 'Fear activates Satan the way faith activates God. Why does the world not accept the logic that if fear, a spiritual force, will make a man sick then faith, the opposite spiritual force, will make him well? If the force of fear can imprison a man, then the force of faith can make him free. Why do men have confidence in fear and not in faith?'[22] Trevor Newport has suggested that Job became vulnerable to the attacks of Satan because he became fearful, and 'fear is faith in the devil'.[23] The fear reveals itself, he argues, in Job's 'constant state of worry' about the spiritual condition of his children (Job 1:5), and in his statement in 3:25: 'Truly the thing that I fear comes upon me, and what I dread befalls me.'

The faith formula

In the end, the process by which faith is put into practice in Word of Faith spirituality can be reduced to a simple, but not rigid, formula: first, find the promise in God's word; secondly, believe in your heart; thirdly, confess with your lips; lastly, act as if the prayer has been answered.[24]

1. Find the promise in God's Word

For a movement that puts so much store by supernaturally revealed knowledge there is at times a remarkable emphasis on the absolute priority of God's Word as the basis for the life of faith. The whole process of believing and confessing must begin with some law or principle or promise from God. Copeland insists: 'The first and most important rule for you to follow in operating in the power of God and living by faith is this: 100 percent committal [sic] to the Word of God and its authority in your life.'[25] Creflo Dollar invokes the Old Testament ideal expressed in Psalm 112:1-3 of the man who fears the Lord and delights in his commandments, in whose house are 'wealth and riches':

> When a man is doing God's Word, He will empower him to prosper. He will give him godly ideas or set him up for favor from men. He will open doors that the man could never have opened by himself. By blessing him at every turn, God has put this man in a position to prosper because he has delighted in His commandments.[26]

By meditating upon the Word of God we may discover specific promises that relate to our current circumstances – the needs we have, the decisions we have to make. But in more general terms we acquire the spiritual understanding necessary to determine whether we are hearing God's voice correctly in areas that are not expressly addressed in Scripture: 'The purpose of meditating is to place you in a position to do God's Word.'[27]

This emphasis is useful for two reasons. It helps to shift the focus away from a preoccupation with material prosperity: Copeland argues, for example, that 'True prosperity is God manifesting Himself to us in His Word.'[28] This is good theology – and, given the low opinion that evangelicals have tended to have of prosperity teaching, good public relations too. We should not disregard the consistent Word of Faith demand for obedience to the Word of God in all areas of life. But it also reinforces the underlying objective, legal basis for Word of Faith teaching, which has set itself the very difficult task of motivating complete and unswerving confidence in the principles that it propounds. Whereas faith in God can easily become a shapeless and subjective notion, the Word of God is fixed and objective – and easily reducible, according to Word of Faith hermeneutics, to a set of unambiguous and infallible rules.

2. Believe in your heart

According to Hagin Mark 11:23 provides the 'unalterable law of faith':[29] "Truly I tell you, if you say to this mountain, 'Be taken up and thrown into the sea,' and if you do not doubt in your heart, but believe that what you say will come to pass, it will be done for you." The Word of Faith movement encourages a quite obstinate and unflinching refusal to accept the failure of confessed faith. The word of faith *must* work, if properly activated, because it is backed up by the unfailing Word of God, and we dishonour God if we suppose his Word to be anything less than utterly reliable. Because there is a fundamental spiritual law at work here, there is no reason to doubt that the prayer will be answered. We have been given the name and authority of Jesus. God is legally bound, therefore, to give us what we ask for: 'I have not prayed one prayer in 45 years...,' Hagin has boasted, 'without getting an answer. I always got an answer – and the answer was always yes.'[30]

To most people, however, this sort of faith does not come easily, and we find various techniques recommended to help the person who prays make the psychologically difficult transition from mere assent to genuine belief that God will answer – or even has already answered – the prayer.

If the mind is unable to grasp how faith is supposed to work, unable to believe, it needs to be renewed, principally by being conformed to the word of God. 'The Word of God produces faith in your heart.... The Word has to be put in for faith to come out.'[31] Through study of God's word we begin to understand the nature and extent of the benefits to which we are entitled by virtue of our redemption. To have faith is to have the right state of mind, the mental attitude appropriate to our new identity in Christ, but it takes rigorous effort and discipline to eradicate the habits of fear and develop the instincts of faith. Copeland's use of a programming metaphor to describe the proper working of the renewed mind perhaps reveals more than was intended:

> When you get your system in proper sequence and your mind renewed to the Word of God where it thinks in line with the New Testament, you will find out that your mind has no pressure on it. It performs as the carefully programmed computer that it really is. You call on it, it goes *di, di, bom, bom,* gets the scripture, shifts it into gear and tells the body, "The Word says

that we are healed! You get yourself straightened up. You are not to operate in sickness." The body does what it is told and receives healing.[32]

Visualization

One of the more controversial techniques encouraged by the Word of Faith movement has been the practice of *visualizing* what one wants from God. How visualization works can be understood in different ways. At one level it is no more than a means of reinforcing a particular state of mind. Paul Gifford quotes from Mensah Otabil's address to the 1999 KICC convention at the London Arena: 'The future doesn't exist out there as something fixed, you design it in your imagination, you desire it, and you go for it, and it becomes a reality for you.'[33] If faith itself is largely a matter of having a state of mind that is able to believe in a certain outcome, then visualization may help a person to come to that state of mind. This, rather than anything more obviously mystical or occult, is probably what Copeland is getting at when he describes the visualization of a healing:

> When you get to the place where you take the Word of God and build an image on the inside of you of not having crippled legs and not having blind eyes, but when you close your eyes you just see yourself just leap out of that wheelchair, it will picture that in the Holy of Holies and you will come out of there. You will come out.[34]

Visualization is regarded as a means of overcoming the controlling effect of false images, which restrict our understanding of the goodness and power of God and inhibit our faith. Copeland explains that we have spent years developing false images that have become 'firmly entrenched in our minds' and need to be replaced with inner images that are consistent with the Word of God.[35]

Sometimes, however, the theory of visualization appears to entail metaphysical novelties. Yonggi Cho has taught the existence of a 'fourth dimension' – a spiritual dimension to existence, linking the subconscious to the Holy Spirit, to which we have access through dreams and visions and which we can manipulate in order to create and control our material existence.[36] 'Through visualizing and dreaming,' he says, 'you can incubate your future and hatch the results.' This is contrasted with the creative power of God: 'The subconscious has certain influence, but it is quite limited, and cannot create like our Almighty God can.'[37] It appears, nevertheless, that this capacity to imagine a future state of affairs into existence is understood in quite realistic terms, not merely as a metaphor for our ability to affect the future by the choices we make. It constitutes an elaboration of the idea of visualization beyond what is generally found in Word of Faith teaching.

3. Confess with your lips

If faith is the power by which the work of God is done in the universe, that power is activated by 'positive confession': 'The force of faith is released by words. Faith-filled words put the law of the Spirit of life into operation.'[38] Words are 'containers of spiritual power'.[39] 'Faith *kept only in your heart* never will bring healing to your body, the infilling of the Holy Spirit, or an answer to prayer. But faith in your heart *released through your lips* will bring results.'[40] In Hagin's succinct formula: 'You can have what you say'.[41]

Word of Faith theology finds the archetypal act of positive confession in the spoken words by which the faith of God was activated in creation: 'Creation did not take place until God released words of faith.' Copeland develops the argument: 'Everything in this material creation, everything you can see, touch, taste or smell came into existence as a result of the Word of God. That means God's Word is the parent substance of all matter.'[42] Just as the 'God-kind of faith' was invested in man at creation, so too the power to affect reality by the spoken word has been transferred from God to man. Charles Capps describes how the principle was revealed to him:

> In August of 1973, the Word of the Lord came unto me saying, "If men would believe me, long prayers are not necessary. Just speaking the Word will bring what you desire. My Creative power is given to man in Word form. I have ceased for a time from my creative work and have given man the book of MY CREATIVE POWER. That power is STILL IN MY WORD."[43]

Various texts are thought to illustrate the power of the spoken word. We are saved by the confession of our lips that Jesus Christ is Lord (Rom. 10:9). We will be justified or condemned according to our words (Mt. 12:37). The words that we speak can affect circumstances around us for good or evil: 'The tongue has the power of life and death, and those who love it will eat its fruit' (Prov. 18:21; cf. 4:20-24; 13:3). We should imitate God, who 'calls into existence the things that do not exist' (Rom. 4:17).[44]

The most important text, however, for the Word of Faith argument is again Jesus' statement about the prayer of faith in Mark 11:23: 'That whosoever shall say unto this mountain, Be thou removed, and be thou cast into the sea; and shall not doubt in his heart, but shall believe that those things which he saith shall come to pass; he shall have whatsoever he saith' (KJV). Copeland develops Hagin's formula: 'You can have what you say! In fact, what you are saying is exactly what you are getting now.'[45] Positive confession will have a positive effect on a person's life, but it is no less true that a negative confession – words that are motivated by fear rather than by faith – will have harmful consequences. Hagin finds the principle in Proverbs 6:2: 'you are snared by the utterance of your lips, caught by the words of your mouth.'[46] Ill-health and poverty can be directly attributed to the way a person speaks.[47] Hagin quotes the words of a Baptist minister: 'You said you could not, and the moment you said it, you were defeated. You said you did not have faith, and doubt rose up like a giant and bound you. You are imprisoned with your own words. You talk failure, and failure holds you in bondage.'[48] John Avanzini applies the principle to personal finances: '...if you constantly speak of the overwhelming size of your debt, and how impossible it will be to overcome, your words will cause your debt to loom high above you. With each negative word, your debt will grow more impossible to overcome.'[49]

Although there is a strong emphasis on the quasi-mechanical function of words and of the Word of God, it is important to recognize that in Faith teaching the Word is backed up – underwritten, guaranteed – by God himself. It is not necessarily a power detached from the person of God. Copeland, for example, makes the typically provocative statement, 'God's Word is as powerful as He is', but he goes on to explain that 'A word is always and only as powerful as the person who gave it.'[50]

4. Act as if it's so

Jesus told his disciples, 'believe that you have received (*elabete*) it, and it will be yours' (Mk. 11:24) – the aorist is taken to mean that receiving coincides with believing. The real test of the faith-filled prayer, therefore, is to act *as though* the prayer has been answered even if the physical evidence is not yet apparent. 'By keeping your actions and your confession in line with the Word, the desired result will come to pass.'[51] This is sometimes called 'corresponding action': one acts in a way which *corresponds* to the expected answer.[52] The young Hagin's determined struggle to get out of bed and walk around his room illustrates the practice. The healing of the ten lepers is often presented as an example: Jesus simply told them to go and show themselves to the priests, and 'as they went, they were made clean' (Lk. 17:14).[53] The principle is no less valid in respect to prosperity, though it may be implemented somewhat differently. Dollar urges his readers: 'Begin to act prosperous, and that's what you'll end up being.' If they stop buying cheap stuff – the polyster dress, the supermarket cologne – they will begin to lose their 'discount mentality' and put themselves in a position to be blessed. 'If you are ever going to receive God's best, you're going to have to break through the wall of containment and think big.'[54]

When the formula does not work

Of course, the formula does not always produce the desired result, not everyone gets what they have confessed; and this has required an apologetic. One way of explaining the discrepancy would be to say that the failure is only apparent: the prayer of faith has been answered but there is sometimes a lag before appearances catch up with the new spiritual reality. For example, JohnAvanzini thinks that he actually became prosperous before he had any money:

> I heard the Word of God and agreed with it and prosperity became a reality for me. But I was tangled up with all those bank notes. I'd taken years to cultivate that patch of notes. And it took some time to get rid of them. In my new mentality, I was free of that debt. It just took some time for that slow process of the natural to catch up with the mega light speed of the Spirit.[55]

Copeland insists that the prayer of faith made in accordance with the word of God must be successful, but it may be necessary to wait: 'through patience, you must hold fast to this Word concerning healing, regardless of symptoms or pain, knowing that patience *will* produce the experience of healing.'[56] Dollar warns against always expecting instantaneous results when a principle of Scripture is applied. God has instituted a 'law of breakthrough' which states that 'if you want a breakthrough, you will have to take the principle and do it over and over and over again until something happens'.[57] The presence of sin in the life of the believer will also be an impediment to effective faith because it means that the Word of God, on which the *word of faith* is based, is not being taken seriously. 'Once you know God's ways and turn your backs on your wicked ways in repentance, total prosperity is available to you.'[58]

More commonly, however, failure is attributed to some defect in the faith of the person praying: 'If it doesn't work,' Hagin insists, 'it's because *I* don't work it.'[59] He draws a distinction between real faith and the sort of hesitant, half-hearted, ineffectual 'mental assent' that believers often mistake for faith – a faith which believes only *after* it has seen. We do not believe in our hearts that God will give us what we ask for; we merely *hope* that perhaps, if it's his will, he will answer our prayers.[60] Real faith is measured by its refusal to accept the symptoms and by its willingness to act *as though* it had already been received.

If the symptoms of the sickness persist after the confession of healing, this may be interpreted as a subterfuge on Satan's part to rob us of what is rightfully ours: if the believer can be tricked into making a negative confession ('See, it hasn't worked!'), the healing will be invalidated. The reality of the symptoms, including pain, must be denied: this is the real test of faith.

> Remember you are *healed by faith*, and not by sight. *Faith* is the *evidence of healing – not the fact* that the cancer has left your body. *Your confession, between the time that you pray and claim your healing until it is seen in your body, is what causes it to come....* Now your body may *scream louder* than ever that you are sick. Fever, pain, nausea, lumps, etc. This is where your *confession* comes in. YOU MUST CONFESS THE WORD OF GOD IN THE FACE OF EVERY SYMPTOM AND EVERY PAIN. This is *faith* versus *sense* knowledge.[61]

> I never have been able to receive physical healing for myself without first believing I have it. Every symptom in my body cries out, "You don't have it." I simply stand firm on what God's Word says about my healing and continue to claim that I am healed. Results are then forthcoming. But if I were to sit around, groan and sigh, gripe, and complain, waiting until every symptom was gone and any feelings corresponded with my faith before I believed, I never would get very far, because *"faith is.... the evidence of things not seen."*[62]

> Get your mind on the answer. See yourself as having received. Constantly affirm, even in the face of contradictory evidence, that God has heard your prayer because the Word says so. That's when you'll get results.... You have to believe you've got

> it before you can receive it.... The believing comes *before* the receiving.[63]

The same argument may account for the recurrence of symptoms after a person has been healed by faith. It is relatively easy to believe at a revival meeting, where there is a 'mass faith' in operation. But if people do not have a proper foundation of faith, a proper grasp of their authority, Satan finds it easy to delude them subsequently and the sickness returns.[64]

Word of Faith teachers argue, finally, that our faith in God is frequently hampered by a number of misconceptions that encourage a defeatist attitude. Copeland points out, for example, that Christians often understand the statement in Romans 8:28 that 'all things work together for good for those who love God' to mean that God can bring good out of the things that go wrong. This, he believes, is merely an excuse for failure. The 'all things' that work for good are not negative or harmful circumstances but the spiritual resources that God has made available: 'the Word of God, the gifts of the Spirit, the Name of Jesus, and the power weapons of the Body of Christ'.[65] A rather more subtle form of the argument is that believers fail to achieve prosperity because their faith is held back by the power of the subconscious mind:

> Most of us have been taught since our childhood that Jesus was poor. Early in our lives, we developed an inner image of Jesus walking around barefoot and penniless. So, every time we begin to build faith for prosperity, our subconscious mind jerks the rug out from under us. It says, "You're supposed to be like Jesus. Jesus was poor – so you have to be poor too." ... You're never going to be able to receive prosperity from God as long as your subconscious mind is filled with misconceptions about Who Jesus was financially, if you're ever going to have the kind of stable faith you need to receive the riches God has for you, you're going to have to dig out the false ideas and replace them with the truth.[66]

* * * *

Proponents of the Word of Faith doctrine hold that faith is effective, in the final analysis, because God is powerful and because he has put himself under an absolute obligation to do for his children what he has promised in his Word. But it is the methodology of faith that especially characterizes the movement's teaching and practice: How do we get it to work? How do we guarantee results? How do we account for the apparent failures? The movement is captivated by the ideal of the man of God who has erased from his mind all fear and doubt, who speaks, prays, commands with supreme confidence in the efficacy of the law of faith, at whose words the demons flee, sickness disappears, and wealth accumulates. This brings us to the next stage in our exposition of Word of Faith teaching: the theology of health and wealth.

4

What you get is health and wealth

'Why did Jesus come?' Kenneth Hagin asks. 'To found a church? To improve on humanity or to give us a code of conduct? No, He came for one purpose: "*...I am come that they might have life, and that they might have it more abundantly*" (Jn. 10:10).'[1] This is the 'God-kind of life' or 'zoe' that the believer receives when she is born again: 'It is, in reality, God imparting His very nature, substance, and being to our human spirits.'[2] The presence of this new life in a person will bring about far-reaching changes of lifestyle and character and thinking. But it will also be manifested in changes in the external and material circumstances of that person's life: above all, it is argued, the God-kind of life is characterized not by sickness and poverty but by health and prosperity.

Health

The Word of Faith movement teaches that the atonement provides not only for the forgiveness of sin but also for the healing of diseases. A person who has been saved should not be sick: 'God wants us to live our full length of time out here below without sickness and without disease. That's His best. Not everybody attains to it, but it's there anyway.'[3]

The main foundation for this belief is found in Isaiah 53:4-5 in the vision of the servant of the Lord who 'has borne our infirmities and carried our diseases' and by whose 'bruises we are healed'.[4] Matthew applies the prophecy to Jesus' healing ministry: 'He took our infirmities and bore our diseases' (Mt. 8:17; cf. 1 Pet. 2:24).[5] On the basis of these texts the Word of Faith movement teaches that the salvation which Jesus brought includes the healing of sickness. Proverbs 4:22 encapsulates the rule by which we attain this healing: the words of God (the reference is, in fact, to the wise words of a father to his son) are 'life to those who find them, and healing to all their flesh'. Hagin argues that by not letting such divine 'words' as Matthew 8:17 escape from our sight, by keeping them within our hearts (Prov. 4:21), we may ensure that we remain free from sickness.[6]

Sickness is regarded not as an accidental or purely physical phenomenon but as symptomatic of a fundamental spiritual disorder, of the control that Satan has over human lives. In many cases the persistence of illness is attributed to the activity of demons. Hagin relates a vision in which an evil spirit responsible for causing cancer in a young girl appeared in the form of 'a small monkey hanging onto her body'.[7] But if sickness is a spiritual disorder, it should be dealt with in much the same way that we deal with sin. 'You need to fight the temptation to be sick,' Kenneth Copeland insists, 'just as you would fight the temptation to lie or steal. Satan will tempt you with sickness, but you don't have to give in. You can resist him with the Word of God like Jesus did.'[8]

Hagin has developed a rather complex classification of the means of healing. First, there is the spiritual gift of healing, which is unpredictable because 'the gifts of the Spirit are manifested as the Holy Spirit wills (1 Cor. 12:11)'.[9] Secondly, there is the option of being healed by faith in the Word of God, which 'will always work for anyone who dares to believe and act on it'.[10] Thirdly, there is the 'anointing of healing power'. This is understood in much more tangible and material terms: it is a power that may be felt by the person who ministers it and transferred by touch or other physical means. It is manifested in Jesus' life in those instances when 'power' is said to have gone out of him (Mk. 5:30; Lk. 6:19) or when people were healed by touching his clothes (Mt. 14:36).[11] Similarly, in

Acts 19:12 people were healed when they came into contact with handkerchiefs and aprons that had touched Paul's body. Hagin claims to have been anointed by Jesus with this healing power.[12]

There is some ambivalence in the Word of Faith movement about the use of medication. The major leaders tend to allow people to seek medical help if they fear that their faith will prove inadequate.[13] Hagin outlines the sort of secondary and supportive role that may be permitted to medical science: 'Doctors often can keep people alive until we can get enough Word in them to get them healed.'[14] Hagin himself appears to have been granted special dispensation for his wife to have an operation to remove a goitre that had not responded to prayer.[15] He also had treatment for an injured elbow, though he believes that the injury was God's way of telling him that he was out of his 'perfect will'.[16]

Prosperity

Just as Christ 'carried our diseases' on the cross, so, it is argued, he also suffered the curse of poverty. Paul's statement in 2 Corinthians 8:9 is interpreted quite literally: 'though he was rich, yet for your sakes he became poor, so that by his poverty you might become rich'. Trevor Newport thinks that Jesus was not actually poor during his life, so this verse must mean that he became poor on the cross in order to deliver us from poverty that we might be rich – 'not just spiritually but financially as well!'[17]

Believers now have a right to prosperity because Christ has won back the resources of the world that were lost to Satan. Hagin tells the story:

> ...the Lord spoke to me and said, "Don't pray for money any-more. You have authority through my Name to claim prosper-ity. I already have put gold, silver, and cattle on a thousand hills for my man Adam, and I gave him dominion over it. After he sold out to Satan, the second Adam, Jesus Christ, came to

> redeem you from the hand of the enemy and to remove you from the curse of the law. Now, instead of praying that I would do it, because I have made provision for your needs, all you need to do is say, 'Satan, take your hands off my money.' Just claim what you need. You reign in life by Christ Jesus."[18]

This entitlement is sometimes expressed in quite immoderate and self-indulgent terms. Hagin assures us that God 'wants His children to eat the best, He wants them to wear the best clothing, He wants them to drive the best cars, and he wants them to have the best of everything.'[19] F.K.C. Price repeats the sentiment: '...by walking in God's financial plan, you can have the $15,000 automobile, wear the $300 suit, and buy the $100 designer shoes. God does not care. He wants His kids to look good.'[20]

Old Testament promises regarding the well-being and prosperity of God's people are appropriated for the new people of God in Christ. The promise that God would bless Abraham (eg. Gen. 17:1-9) is especially important because it can more easily be shown to have relevance for those who are Abraham's descendants through faith (Gal. 3:14, 29). A prominent aspect of this blessing, in keeeping with the principle established in such texts as Proverbs 10:22 ('The blessing of the LORD makes rich, and he adds no sorrow with it'; cf. Ps. 112:1-3), was that Abraham became extremely wealthy (eg. Gen. 24:35).[21] The Mosaic covenant, with its repeated assurances that God would prosper Israel if the people remained faithful to the covenant (eg. Ex. 23:25-26; Deut. 6:1-3; 7:12-15; 15:4-6; 28:1-14; 29:9; Is. 1:19), is regarded only as a particular application of the seminal promise that God would bless Abraham and his descendants. Deuteronomy 8:18 is understood to encapsulate a universal principle of divinely guaranteed prosperity: 'But remember the LORD your God, for it is he who gives you power to get wealth, so that he may confirm his covenant that he swore to your ancestors, as he is doing today.'

The Old Testament Wisdom literature endorses the 'good life' as a gift from God: 'Likewise all to whom God gives wealth and possessions and whom he enables to enjoy them, and to accept their lot and find enjoyment in their toil – this is the gift of God.' John Avanzini insists that an impoverished lifestyle is a fundamental denial of the goodness of God: 'let me assure you, that is not God's way. He says, "There is more than enough." He says, "The good life is your portion!"'[22]

The covenant with Abraham was an 'eternal covenant', established with all the generations of his 'offspring' (Gen. 17:7). Christians, therefore, although they have not always appreciated the fact, are heirs to the same prosperity: 'God has obligated Himself to bless you as He blessed Abraham. The promise to you is that God will establish His covenant with you in this generation. He has given His Word to prosper you in the same way He prospered Abraham.'[23] This is not an optional extra for Christians: 'The covenant cannot be established in your life unless you believe God's Word concerning prosperity. Let there be no doubt about God's will. God's will is to establish His covenant in the earth. Prosperity is a major requirement in the establishment of God's will.'[24]

What is expressed biblically through the language of covenant can be restated in terms of spiritual laws: they are an expression of the consistency of God. The law of prosperity which God revealed to Abraham will also work for the Christian today. By putting these laws into operation we glorify the God who spoke them and add 'one more defeat to Satan who said it would not work'.[25] As with the law of faith, however, the implementaton of the law of prosperity is not restricted to Christians: 'God didn't bless him because he was a sinner. He received God's blessing because he honored God. God has a certain law of prosperity and when you get into contact with that law and those rules, it just works for you – *whoever you are*. When you come into contact with God's laws, they work.'[26]

Jesus told his disciples that not one of them who had left home or family or friends or possessions for his sake and for the sake of the gospel would fail to 'receive a hundredfold now in this age… and in the age to come eternal life'

(Mk. 10:29-30). According to Word of Faith teaching this illustrates a key, universal law of prosperity: whatever you give for the sake of the gospel, you will receive a hundredfold in return.[27] Programmed into the economy of the kingdom of God is a formula which ensures a very high rate of return on any investment made. If the full return does not materialize immediately, Gloria Copeland suggests that Jesus promised only that the money would come sometime 'in this life' (*en tōi kairōi toutōi*, translated 'in this age' in the NRSV).[28]

Finally, appeal is frequently made to John's expressed wish to Gaius 'that thou mayest prosper and be in health, even as thy soul prospereth' (3 Jn. 2 KJV), which is taken to mean that true spiritual well-being consists of mental, bodily and financial prosperity.[29]

On the basis of these texts Word of Faith teachers conclude that, just as it is an abnormality for a believer to be sick, so we dishonour God by not laying claim to the wealth that has been vouchsafed to us in Christ, who has redeemed us from the bondage of poverty. Sovereignty over the earth, they argue, has been restored to the church, and with it comes the right to possess the riches of the earth. Poverty is not a mark of spirituality or holiness but a symptom of the failure to attain the prosperity which God wishes to give us.[30] The Word of Faith critique of traditional Christianity is quite stark: by its ideological distrust of prosperity the church has allowed the wealth of the world to fall into the hands of Satan and as a result now finds itself at the mercy of an ungodly financial system.[31]

A divine economy

On the basis of the belief that God wishes to bestow material prosperity upon his children, the Word of Faith movement has gone some way towards describing a 'divine economy' – a thoroughgoing alternative to the secular economy, powered, it claims, not by the profit motive but by faith in the goodness of God and the dynamic of giving and receiving.

True prosperity

Word of Faith teachers insist that the economy of God demands a way of thinking that is quite contrary to worldly systems of economics. On the one hand, it is driven not by human greed but by the generosity of God. On the other, godly prosperity is much more than financial success. So Creflo Dollar writes: 'Say all the time that the Lord takes pleasure in prospering His people in their spirits, souls, bodies, marriages, and everything that affects them in this life. Say that God wants you to be in control of all circumstances, not only financial ones.'[32] Copeland insists: 'The absolute priority in studying prosperity is that you should *never* think of it from a carnal viewpoint, from the world's attitude.... If you're not careful, when you think of the laws of prosperity, all you will see is money – only a very small part of prosperity. *True prosperity is God manifesting Himself to us in His Word.*'[33] Kenneth Hagin Jr. warns new students at Rhema Bible Training Center: 'If you came here with ears itching to get faith so you can drive Cadillacs, fly airplanes, or have million-dollar homes, go home.'[34] The person whom God blesses with prosperity should take care not to allow his wealth to usurp the place of God in his life. But anxieties about the corrupting influence of wealth should not lead the church to embrace an economy of poverty and insufficiency. If Satan can seduce us with visions of great riches, he can also incapacitate us with a false ideology of self-denial. Prosperity teaching repudiates the deeply ingrained religious premise that poverty is inherently godly:

> Abject poverty, ignorance, and starvation are *not* God's perfect will for His children. He did not create a world of lack. He did not envision a Kingdom of want; He created a world of abundance! The poverty and insufficiency that we now witness in the world are the creation of the evil one: want, hunger, disease, and death are the best that his depraved nature could bring forth.[35]

Sowing and reaping

Although individual prosperity, as with healing, may be confessed and claimed by faith, the fundamental principle undergirding the economy of the kingdom of God in Word of Faith teaching is the law of 'sowing and reaping' – a 'universal law of divine reciprocity', as Price calls it.[36] Galatians 6:7 is seminal: 'Do not be deceived; God is not mocked, for you reap whatever you sow'. Similar statements are found in Luke 6:38; 2 Corinthians 9:6-12; Philippians 4:19.[37] Copeland gives the example of the boy who brought the five loaves and two fish to Jesus (Jn. 6:5-13), arguing, on the one hand, that the miracle could not have taken place if the boy had not been willing to give *his own* meal, and on the other, rather more speculatively, that he was rewarded with the twelve baskets of leftovers. The story is presented as a paradigm for giving today: 'God's way is for goods to come into the ministry – for the ministry to receive it, handle it, bless it and distribute it, or sow it – then for it to go out, multiplied in greater number than when it came in. That's the anointing of increase.'[38]

The principle of sowing and reaping is frequently presented in very formulaic and utilitarian terms: the practice of naming a seed in order to gain a particular material blessing is an example.[39] But behind it lies a far-reaching and quite radical understanding of how the economy of the kingdom of God might work. The argument is that whereas the secular economy is governed by rules of earning wealth and keeping it, within the kingdom of God the controlling principle must be one of *giving*: we work in order to give (cf. Eph. 4:28) and we give with the expectation of receiving from God. What drives this economy is not the compulsion to accumulate wealth and possessions but the desire to give and the willingness of God to bless *his children*.[40]

Prosperity teaching insists that believers are under a covenantal obligation to tithe and that this constitutes the cornerstone of biblical prosperity: 'God's financial blessings are reserved for the tither alone.'[41] Ten per cent of gross income belongs not to us but to God (cf. Lev. 27:30); if we withhold it, we are robbing God (Mal. 3:8), and, technically at least, owe twenty per cent interest on the tithe that is unpaid (Lev. 27:30).[42] However, because the tithe belongs to God already, it is not something that we actually *give* and cannot be factored into the 'give, and it will be given to you' equation (Lk. 6:38). Avanzini argues that tithing merely opens the windows of heaven. It is the offerings that we give over and above the tithe that determine the abundance of blessing that is actually poured out.[43]

By giving to God and to others we store up money for ourselves in a heavenly account that is beyond the reach of thieves and invulnerable to the vagaries of the world's financial system.[44] Believers should realize that they are in a position simply to claim the prosperity which now rightly belongs to them. When Jesus told his disciples to 'store up for yourselves treasures in heaven', he did not mean that these savings would not become available to them until they died. He meant, Copeland argues, that the 'wealth' that they acquired through their faithfulness and obedience was deposited there, rather than in some earthly bank, for safe keeping *until it was needed on earth*. That wealth could then be withdrawn from the disciple's heavenly account through positive confession.[45]

Undoubtedly the arguments about giving can be self-serving. The tacit assumption is that a good proportion of people's giving will be channelled into the Word of Faith ministries.[46] We are also frequently left with the impression that giving has been made just another excuse for greed: 'If you want a nice watch, why don't you give one away and be expectant for your nice one to come in? If you want a nice car, why don't you sow for one, then you can be expectant for a new car?'[47] But alongside this we find a strong, and seemingly genuine, appreciation of how much could be done in terms of evangelism and the alleviation of suffering if the church had the faith and boldness to assert its right to greater financial resources. God will bless his people in every respect so that they may be a blessing to others.[48] To the question 'how much money is enough?' Avanzini answers: enough to do what God requires. He lists twelve things that God asks us to do with our money:

tithing joyfully, funding global evangelism, contributing toward 'a better-than-average standard of living for your minister', provision for one's own household, giving good gifts to our children, keeping a good savings account, funding a proper retirement plan, paying bills on time, paying taxes, avoiding debt, giving generously to the poor, and lending to every believer who asks.[49]

This intention is often overlooked by the critics. Copeland maintains that prosperity is properly 'the ability to use the power of God to meet the needs of mankind'.[50] He argues that for believers to be satisfied with a simple lifestyle is not humility but, paradoxically, selfishness: 'They could ask God for a million dollars, take out just enough to meet their simple needs, and give the rest away. But that doesn't even occur to them because, when it comes to money, they've been brainwashed by a world that says if you have it, you have to keep it!'[51]

John MacArthur accuses the 'advocates of the prosperity gospel' of teaching that wealth is a sign of God's favour.[52] The accusation is not entirely unfounded, but it is misleading. An authentic prosperity theology holds that wealth is given to us when we are obedient to the terms of the covenant, above all when we give out of 'love for the Lord and our desire to bless Him and His people'.[53] Prosperity teachers would fully endorse MacArthur's argument that 'God's plan for the believer's genuine prosperity… is simply this: *You and I must give away what we have*.'[54] They would merely add that such giving raises the expectation of receiving a much greater return from God.

Practical instruction

Alongside the overtly faith-based methods of achieving prosperity we also find a good deal of practical instruction about managing personal finances and generating wealth. Texts from Proverbs have been found in support of such mundane practices as working longer hours, taking a second job, or seeking promotion.[55] In particular, the Word of Faith movement is strongly opposed to borrowing because it makes the debtor a slave to the world's financial system (cf. Prov. 22:7), the tail rather than the head (cf. Deut. 28:12-13). Instead, the believer should ask God for whatever money he needs.[56] The emphasis on debt reduction in prosperity teaching is clearly a response to a serious and widespread social problem. Avanzini argues that freedom from debt should be normative for the kingdom of God: God wants us to live debt-free lives. The biblical basis is found in such stories as the miraculous provision of oil to pay off the widow's debts (2 Ki. 4:1-7), the recovery of the borrowed axe-head (2 Ki. 6:1-7), and Nehemiah's financial reforms (Neh. 5:1-13). The Word of Faith methodology is applied to debt management in a quite formulaic and practical manner: 'This dynamic Bible truth will divinely energize your out-of-debt program. Your new attitude will work *for* you instead of *against* you. Start this very day to speak words of death to your debt and words of life to your out-of-debt program.'[57]

The end-time transfer

There is, finally, an important eschatological dimension to the Word of Faith argument about prosperity. The wealth that is now being created and amassed by the world, which the church should have claimed for itself, is currently being used to finance the kingdom of darkness. In the end-times, however, it will be transferred to the church: 'the sinner's wealth is laid up for the righteous' (Prov. 13:22; cf. 28:8; Job 27:13-17; Eccl. 2:26; Is. 61:5-6).[58] James' warning to the rich that they have laid up treasure for the last days is understood as a reference to this transfer of wealth. This supposed redistribution of the world's wealth is sometimes taken to be the means by which God will finance the preaching of the gospel to the world in the last days.[59] Gloria Copeland quotes a prophecy given by Charles Capps in 1978: 'Yes, there's coming a FINANCIAL INVERSION in the world's system. It's been held in reservoirs of wicked men for days on end. But the end is nigh. Those reservoirs shall be tapped and shall be drained into the gospel of Jesus Christ.'[60] Some prosperity teachers envisage the formation of an elite corps of spiritual financiers who will receive the wealth that has been transferred from the world and use it to fund the end-time harvest.[61]

* * * *

It is easy for critics of the Word of Faith movement to complain about the preoccupation with wealth, the subtle exhortations to give to this or that Word of Faith ministry. It is easy enough, as we shall see later, to cite examples of how Scripture has been bent out of shape to support the principles and goals of prosperity teaching. But in our haste to denounce the errors, we can easily miss some of the quite sensible, even biblical, qualifications and safeguards that have been incorporated into the teaching. A more sympathetic appraisal of the message will take note of the generally consistent determination to connect prosperity with righteousness and godliness. If we are going to quote Gloria Copeland's extravagant principle of a hundredfold return on our giving, we should also quote her statement that 'Godly prosperity is the result of putting God's Word – all of it, not just the parts about financial prosperity – first place in your life.'[62]

The argument, at its best, is not that the pursuit of wealth is a good and godly thing, but that when we first seek the kingdom of God and his righteousness, all these other things – family, friends, property, possessions, money – will be given to us *in abundance* – because the new life in Christ is a prosperous life. In Gloria Copeland's words, when you obey the Word of God, you become a 'candidate for increase'.[63] 'Prosperity,' as Price writes, 'ought to be the result of a quality of life, commitment and dedication that is in line with God's Word.'[64] Of course, we may still not agree with the basic premise and we may have doubts about the motivation behind even the more moderate and balanced statements, but it is important that we do not disconnect the central doctrinal claims of the movement from this wider body of practical and often quite reasonable teaching.

5

The debate about origins

The origins of the Word of Faith movement have been a matter of some controversy and, indeed, have been a decisive consideration in the argument over whether or not the movement should be considered heterodox. The movement was born and raised somewhere on the margins of the extended family of Pentecostalism, and although the family has not always approved of the child's often reckless and extravagant lifestyle, they have generally remained on speaking terms. In recent years, however, doubts have been raised about the *paternity* of the child. Some scholars have ventured to question whether the more eccentric personality traits might not be attributable to a theological indiscretion, an illicit union, resulting in the introduction of foreign genetic material into the lineage. A little investigation has led to accusations that there are one or two skeletons in the Word of Faith closet.

The Pentecostal ancestry

The American Holiness Movement

The revivals of the early nineteenth century in America anticipated later Pentecostalism in a number of ways. Of particular importance for this study was a common emphasis on the work of the Spirit in sanctifying and 'perfecting' the believer through a 'second work of grace'. The writings of John Wesley and the ethos of Methodism provided the basis for the later Holiness movement with its stress on the transformation of the inner life.

Several of the distinctive emphases of the Word of Faith movement began to emerge in this intense revivalist environment. The perfectionist doctrine was developed further by the the evangelist Charles Finney (1792-1875), who also defined many of the principles of 'prevailing' or 'effectual prayer'. Finney maintained that if prayer was definite in its objectives, in accordance with the will of God, and accompanied by unswerving faith, it would always be successful.[1] The 'altar theology' of Phoebe Palmer (1807-1874) included the idea that sanctification came about not through arduous self-discipline but through faith in the Word; that faith had the predictability of a 'spiritual law'; that it was not an inner disposition only but needed to be confessed and acted upon; and that the promises of God might overrule the evidence of the physical senses.[2]

In 1846 E.O. Allen explicitly linked the Holiness doctrine of Christian perfection with the belief in divine healing.[3] If sickness was a consequence of sin, he argued, the experience of sanctification – the progressive or, according to some, instantaneous removal of sin from a person's nature – should result in the elimination of illness.[4] Allen's account of his own healing reveals an obstinate refusal to accept the contrary evidence of symptoms, a tenacious adherence to the conviction that God had healed him. The Word of Faith emphasis on acting according to one's professed faith can be found in the teachings of Elizabeth Mix, a highly respected and successful black evangelist, who had been healed of tuberculosis through Allen's ministry. Mix told her patients that, regardless of how they felt, they should act out their belief that they had been healed.[5] She wrote to the young invalid, Carrie Judd: 'I want you to pray for yourself, and pray believing, and then *act faith*. It makes no difference how you feel, but get right out of bed and begin to walk by faith.'[6]

The most influential figure in the Faith-Cure movement was the Episcopalian Charles Cullis (1833-1892). Cullis, a homeopathic practitioner from Boston, set out to replicate the 'faith principles' of George Müller in founding homes for 'indigent and incurable consumptives'. Through contact with German faith-healers Cullis became convinced that radical faith should also be exercised towards divine healing. Others picked up on this. W.E. Boardman, who went on to become a leader of the Keswick Holiness movement, found in Psalm 103:2-3 a powerful argument for the view that healing was an integral part of redemption in Christ: 'Bless the LORD, O my soul, and forget not all his benefits: Who forgiveth all thine iniquities; who healeth all thy diseases' (KJV).[7] Carrie Judd Montgomery published a monthly magazine, *Triumphs of Faith*, which was 'devoted to faith-healing and to the promotion of Christian Holiness'.[8] In the opening editorial she wrote: 'Christ bore our sickness as well as our sins, and if we may reckon ourselves free from the one, why not from the other?'[9]

The teachings of this healing movement were articulated most clearly and most radically in the writings of A.J. Gordon (1836-1895), A.B. Simpson (1844-1919), and Captain R. Kelso Carter (1849-1928). Gordon's important work *The Ministry of Healing: Miracles of Cure in All Ages* countered the arguments of the cessationist consensus, but also sought to differentiate authentic Christian healing from the teachings of the burgeoning Christian Science movement.[10] Simpson, who founded the Christian and Missionary Alliance, added to the belief that healing was provided in the atonement an objection to the use of the 'means' of modern medicine. His argument for the necessity of confession constitutes a powerful apologetic for the modern Word of Faith movement:

> Faith drives the nail, but confession clinches it; and until we step out, committing ourselves and making our attitude irrevocable and public, we are liable to be moved and shaken.... Christ required confession from those whom He healed, and He still requires it. If we would make any advance in spiritual blessing, we must commit ourselves irrevocably to what faith claims, and go forward without doubt or calculation. It is a

> sublime spectacle to behold a human spirit that has committed itself to God's Word before all the universe, standing and waiting upon heaven to help and answer. For such a spirit all heaven must be concerned, and we can imagine God upon His throne, saying, "Something must be done for this heart that thus fully trusts me." Beloved, are you wholly committed to God, and have your lips sealed your covenant and claim?[11]

Carter later retracted two of the more extreme positions: the view that healing was automatically provided in the atonement, with its corollary that the continued presence of sickness was indicative of sin or a lack of faith; and the repudiation of medical procedures. This change of mind, which came about after he needed medical treatment for an 'attack of brain prostration', proved liberating, for, as Dayton quotes him, he 'no longer felt called upon to ransack the universe for a reason for any ache or pain that came along. It did not follow that he was a transgressor because he was a sufferer.' He came in the end to the more moderate opinion that healing was not an automatic entitlement but a 'special favour', to be granted or withheld according to the sovereign will of God.[12]

The ministries of these faith-healers also had a strong practical and social orientation. In addition to his homes for consumptives, Cullis set up orphanages, various other homes for the seriously ill, a faith-cure home, a home for 'fallen women', a home for the insane, and a college and orphanage for southern black students. Impressed by Cullis' compassion for the needy and destitute, Gordon was instrumental in founding the Boston Industrial Temporary Home for the care of drunkards and participated in a range of social and political activities including the Prohibition Party, the women's rights movement, relief for the unemployed, and the protection of Chinese immigrants. A.B. Simpson established rescue missions, a home for the rehabilitation of prostitutes, temperance homes, a free dispensary, an orphanage and a prison reform ministry.[13] It is worth drawing attention to this dimension of the nineteenth century faith ministries because social action does not always feature high on the agendas of their modern counterparts.

Out of Zion

Towards the end of the nineteenth century the arguments about divine healing were somewhat radicalized, most notably through the influence of J.A. Dowie (1847-1907)[14] and the nascent Pentecostal movement. Dowie reinstated the connection between sin and sickness: 'Sin is a cause, of which Disease, Death and Hell are the inevitable effects and consequences.... Holiness is a cause, of which Health, Eternal Life and Heaven are the glorious effects and consequences.'[15] He believed that divine healing was always accomplished instantaneously and that medical doctors, whether they knew it or not, were in league with the devil. A year at medical school in England had convinced him that contemporary medicine was a dangerous amalgum of ignorance and hypocrisy.

Influenced by the proto-Pentecostal Irvingites, Dowie developed a successful healing ministry, first in Australia, then later in America. In 1890 he moved to Chicago where he founded the massive 'City of Zion' with the intention that it should provide a working model of a godly society.[16] Dowie's antagonism towards medicine, his universalist position on salvation and his radical social policies attracted severe criticism.[17] But in the short term, at least, Zion was a success, and by 1898 he had established two hundred local congregations across the country. The movement's social impact is recorded by P.G. Chappell:

> His church members canvassed the poorer tenements of Chicago to care for the poor and elderly, distributing food, clothing, and fuel; cooking meals; scrubbing floors; finding employment, etc. As a social reformer he campaigned for a free national system of education, and fought discrimination, racism, anti-semitism, pornography, birth control measures, gambling, drugs, tobacco, breweries, saloons, and secret organizations.[18]

Dowie suffered a stroke in 1905 which left him paralyzed, but the reins of leadership were taken up by Charles Fox Parham

(1873-1929), who fused the doctrine of divine healing with the Pentecostal belief in the baptism of the Holy Spirit. Out of Zion came a number of influential Pentecostal healing evangelists, perhaps the most important of whom was F.F. Bosworth (1877-1958).[19] With his large-scale healing campaigns, his Radio Revival Ministry, and a well-organized administrative staff handling donations and requests for prayer he established a format for Pentecostal evangelistic organizations that was replicated to great effect by a multitude of successors.

Most of the Word of Faith arguments about faith and healing can be found in Bosworth's influential book, *Christ the Healer*.[20] Bosworth taught that the sick person must first know with certainty that it is God's will to heal her. She should then believe that her prayer has been heard even if the healing is not yet physically apparent. If these rules are followed, 'we can *always* bring to pass the fulfilment of any Divine promise'.[21] Bosworth held that healing is included in the atonement and is currently available to the believer on that basis (14-39), that there can be no intrinsic spiritual benefit in suffering (59-61), and that healing is available to all who seek it (41-61).

The post-war healing revival

In May 1946 an angel reportedly appeared to William Branham (1909-1965) and promised that he would receive the gift of healing and preach to thousands. The campaigns that ensued sparked off a major healing revival. The controversial Latter Rain movement was a direct product of Branham's ministry and bore the imprint of his rather eccentric beliefs.[22] The other outstanding figure of this revival was Oral Roberts (1918-), described by the historian David Harrell as 'one of the most influential religious leaders in the world in the twentieth century'.[23] Although at heart a crusading evangelist, Roberts more than anyone else exploited the emerging medium of television in order to promote a gospel of faith and healing across America. Deeply impressed by the apparent assurance of prosperity in 3 John 2 Roberts devised a 'Blessing-Pact', which promised financial blessing for people who gave $100 to his ministry.[24] Phrases such as 'God is a good God', 'expect a miracle', and 'seed-faith' gained widespread currency as a result of Roberts' teaching, preparing the ground for the emergence of the modern Word of Faith movement.

In a more sociologically oriented analysis Hollinger suggests three general reasons for the growth of the Word of Faith movement at this time. He points, first, to the disadvantaged social and economic context in which the movement developed: 'Coming from such marginal contexts, the faith preachers have often despised their early poverty and deprivation. A gospel of economic and physical well-being was appealing to such persons and continues to provide hope for the thousands of followers who seek release from a life of socio-cultural disenfranchisement.'[25] Secondly, the pursuit of physical well-being and material prosperity had become a dominant theme in American culture. Thirdly, there was the fund-raising imperative. The big independent evangelistic organizations were unhampered by the constraints and bureaucracy of denominational oversight, but they were also on their own financially at a time when radio and television were proving indispensable but very expensive tools for ministry. David Harrell comments: 'In the early stages of the revival, the ability to inspire large collections in the meetings was crucial. The nightly offerings were a highlight of the services.'[26]

In this context, many of the principles that had been developed to account for and validate the practice of divine healing were transferred to the financial realm. A.A. Allen (1911-1970), for example, claimed on one occasion that he had been able to pay a $410 printing bill when God turned one dollar bills into twenty dollar bills. 'I believe I can command God to perform a miracle for you financially,' he boasted. 'When you do, God can turn dollar bills into twenties.'[27] If God could heal the sick, he could also provide finances for overstretched evangelistic organizations. But there was an important difference between health and wealth: people had control over their money. While the evangelist or teacher might believe in *faith* that God would provide the financial resources necessary to keep the organization afloat, the whole process could be made much more reliable if people had a good incentive to respond to the promptings of the Holy Spirit and give to the ministries. The belief that God would abundantly bless those who gave generously to support the work of the kingdom provided just that incentive – and at the same time justified a certain ostentation on the part of those who had discovered this secret of divine success. The wealth of the evangelist was the clearest possible sign that the laws of divine prosperity worked.

The potential for abuse, it hardly needs to be said, was enormous. In 1949 Gordon Lindsay, one of the most respected leaders of the healing revival, issued a passionate warning: 'This revival can be greatly retarded if there is a continual auctioneering for money in the campaigns. There are some who are short-sighted enough to have destroyed their usefulness to the kingdom of God by an offensive handling of finances.'[28] In the early 1950s the Assemblies of God began to dissociate itself from the revivalists, worried about the detrimental effect of the independent evangelistic campaigns on the ministry of local churches and alarmed by the dubious fund-raising techniques and the promises of financial blessing.[29] Despite the criticism, by the 1960s, in Harrell's words, 'the promise of prosperity had come to rival healing as a major theme of the revival'.[30] Around this time, however, Pentecostal revivalism began to give way to the new charismatic movement. Kenneth Hagin was one of those who made the transition to this 'less-separatistic and less-legalistic expression of faith'.[31]

It is apparent that many of the characteristic teachings and practices of the Word of Faith movement have their antecedents in the Holiness-Pentecostal tradition: the attribution of sickness to sin and the work of Satan; the inclusion of healing in the atonement; the denial of the physical symptoms of disease; the disapproval of healing by means of medical science; the understanding of faith as a spiritual law; the activation of faith through positive confession; the professed reliance on faith for funding.[32] In their organization and style the major Word of Faith ministries can be seen as a natural development of the high-profile healing ministries.[33] There is the same dependence on a charismatic preacher, the same tendency towards megalomania and expansionism, the same enthusiastic adoption of new technologies. The predilection of the Word of Faith movement for grandiose and utopian building projects, such as Kenneth Copeland's ambition to create a revival capital of the world, has its antecedents in the Holiness-Pentecostal tradition: the homes of healing established by men such as Cullis and Gordon, Dowie's City of Zion and Oral Roberts' university and medical centre.

There are certain elements of Word of Faith teaching, however, that do not appear in the mainstream of the Holiness-Pentecostal tradition: for example, the peculiar atonement mythology of two deaths and the punishment of Christ in hell, and the elaborate 'metaphysics' of faith. The preoccupation with prosperity is anticipated in the teaching of Pentecostals such as Thomas Wyatt, A.A. Allen and Oral Roberts,[34] but the theoretical underpinning is missing. Where did these extraneous elements come from? If Pentecostalism gave birth to the Word of Faith movement, we now need to consider the delicate and rather complex question of who the father was.

Word of Faith and the metaphysical cults

The argument has been put forward that the distinctive doctrines propounded by Hagin, Copeland and others have much in common with the teaching of New Thought metaphysics.[35] Daniel McConnell's book, *A Different Gospel*, first published in 1988, has been especially influential in this regard, with its rigorous thesis that the Word of Faith movement is a cultic wolf dressed in Pentecostal sheep's clothing.

The bewildering array of cultic movements that emerged in the US in the nineteenth century can be sorted into two general categories: on the one hand, the historically or eschatologically oriented cults such as Mormonism, the Jehovah's Witnesses, and the Worldwide Church of God, spawned by the Adventist fervour that swept America in the early part of the nineteenth century; and on the other, the a-historical or 'gnostic' cults, which had their origins in a widespread fascination with the powers of the mental and spiritual worlds, ranging from transcendentalism to the occult. New Thought belongs to this latter group.

The aetiology of these gnostic movements takes us back to Phineas P. Quimby, a 'mental healer' who believed that illness could be cured through 'healthy attitudes' and positive thinking. 'If I believe I am sick,' he said, 'I am sick, for my feelings are my sickness, and my sickness is my belief, and my belief is my mind. Therefore all disease is in the mind or belief.'[36] Quimby's ideas were transmitted and developed by his patients, the best known being Mary Baker Eddy, who later founded the Christian Science movement. 'P.P. Quimby rolls away the stone from the Sepulchre of error,' she enthused, 'and health is the resurrection.'[37] In the 1880s Julius Dresser and Warren Evans, both also former patients of Quimby, organized a movement known as the Church of Divine Unity. Unity, in fact, proved not to be one of its strong points: the movement quickly fragmented and became a loose association of groups under the general rubric of 'New Thought'. In 1914 the International New Thought Alliance was founded.

The waters of New Thought metaphysics flowed out across the confused landscape of twentieth century American life in several directions. A multitude of quasi-Christian groups appeared, the best known of which was the Unity School of Christianity, founded by Charles Fillmore (1854-1948).

New Thought was 'transcendentalist' in the sense that it attributed to the human mind the intrinsic capacity to attain a transcendent perspective and knowledge. The result was both a diminution of the transcendent and an elevation of humanity. New Thought was strongly opposed to the traditional religious debasement of the creature before an Almighty God and decried the negativism and weakness of thought that such a posture engendered. 'New Thought came as the corrective to this abject submissiveness. It substituted self-realization for self-sacrifice, and development for self-effacement. It is nothing if not an affirmative thought, and this positiveness has come to stay.'[38] Its stated purpose was: 'To teach the infinitude of the supreme one. The divinity of man and his infinite possibilities through the creative power of constructive thinking and obedience to the voice of the indwelling Presence, which is our source of Inspiration, Power, Health and Prosperity.'[39]

The central belief was that a person's material and spiritual circumstances may be changed by the power of the mind. This power is either internal to the mind itself or works by activating a transcendent power. H. Emilie Cady wrote: 'Our affirming, backed by faith, is the link that connects our conscious human need with His power and supply.'[40] Cady also claimed that 'there is power in our word of faith to bring all good things right into our everyday life'.[41]

The gnostic system developed by Emmanuel Swedenborg (1688-1772) included the idea that the universe, in both its physical and spiritual dimensions, operates according to certain laws: the 'law of attraction', for example, determines that like attracts like.[42] New Thought took up this idea and used it to explain how mental phenomena – attitudes and ideas – could affect physical reality. So Fillmore argued that Jesus' healings were not miracles but simply the application of a universal law:

> Few have dared even to suggest that Jesus applied universal law in His restorative methods; for on the one hand it would annul the miracle theory and on the other it would be sacrilegious to inquire into the miracles of God.... But in recent years a considerable number of Jesus' followers have had the temerity to inquire into His healing methods, and they have found that they were based on universal mental and spiritual laws that anyone can utilize who will comply with the conditions involved in these laws.[43]

New Thought was largely responsible for introducing the ideology of success into the modern American psyche.[44] At one end of the metaphysical spectrum Orison Swett Marden (1850-1924) wrote a number of books on how to make use of spiritual laws and the power of the mind to achieve social and business success. He is a natural forebear of writers such as Dale Carnegie and Norman Vincent Peale, whose book *The Power of Positive Thinking* has come to define the genre. Somewhat closer to the biblical tradition, Charles Fillmore and Ralph Waldo Trine (1866-1958) argued that faith in God or universal Mind would necessarily lead to personal prosperity.[45]

Many of the precepts and axioms of modern prosperity teaching can be found with minimal variation of language and argument in Fillmore's book *Prosperity*. Here we have the proposition that 'there is a kingdom of abundance of all things, and it may be found by those who seek it and are willing to comply with its laws' (16); that 'God's world is a world of results that sequentially follow demands' (18); that 'when there is an appearance of poverty anywhere, it is our duty to deny it' (37-38); that 'all affirmations that carry ideas of abundance will lead one into the consciousness that fulfills the law' (41); that 'God had faith when He imaged man and the universe and through His faith brought all things into being'; that 'Man, being like God, must also base his creations on faith as the only foundation' (42); that 'Faith is the perceiving power of the mind linked with a power to shape substance' (43); that 'your word is charged with great spiritual life force' (47-48); that 'If you talk about substance in a negative way, your finances will be decreased, but if you talk about it in an appreciative, large way, you will be prospered' (48); that 'It is a sin to be poor.... a sin to wear poor clothes' (60-61); that 'As we sow in mind so shall we reap in manifestation' (67); that 'There is a universal law of increase'; that 'God's will is health, happiness, and prosperity for every man' (111); that 'Debts exist in the mind, and in the mind is the proper place to begin liquidating them' (121); that 'There is a law of giving and receiving' (145); and that 'A part of the divine plan is substantial provision by the Creator for all the mental and physical needs of His creation' (161).

Word of Faith methodology is not merely 'humanistic': it turns not around the power of the mind but around the two poles of God and Satan, who between them ultimately determine the possibilities and limits of faith. There is, nevertheless, the same elevation of humanity and emphasis on our capacity for shaping our own destiny, the same belief in the power of thought and language to influence material circumstances for better or for worse. Extensive use is made of the notion of spiritual laws to reinforce the trustworthiness and efficacy of faith. The fact that New Thought developed alongside the rediscovery of divine healing within the Holiness movement also suggests a strong affinity between these two metaphysics.

The question, however, is: Does this amount to a genetic dependence? Has the Word of Faith movement been directly influenced by New Thought metaphysics? What is the nature of the correspondence between these two systems of thought? Writers such as Fillmore and Trine are like big game hunters who have stalked the forests of biblical truth; they have shot many of the wonderful beasts that live there, stuffed them with the platitudes of transcendentalist metaphysics, and installed them in the gloomy halls of New Thought to give the impression of divine life. Are the Word of Faith teachers guilty of the same lack of respect for the integrity of biblical truth? Or have they perhaps inadvertently released some alien species into the biblical landscape? Are they poachers or merely careless game-keepers?

Is E.W. Kenyon the missing link?

The key to this puzzle appears to lie in the work of E.W. Kenyon (1867-1948), a figure who holds a rather dubious position in the family annals of the Word of Faith movement. His influence has not always been acknowledged by Word of Faith teachers, but many critics would argue that he provided the conduit by which New Thought metaphysics was channeled into the fast-flowing stream of American Pentecostalism;[46] and in McConnell's view it is Kenyon, not Hagin, who is the true father of the Word of Faith movement.

Essek William Kenyon began his ministry in 1893 as a Free Will Baptist pastor in New England and parts of Canada.[47] In response to repeated requests to run Bible studies he founded

Bethel Bible Institute in 1900. Impressed by such faith-based ministries as George Müller's orphanages and Charles Cullis' hospices, he sought to operate Bethel on similar lines, insisting that 'no teacher or head of Department or anyone however connected with the Institution shall ever receive a salary'.[48]

Kenyon severed all links with Bethel in 1923 following a decline in student numbers and a clash with the board over the policy of faith-based funding.[49] He moved to California where he continued a wide-ranging interdenominational evangelistic ministry before eventually settling into a series of pastorates. Although Kenyon was suspicious of Pentecostalism, his healing ministry brought him into contact with prominent Pentecostal figures such as Aimee Semple McPherson and F.F. Bosworth, and he later had a significant influence on the thinking of post-War healing evangelists such as Branham, Roberts and Osborn. In 1931, following a divorce from his second wife, he moved to Seattle where he started the New Covenant Baptist Church and a pioneering radio program called 'Kenyon's Church of the Air'. He died in 1948 at the age of 80.

In its broad outlines the biography is not especially controversial. McConnell argues, however, that there is abundant evidence in Kenyon's educational background and in his writings to make us think that his theology was shaped to a significant degree by New Thought and other transcendentalist ideologies.

First, Kenyon admitted to having regularly attended services at the Unitarian church of Minot J. Savage in Boston. McConnell regards this as suspicious behaviour not only because Unitarianism, with its rejection of the Trinity and of the divinity of Christ, comes some way short of orthodox Christian doctrine, but also because, for many Christians falling out of love with orthodoxy in the nineteenth century, it was a convenient staging post on the way to Transcendentalism and New Thought.

Secondly, in 1892, during an agnostic period when he had ambitions to be an actor, Kenyon had enrolled at the Emerson College of Oratory.[50] Charles Emerson was only one of a horde of intellectuals on a journey from traditional theism to metaphysics in the nineteenth century. Having started out as a Congregationalist, he shifted towards Unitarianism, but before long was mixing his own metaphysical potion from a variety of readily available New Thought ingredients. In 1903 he converted to Christian Science. McConnell thinks it highly improbable that Kenyon would have studied at Emerson College without being affected by the erratic religious thinking of such a vigorous propagandist as Emerson.

McConnell suggests, thirdly, that although Kenyon frequently criticizes and repudiates the teachings of the metaphysical cults, he has nevertheless assimilated much of their thinking and terminology – a classic example of religious syncretism. McConnell's conclusions are not uncharitable. He suspects that Kenyon moulded his rather elementary theology to the intellectual contours of New Thought and its derivatives somewhat innocently, perhaps even understandably, because he had seen both the success of these new religious movements and the failure of mainstream Christianity to respond effectively to the crisis of faith. He concludes: 'Although his intent was to help the church, Kenyon's syncretism of cultic ideas resulted in a strange blend of evangelical fundamentalism and New Thought metaphysics. In his attempt to correct one error, Kenyon created another.'[51]

If it is the case that Kenyon's theology was infected by the presuppositions of the metaphysical cults, the question then arises whether this contagion was transmitted through Kenyon to the founders of the Word of Faith movement. McConnell argues his thesis on two fronts. He points, first, to clear instances where Hagin has plagiarized large sections of Kenyon's writings.[52] There is an obvious ethical problem here, though Hagin claims, presumably by way of defence, to have been able to recite whole chapters from books after one reading while at school – 'because I looked to my spirit'.[53] But the more fundamental difficulty for Hagin lies in the fact that he always claimed that the distinctive doctrines of the Word of Faith movement came to him by direct revelation from Jesus.[54]

Secondly, McConnell draws attention to conceptual parallels between Word of Faith doctrines and the teachings of Kenyon and the earlier exponents of New Thought.[55] So, for example, Hagin's dictum that the believer is 'as much an incarnation as Jesus of Nazareth' derives from Kenyon's doctrine of identification, although Kenyon himself recognized that 'Christian Science, Theosophy, New Thought and Modern Unitarianism teach, consciously or unconsciously, the Incarnation of the human family, that is, they teach that every man has a God in him.'[56] Likewise, Hagin taught that all disease is spiritual in origin, which is why Christ had to suffer not only physically on the cross but also spiritually in hell. The same idea is found in Kenyon: 'sickness is a spiritual condition manifested in the physical body'; and before that in the New Thought teaching of Ralph Waldo Trine, who believed that 'everything in the visible, material world has its origins in the unseen, the spiritual, the thought world'.[57] Copeland's belief that there are certain universally applicable spiritual laws governing prosperity which can be controlled by faith seems not very far from Trine's position:

> If one holds himself in the thought of poverty; he will be poor, and the chances are that he will remain in poverty. If he holds himself, whatever present conditions may be, continually in the thought of prosperity; he sets into operation forces that will sooner or later bring him into prosperous conditions. The law of attraction works unceasingly in the universe.[58]

Kenyon was perhaps too much of a mystic and a romantic to be such an unabashed advocate of material prosperity, but McConnell has no doubt that his belief in 'the great spiritual laws that govern the unseen forces of life' slots naturally into the gap between Trine and Copeland.[59]

Criticism of McConnell's argument

More recently, attempts have been made to show that McConnell has misrepresented the nature of Kenyon's influence on the Word of Faith movement.

William DeArteaga admits that Hagin has been less than candid about his intellectual debt to Kenyon.[60] But he also maintains that Kenyon's influence has not been entirely unhealthy. He points to Kenyon's explicit repudiation of many of the core principles of New Thought[61] and suggests that he was one of a number of teachers who poured away the heretical bathwater of New Thought metaphysics but kept the baby of faith in God's abundant provision. DeArteaga argues that God used the idealism of New Thought, modified by Kenyon, to highlight and correct the failings of the cessationist and materialist consensus that prevailed in the church, and to strengthen orthodox faith against the corrosive effect of higher criticism.[62] In a foreword to the original edition of Kenyon's *The Father and His Family* (1916) Francis Bernauer expressed his belief that if Kenyon's ideas had been published a few years earlier, the metaphysical cults would not have had the same popularity.[63] Joe McIntyre has taken the argument a step further by suggesting that, in fact, Kenyon actively opposed New Thought and challenged 'those deceived by the metaphysical cults to return to the simple truths of the Bible'.[64] He quotes an article written by Kenyon in which he states: 'There are several Jesus' [sic] today whose advocates are challenging us to worship. The Jesus of the various cults has very little resemblance to the Jesus of the apostle Paul.'[65]

The argument that Kenyon unwittingly absorbed elements of New Thought teaching is not entirely convincing. There are certainly echoes in Kenyon's writings of the idea that the spiritual realm is tractable to a kind of spiritual 'science', and that by means of this knowledge – or *gnosis* – the powers of the spiritual world may be manipulated for personal benefit.[66] But it is not always easy to differentiate between the rhetoric and the substance of the argument. When Kenyon speaks, for example, of 'God breaking into the sense realm', is this evidence of a latent metaphysical dualism, as McConnell argues, or is it just the rather crude conceptualization of popular Christianity?[67] In any case, it is not unusual for a Christian apologist (Paul, for example) to adopt the language and thought-forms of his antagonists for rhetorical reasons.

It is difficult to tell for certain from this distance whether Kenyon was trying to drag the church *out* of the dead-end of anti-supernaturalism or *into* the noisy thoroughfare of transcendentalism. But it is clear that the rhetorical and polemical framework must be taken into account if we are properly to understand the overlap between Kenyon's teaching and that of the metaphysical cults.

It has also been suggested that Kenyon was influenced much more by the Higher Life and Faith-Cure teachings than by New Thought; and more intriguingly, that many of the parallels with New Thought in Kenyon's writings are attributable to the remarkable degree of overlap between these two movements. 'Kenyon's theology may *seem* dependent on Christian Science and New Thought,' DeArteaga writes, 'but only because the Faith-Cure movement shared a general idealist perspective with the other non-Christian groups.'[68] There is an important difference between a mental idealism and a spiritual idealism, but the potential for confusion is apparent. In Robert Bowman's view 'McConnell's quick dismissal of the idea that Kenyon should be placed in the non-Pentecostal evangelical healing tradition is perhaps the greatest weakness of his book.'[69]

The influence of Emerson College on Kenyon's thinking may also have been exaggerated. On the one hand, Kenyon attended the college during a period of backsliding. On the other, McIntyre cites evidence that the college was endorsed by leaders of the Holiness movement such as Cullis and, if anything, may have been too conservative for Kenyon's intellectual tastes at the time.[70]

Finally, DeArteaga stresses the fact that Kenyon's eventual spiritual 'breakthrough' and call to Christian ministry occurred during a visit to A.J. Gordon's Clarendon Street Baptist Church in Boston, and that he was later closely associated not with the religious off-shoots of New Thought but with Pentecostalism.

The question of origins is not irrelevant to a responsible evaluation of the Word of Faith movement. The relation of the past to the present, however, is never easy to describe.

Similarities do not necessarily indicate dependence, and dependence does not always indicate a common purpose. Ideas may come to us directly from their source, or they may take a more circuitous route, being reshaped along the way by other hands. Sometimes it is only the outer casing of an idea – the language and imagery – that gets transferred. Somewhere along the way the original thought has been discarded, and something new has been put in its place. To judge the Word of Faith movement according to its past, therefore, is not entirely inappropriate, but it is hazardous. The past provides part of the interpretive context and may help us to resolve some of the puzzles and ambiguities of Word of Faith teaching. But DeArteaga is right to warn against the 'genetic fallacy' of 'rejecting an idea because of where it comes from rather than disproving the argument'.[71]

Probably all the distinctive elements of Word of Faith teaching can be found within the two broad currents of American religious experience represented by the Holiness/Faith-Cure/Pentecostal movements and the metaphysical cults. These two currents were not entirely distinct. They intermingled at places; they shared common interests; they exchanged terminology and arguments.[72] Kenyon was perhaps the best example of that confluence.

The fundamental objective of New Thought metaphysics was to enhance humanity's innate capacity for self-betterment and control over its circumstances, and to develop a notion of transcendent reality that permitted this sort of manipulation. So, on the one hand, there is the elevation of humanity to a quasi-divine status and the cataloguing of various mental and spiritual techniques by which we may transform physical reality. These thoughts are at least *analogous* to the Word of Faith doctrine of Identification and the understanding of faith as a positive force that can be utilized to bring about healing and prosperity. On the other hand, the exposition of the metaphysical rules which make this sort of control possible provides a much more plausible backdrop to the Word of Faith argument about spiritual laws than anything in Pentecostalism.

* * * *

The potential to develop a doctrine of prosperity was probably latent in the earlier 'faith' movements, partly as a result of the ideal of funding ministry through faith alone, partly as a natural extension of the well-being achieved through bodily healing. Some other factor, however, must be invoked in order to explain how this potentiality developed into full-bloodied prosperity teaching. The financial demands of high profile evangelistic ministry provide part of the answer. But it seems certain that the ideology of success and self-fulfilment, going back to the metaphysical cults and New Thought, has had some part to play in shaping this distinctive element in Word of Faith teaching.

But it also seems broadly correct to say that the modern Word of Faith movement is in the first place an offshoot of post-war Pentecostal revivalism. To whatever extent it may have deviated from classic Pentecostalism and drawn on other sources, it would be a mistake to regard it as being essentially the product of a non-Christian tradition.[73] Some weight should be given to disclaimers issued by Word of Faith teachers. Hagin writes, for example: 'Some have misunderstood this type of teaching, thinking I tell people to deny all symptoms and go on as if they weren't even there. They think I am teaching Christian Science. However, this is not Christian Science; this is Christian sense. We do not deny pains and other symptoms, for they are very real. Instead, we look beyond them to God's promises.'[74] Bowman seems close to the mark when he concludes that it was Hagin's peculiar synthesis of Kenyon's teaching with Latter Rain Pentecostalism that produced the modern Word of Faith movement.[75]

PART TWO

An evaluation of Word of Faith teaching

6

Problems of interpretation and theology

Most of the misreadings of Scripture that have been detected in Word of Faith teaching can be traced back to a number of persistent flaws in the movement's hermeneutic – the largely undeclared set of presuppositions and rules that governs interpretation. These flaws are not unique to Word of Faith teaching – they can also be illustrated to a greater or lesser degree from much popular evangelical exposition, and it may be debatable whether the Word of Faith hermeneutic is really so much worse than that of other forms of popular Christian exposition. One is inclined to think that the hermeneutical shortcomings have been noticed only because the content of the teaching has been controversial. Poor exegesis that supports the doctrinal consensus tends to be excused.

The Word of Faith movement has developed a somewhat idiosyncratic set of doctrines within the framework of a narrowly focused pastoral and evangelistic ministry, isolated to a large degree from the wider Christian community and without any real impetus to satisfy the more rigorous requirements of scholarship.[1] Although it is still fashionable in some Christian circles to disregard or even deride biblical scholarship as being irrelevant to the interests of ordinary believers,[2] we cannot simply ignore the question of whether a passage of Scripture has been correctly or appropriately interpreted. No amount of faith or conviction will make a wrong interpretation right.

In this chapter we will sketch out and illustrate the main intellectual precommitments and failings that appear to have generated the various errors of interpretation that have been found within Word of Faith teaching.[3] First, Word of Faith teachers bring to the reading of Scripture – naturally enough – a strong attachment to the principles of prosperity teaching. On the one hand, this has resulted in a selective and tendentious use of Scripture; on the other, it has produced forced and unnatural readings of the texts. This is made worse, secondly, by a highly utilitarian use of the biblical texts. Scripture is treated as a contractual or covenantal document whose practical value lies almost entirely in the fact that it comprises a set of promises, rules, laws, conditions, etc., which must be appropriated and activated by the believer in order to achieve spiritual and material success. Thirdly, Word of Faith teaching, like many forms of popular Christian exposition, operates with a naïve hermeneutic which largely disregards historical and literary distinctions within the text and refuses to engage in dialogue with the scholarly community. This is in quite marked contrast to mainstream Pentecostalism, which has in recent decades developed a significant body of critical scholarship.[4] This insularity has been exacerbated, fourthly, by the high value placed on revelation knowledge and the interpretive insight of the inspired teacher.

However, while it is undoubtedly the case that these factors have led to misreadings of Scripture and what we are bound to call doctrinal errors, we also need to take into account the quite distinctive form in which Word of Faith teaching is communicated. The Word of Faith movement has its own peculiar rhetoric, and it seems likely that some confusion has arisen because critics have failed to distinguish between *what* is being said and *how* it is being said.

Ideological bias

Selecting the evidence

The interpretation of scripture in Word of Faith teaching is controlled, in the first place, by the eccentric story about salvation and the argument about prosperity. There is an inevitable circularity to interpretation: historically, it is very difficult to determine whether the chicken of exegesis preceded the egg of doctrine, or vice versa. The problem now, however, is the *degree* to which the reading of Scripture is controlled by the established doctrinal position. Colossians 1:18, for example, is taken by Kenneth Copeland as evidence for the belief that Jesus was born again in hell: 'It is important for us to realize that a born-again man defeated Satan.... Colossians 1:18 refers to Jesus as the firstborn from the dead.... He was the first man to be reborn under the new covenant.'[5] Normally 'first born' would be understood as a metaphor for the resurrection, as 'first fruits' is in 1 Corinthians 15:20; it certainly does not mean 'born again'.[6] It seems clear that the Word of Faith gloss on this verse has been motivated by the need to find support for the doctrine of Christ's spiritual death and contest with Satan.

The interpretive control is sometimes made explicit. Copeland advises his readers to commit themselves to the 'absolute truth' of John 10:10 before they begin meditation in the Word: 'The thief comes only to steal and kill and destroy. I came that they may have life, and have it abundantly.' The principle of receiving an abundance of life is then made the benchmark for the interpretation of passages such as the story of the rich young ruler which appear to contradict the argument about prosperity.

> Whenever I read something that seems contradictory to this, I immediately stop and straighten out my thinking. The truth is hidden in some way, and I rely on the Holy Spirit to reveal it to me. God is not our problem. He does not steal from us. He is the giver of all good things! When you commit yourself to this basic truth, you block Satan and deal a deadly blow to deception. As long as you are open to it, Satan will prove that God wants you to live in poverty and in sickness to teach you humility. He will try to convince you that the rich young ruler couldn't receive eternal life because he had money, but Satan is a liar and the father of lies![7]

There are fundamental difficulties with this argument. Has the principle of an abundance of life been properly interpreted? Does it include material prosperity? We will have more to say on this theme later, but we are hard-pushed to find anything in John's Gospel that would justify the view that this statement guarantees material abundance. Is it appropriate, in any case, to use a *single* principle in this way as a blunt hermeneutic instrument with which to hammer unaccommodating texts into shape? It is certainly true that God does not 'steal and kill and destroy', but this is only one guiding principle among many in Scripture. It emerges out of a particular argument about the relation of Jesus to the 'thieves and bandits' who went before him (Jn. 10:8) and the 'hired hand' who flees from the wolf (12-13); and it is bound to interact with other principles in a complex way. Prosperity teaching tends to overlook the willingness of the apostles to forego comfort and health and prosperity for the sake of the gospel. Why should we not find in the story of the rich young ruler the 'basic truth' by which we interpret John 10:10?

The practical requirements and limitations of Word of Faith ministry have also exerted a controlling influence on the selection and interpretation of biblical texts. Although Copeland's writings, in particular, exhibit some of the characteristics of a systematic theology, they are nevertheless geared towards underpinning a populist and spiritually utilitarian message. Texts are selected and interpreted in order to address the issues and controversies raised by the practice of a Word of Faith ministry.

Squeezing through exegetical loopholes

One of the strongest indicators of the weakness of the Word of Faith argument is the reliance on a small number of texts that need to be very carefully – we might say casuistically – interpreted in order to extract from them the required meaning. Mark 11:22 is a case in point. The idea that God acts by faith hangs virtually by a single frayed exegetical thread – the argument that *echete pistin theou* in this verse means not 'have faith in God', as it is usually translated, but 'have the faith of God', have the God-kind of faith.[8] At first glance this is not implausible: the genitive construction is at least ambiguous. But we shall see later that it is grammatically unlikely and makes no sense contextually.

F.K.C. Price deals with the obvious stumbling block of Jesus' instructions to the rich young ruler in Mark 10:17-22 by pointing out that he does not actually tell the man to give *all* the proceeds from the sale of his possessions to the poor. 'Jesus wanted this man to turn all of his solid assets into liquid assets so he could carry them with him.'[9] Only part was to be given away. For this man, who had kept the covenant, to have been left with nothing would have constituted a 'denial of God's provision'.[10]

Again, technically, Price has a point: the text literally reads 'whatever you have sell and give to the poor'. But the argument hardly makes sense. Would merely liquidating his assets have left the man so disconsolate? Would Jesus really have expected him to carry such a large sum of money with him when they were so close to Jerusalem and the turmoil of the final days? The second imperative ('give'), which has no immediate object, naturally presupposes the result of the first clause ('sell what you own'). If Jesus had meant that he was to give much less than the total proceeds from the sale of his possessions, we would expect this to have been made explicit: 'give *part of it* to the poor...'. Luke, moreover, has the verb *diadidōmi* which is used elsewhere in the New Testament for the *division* of spoils (Luke 11:22) and for the *distribution* of food (Jn. 6:11) and of the proceeds from the sale of the disciples' possessions (Acts 4:35). Luke certainly meant that *all* the man's wealth would be distributed to the poor.[11]

In the end, the doctrinal position is sustained only in appearance, by means of a grammatical loophole – a hole no bigger than the eye of a needle through which the interpreter has tried to force a strange theological camel. This sort of highly questionable micro-exegesis, which focuses on a grammatical or semantic anomaly to the exclusion of the wider interpretive context, is characteristic of the cultic mentality. Nevertheless, a word of caution is still in order. The prevailing consensus is not always right; and sometimes the narrow field of vision of marginal or sectarian groups may uncover insights that the consensus has overlooked.

A failure of perspective

The reliance on exegetical loopholes is illustrative of a more general failure of interpretive perspective. Many of the distinctive Word of Faith doctrines are built around texts plucked from obscurity rather than central biblical arguments. The argument about a massive transfer of wealth from the world to the church in the end-times is based largely, as we have seen, on a few isolated verses in the Wisdom literature which speak of the wealth of the wicked being transferred to the righteous. The problem is that there appears to be no reference to this extraordinary occurrence in the many lengthy apocalyptic texts in the New Testament. We must be suspicious of odd doctrines that are 'discovered' in remote corners of the Bible but do not appear where we would expect to find them. James' statement about the unrighteous wealthy having laid up treasure for the last days (Jas. 5:3) does not describe some end-time transfer of wealth to the church. The argument has been misread. First, this wealth has been corrupted and has become worthless (2-3). Secondly, it is the means by which they will be judged: 'it will eat your flesh like fire' (3). This is the sense in which it has been 'laid up for the last days'. The peculiarities in the Word of Faith doctrines of atonement and faith arise from a similar focus on peripheral texts which are either misinterpreted or have only a tenuous relevance to the theme.

Jumping to the wrong conclusions

There are many instances where a prior commitment to Word of Faith dogma has resulted in false, or at least highly speculative, inferences being drawn from a text. For example, Peter Gammons argues from Genesis 2:12 that there was gold in Eden and that the Bible says, 'the gold of that land is good'.[12] The gold, however, is not in Eden but in Havilah (possibly Arabia), around which the river Pishon flows; and the assertion that this gold was good is probably not a moral but a mineralogical judgment, though it may also reflect the importance of gold for the decoration of the tabernacle.[13] In Genesis 26:12 we are told that 'Isaac sowed seed in that land, and in the same year reaped a hundredfold.' The story clearly resonates with prosperity themes, and Trevor Newport cites the passage in support of the principle of a hundredfold return on giving.[14] But although this is certainly an instance of God prospering one of the patriarchs, the basis for this is the promise which God made to Abraham (3-5). The argument that Isaac was seeing 'an hundredfold return on all his giving' is entirely unfounded, and there is no basis at all for the assumption that he had continued a practice of tithing from Abraham's encounter with Melchizedek (Gen. 14:20). Creflo Dollar insists that there is 'a direct connection between your mouth and prosperity' and quotes Psalm 35:27-28 KJV in support of his contention.[15] In fact, he has read the argument back to front. The psalmist does not make 'prosperity' the result of speaking: rather a person speaks out in praise of God *because* he 'hath pleasure in the prosperity of his servant'. The issue in Nehemiah 5:1-13 is not the management of debt but the exploitation of the people by the wealthy. The story cannot be made the basis for a programme of debt-cancellation: it illustrates rather the need for justice among the people of God.[16] In Matthew 17:27 Jesus tells Peter that he will find a coin in the mouth of the '*first* fish' that he catches. Copeland, realizing that this was a 'financial operation' and having claimed 'the revelation on it', comes to the entirely unwarranted conclusion that Peter went on to catch a lot more fish at Jesus' behest and made a healthy profit on the transaction.[17] Kenneth Hagin takes John 10:18 as evidence that before Jesus died spiritually in Gethsemane, his body was not mortal.[18] But the statement means only that he laid down his life voluntarily. Benny Hinn argues from Acts 4:34 that God not only saved large numbers of people but also caused them to prosper.[19] But there was no *increase* of wealth, merely a redistribution.

The contractual function of Scripture

Most evangelicals now would probably recognize that the Bible is God's Word to mankind in a rather complex and variegated sense: it cannot be read and applied properly without taking into account the different historical contexts within which the parts arose, the different literary styles that it exhibits, the different purposes for which the various documents were written. The Word of Faith movement, however, tends to regard the Bible as a uniform contractual document containing the detailed legal basis for the life of faith.[20] So Copeland advises someone facing a personal difficulty first to search the Word for the promise of God that covers the situation, then to focus attention on it: 'Keep it in the forefront of your thinking. Don't spend your time looking at the problem and listening to the negative words of those around you. Instead fix your mind on God's Word.'[21] To give a concrete example: 'Isaiah 53:5 assures me that Jesus already provided healing for me on the cross. So I say, "I am thanking You, Lord, for providing healing for me. By faith I receive that provision now, in Jesus' Name. I set myself in agreement with Your Word which says, 'by His stripes I was healed'"....'[22]

The loss of historical context

In contrast to the more familiar fundamentalism that regards Scripture as a body of inerrant propositional truth, the Word of Faith movement has developed a fundamentalism of promise. On this basis it becomes a quite straightforward matter, requiring only a little exegetical ingenuity and selectivity, to apply the many promises and warnings regarding 'prosperity' found in the Old Testament directly to the circumstances of the church today: 'Anything God taught Abraham or his descendants about operating financially will work just as well today as it did several thousand years ago.'[23] Statements and promises are translated into universal laws for the successful management of a person's material and spiritual life.[24] But the reluctance to discriminate between different historical – and more importantly, different covenantal – contexts has given rise to a number of distortions and anomalies.

First, there is the basic question of whether the terms and conditions of the older covenants apply at all to the Gentile church. If the believer is not subject to the law of Moses, is there any reason for supposing that the *legal* provisions which directly connect material prosperity with covenantal obedience (and material deprivation and suffering with disobedience) have validity for those who are in Christ?[25]

Secondly, there is confusion regarding the nature of any blessing or judgment that might be carried over from the covenants with Israel to the new covenant in Christ. Does the church inherit the material circumstances of Israel or are the blessings and judgments consistently spiritualized? What does it mean to be a descendant of Abraham? If the church has not inherited the *land*, on what basis might we claim the wealth which accrued to Abraham *from the land*?[26] It is noteworthy that the land is missing from Paul's list of benefits in Romans 9:4-5. If we want to claim the blessings promised in the law, are we not then bound to keep the *whole* law (cf. Gal. 5:3)?

Proper consideration should be given, thirdly, to the argument that healing was a unique aspect of the ministry of Jesus and the apostles and was never intended to be a feature of the post-apostolic church. Douglas Moo warns that those who advocate miraculous healing 'frequently fail to take seriously enough the discontinuities that are the product of salvation history'.[27]

Finally, the relation of prosperity statements to particular acts of divine judgment is invariably overlooked. Jeremiah 33:9, for example, is sometimes cited as evidence that God wishes to bless the church with material prosperity: 'And this city shall be to me a name of joy, a praise and a glory before all the nations of the earth who shall hear of all the good that I do for them; they shall fear and tremble because of all the good and all the prosperity I provide for it.' The passage speaks, however, of the restoration of Jerusalem after the desolation of the exile: 'For I will restore the fortunes of the land as at first, says the LORD' (Jer. 33:11).[28] Even if we were to accept the general applicability of Old Testament promises to the church, we would still have to reckon with the fact that it is after the particular poverty of divine judgment that the city will be made prosperous again; we cannot simply infer from this that the church, which has not suffered the disaster of military invasion as punishment from God, will enjoy material prosperity.[29] If we argue that the church is the new, restored Jerusalem, then there is again the problem of interpreting this prosperity in material terms when the 'Jerusalem above' (Gal. 4:26) is essentially a spiritual entity.

The loss of particularity

It is characteristic of the strongly 'contractual' hermeneutic of the Word of Faith movement that statements of various types which have only a localized or particular frame of significance in the text are reconfigured as universal rules and deployed as personal promises for the believer. Although in many instances this will appear unexceptionable, as a general principle it cannot be defended. By reducing the whole of Scripture to the uniform function of a contract Word of Faith teaching removes the main criterion by which we must distinguish between the particular and the universal, between what is contingent and what is normative, between what passes away and what remains.

This is the equivalent at the level of hermeneutics of Charles Farah's axiom that one man's faith is another man's presumption.[30] The fact that God blessed certain individuals in the Old Testament with great wealth and possessions does not mean that every Christian can expect the same preferential treatment.[31] In any case, we can hardly make a general inference from the example of the patriarchs and kings of Israel. Joseph prospered in the house of Pharaoh because the Lord was with him and he had the Spirit of God (Gen. 39:2-3, 23; 41:37-46). The point is not that Joseph was personally entitled to wealth but that his prosperity was to be the means by which God would safeguard the family of Jacob and keep his covenant with Abraham. Joseph's prosperity was the means to a particular end: we cannot infer from this story a general rule which states that any child of God may attract wealth to himself in the same way.[32]

John Avanzini provides us with another example. In support of his argument that God will help us get out of debt he adduces the stories of the widow's inexhaustible supply of oil (2 Ki. 4:1-7) and the floating borrowed axe head (2 Ki. 6:1-7).[33] But these are at best *occasional* instances of God's provision for those in debt. It is not at all clear that *ad hoc* miracles of this sort provide the basis for a systematic expectation of debt-cancellation.

We have seen already that John's personal and perhaps conventional greeting to Gaius ('Beloved, I wish above all things that thou mayest prosper': 3 Jn. 2 KJV) is widely regarded within the Word of Faith movement as evidence for a universal principle of material prosperity. Price attempts to justify the extrapolation from this particular 'wish' to a general rule applicable to all believers who obey God on the grounds that God is no respecter of persons (cf. Rom. 2:11): 'If He blesses one person, then He has obligated Himself to bless you or me or anyone else who will make a stand on His Word of promise.'[34] The argument makes at least two false steps. First, Paul's statement in Romans 2:11 has to do with judgment: it is illegitimate to infer from the fact that God shows no partiality in judging Jews and Gentiles that there will be no discrimination with regard to material provision. Secondly, whatever John may have wished regarding Gaius' personal circumstances cannot be read as a promise from God applicable at all times to all believers.[35] God may wish to bless, but he also wishes to use those whom he has chosen, and we must surely allow for the possibility that God's purposes will at times *preclude* material prosperity.

A simplistic hermeneutic

Failure to recognize argumentative context or genre

Most critics have noted that Word of Faith teaching frequently interprets a biblical statement without reference to the literary or argumentative context in which it was set. The problem is that taken out of context a statement can be made to mean many different things according to the whim of the interpreter.

The crude contractual hermeneutic encourages the view that Scripture consists of statements directed at the believer. Little consideration is given to the basic rules of an historically and critically aware hermeneutics. Obviously we are dealing here with some fundamental differences of opinion with regard to how we apply Scripture in personal and practical situations. Nevertheless, even a conservative hermeneutic should recognize that the meaning of statements, like the meaning of words, is dependent both on internal semantic and grammatical relations and on external relations determined by argumentation, genre, and historical setting.[36] There are inherent dangers in the atomized extraction and application of proof-texts and promises. 'By neglecting contextual, scientific exegesis,' Farah writes, 'people are brought into bondage to Scriptures which do not teach what they think is being taught.'[37]

A preference for literalism

The argument over whether any particular biblical statement should be interpreted literally or figuratively is always going to be a difficult one. The problem of literalism generally arises in the absence of an historical or literary imagination when the Bible is treated as a flat, two-dimensional text whose meaning for the modern reader can be lifted directly off the surface.[38] The complexity introduced by the nature of the Bible as a set of diverse, historically conditioned documents – the third dimension of depth – is overlooked. The result is a failure to recognize the extent to which judgments about genre, literary style, rhetorical purpose, historical context, and so on, must be included in the process by which we determine the 'meaning' of a passage. Isolated clauses and verses become more important than arguments; dialogue is reduced to divine pronouncements; surface patterns are given precedence over deeper structures of meaning; passages are selected, strung together, and interpreted according to the occurrence of key words (eg. 'sowing', 'reaping', 'prosper'). The rich, multifarious chronicles of a covenant people are reduced to the univocal clauses and conditions of a legal contract.

Hank Hanegraaff draws attention to Copeland's '*hyperliteral* reading of Isaiah 40:12' as the basis for his highly anthropomorphic conception of God.[39] If God literally 'marked off the heavens with a span', does he also literally 'gather the lambs in his arms', as the preceding verse has stated? Copeland's very 'literal' interpretation of Isaiah 53, which is taken as a direct and detailed description of the crucifixion, is another example:

> You see, when Jesus received into His own spirit all the sin and sickness of the ages, it so pulled and stretched and disfigured His body that it astounded that centurion. He knew that wasn't the result of the process of crucifixion. So the only thing he could figure was the Jews must be right. This man must have been the Son of God – and He must have blasphemed and so displeased His Father that God was cursing Him right before their eyes.... We know that's what people thought because Isaiah says, "Surely he hath borne our griefs, and carried our sorrows: yet we did esteem him stricken, smitten of God, and afflicted" (Isaiah 53:4).[40]

A more historically oriented hermeneutic would want to allow for a degree of indirectness in the manner of reference that would make this sort of detailed literalism inappropriate. This does not make the prophecy any less true; it merely adjusts the function of truth to suit the genre. There is, of course, nothing in the Gospel narrative to suggest that the centurion was startled by the extreme disfigurement of

Jesus' body or that he recognized the fulfilment of Isaiah 53:2-5.

Misleading English translations

Although prosperity teaching will sometimes make reference to the original Hebrew or Greek in support of its arguments, mistakes often arise as the result of reliance on a misleading English translation. For example, when Paul says that 'godliness is profitable unto all things' (1 Tim. 4:8 KJV), he does not mean that there is money to be made out of it.[41] Godliness is 'profitable' or 'useful' (*ōphelimos*) because it holds a 'promise of life' both for the present and for the age to come.[42]

The most common instance of this rather basic interpretive error, however, is the assumption that the 'prosperity' word-group in English, particularly in the KJV, has the narrow meaning of financial prosperity. This is partly a failure to realize that the verb 'prosper' tends to have a wider semantic field than the noun 'prosperity' – that all that prospers is not necessarily prosperity. For example, Psalm 35:27 KJV states that the Lord 'hath pleasure in the prosperity of his servant'. The Hebrew word translated 'prosperity' in this case is *šālōm*, which means more than just peace, the absence of conflict, but also rather more than material prosperity.[43] The KJV has 'prosper' in Deuteronomy 29:9 ('Keep therefore the words of this covenant, and do them, that ye may prosper in all that ye do'), but the underlying sense appears to be that of acting wisely, having insight (*śāḵal*). The Greek text has *synēte*, meaning 'understand, perceive clearly'.[44]

Joshua 1:8 has a paradigmatic resonance for the Word of Faith movement because it attributes 'prosperity' to confessing, meditating upon, and obeying the Word of God: 'This book of the law shall not depart out of your mouth; you shall meditate on it day and night, so that you may be careful to act in accordance with all that is written in it. For then you shall make your way prosperous, and then you shall be successful.' The Hebrew verb translated 'you shall make your way prosperous' is *ṣālēaḥ*, the root meaning of which is to 'accomplish satisfactorily what is intended':[45] such prosperity is found not in the accumulation of wealth but in the fulfilment of a goal. If Joshua is obedient to God, he will achieve the task set for him: 'you shall put this people in possession of the land that I swore to their ancestors to give them' (6). Nehemiah's prayer, using the same verb, that God would 'prosper' his servant this day (Neh.1:11 KJV) is not a model for the sort of prayer for general material prosperity advocated by the Word of Faith movement.[46] Nehemiah simply prays that he will have success in petitioning king Artaxerxes. When later he proclaims, 'The God of heaven, he will prosper us' (2:20 KJV), he does not mean that they will all become rich but that despite the opposition they will succeed in rebuilding the wall of Jerusalem.[47]

When the elder prays for Gaius that 'thou mayest prosper and be in health, even as thy soul prospereth' (3 Jn. 2 KJV), the word translated 'prosper' is *euodoō*, the basic meaning of which is something like 'to lead along a good path': in the Greek text of Genesis 24:27, for example, Abraham's servant thanks God that he has 'led him well' to the house of Nahor, Abraham's brother.[48] Paul prays that he may 'succeed' (*euodōthēsomai*) in his ambition to visit the believers in Rome (Rom. 1:10). In 1 Corinthians 16:2 the verb has some reference to financial gain, but we cannot assume that it always has this narrow context-dependent connotation. John's prayer, therefore, is that Gaius may not only prosper spiritually but also that he may 'do well' in the outward circumstances of his life.[49] Such success may naturally have a financial component to it, but this is not intrinsic to the meaning of the term. Having said that, it is worth underlining the fact that the prayer appears to be a response to the generosity that Gaius had shown towards itinerant Christian workers (5-8). This is fully in keeping with the Word of Faith argument that those who give willingly to support Christian ministry may expect God to 'prosper' them – not only spiritually but also materially and practically.

Revelation knowledge

Revealed doctrine

Word of Faith teachers rely heavily on supernatural insight – revelation knowledge – into the meaning of Scripture.[50] The Word of God, in whatever form it takes, is understood to speak fundamentally not to the mind but to the spirit: what we understand *in the spirit*, therefore, takes precedence over any understanding acquired through the exercise of reason.[51] Technically this position may be classified as a form of 'fideism', a theological position which takes the operation of faith to be entirely independent of human reason.

Major points of doctrine, especially where there is divergence from traditional Christian teaching, are commonly attributed not in the first place to exegetical insight but to revelation. For example, Copeland attributes remarks he made to another pastor about the meaning of Romans 8:26-28 to the Spirit of God speaking through him.[52] Hagin relates how during a tent meeting in Texas in 1950 he was taken up in the Spirit to the throne of God where Jesus discussed many matters with him that had a bearing on Hagin's own ministry. Jesus explained, for example, that he was not only anointed by the Holy Spirit to minister: 'I also had this other phase of ministry. I was also anointed with healing power.'[53] He then told Hagin that he too would move into a new phase of ministry when he would be anointed with a healing power that would be transmitted through touch.

In the same vision Jesus drew attention to Mark 6:5, pointing out that he could heal only a few people in his home town, and they 'didn't have much wrong with them'.[54] Hagin was taken aback by this. 'Now you talk about shocking a fellow! That shocked me out of some of my tradition. It just shot it full of holes. So I answered, "Lord, I've read the New Testament through 150 times and portions of it more than that. And I didn't know that was in there."' He then observes that one translation of this verse refers to 'a few sickly folk', as though this provided exegetical confirmation of Jesus' commentary. He explains: 'And you know, if you're just sort of sickly, you don't have too much wrong with you.' Hagin then makes use of this insight in his response to accusations that his healing ministry was not as effective as that of Jesus and the apostles: not even Jesus could heal everyone who came to him.[55]

Sometimes Hagin's Jesus appears to get things a little muddled. In explaining why he healed only one person at the pool of Bethesda, Jesus reminds Hagin that although there were many widows in Israel, Elijah went only to the widow of Zarephath; and although there were many lepers in Israel, none of them was healed except Naaman the Syrian (Lk. 4:25-27). The significance of these incidents, of course, if we may presume to contradict Hagin's Jesus on this point, is not that one was healed rather than many but that foreigners and not Jews were the beneficiaries of God's grace. The stories hardly constitute a proper analogy for the healing at the pool of Bethesda.

The dangers inherent in bringing such 'revelation' to bear on the interpretation of Scripture are obvious.[56] Although in principle a person may always check the content of these disclosures against Scripture, in practice when a successful, high-profile teacher who is not afraid to anathematize dissenters claims to have received supernatural insight, few within the movement will beg to differ.

Beyond criticism?

Is there any justification for the sort of authoritarian and 'inspired' interpretation of Scripture that is found in the Word of Faith movement? Evangelicalism has become accustomed to the idea that biblical interpretation and the systematizing of beliefs are collective activities. The work of scholars past and present is open to review and correction by the whole community. Preachers and teachers must be held accountable for what they say (cf. Rom. 16:17-18; 1 Tim. 1:3-4). Even the strongest prophetic statements should not be accepted uncritically but should be weighed by others (cf. 1 Cor. 14:29).

The text that is most often invoked in defence of the authoritarian position is Ps. 105:15 (cf. 1 Chron. 16:22). The verse relates to the period from Joseph's departure into Egypt to the Exodus, during which the descendants of Jacob wandered 'from nation to nation, from one kingdom to another people' (13). God allowed no one to oppress his people and 'rebuked kings on their account, saying, "Do not touch my anointed ones; do my prophets no harm"' (14-15).[57] The statement, therefore, is an assurance of divine protection over the people *as a whole* during this period. In any case, there is no basis on which this verse can be applied directly to the circumstances of the church. We may choose to make use of it analogically, but *analogies* are very malleable things. If the argument is not to be merely arbitrary, there must still be a good biblical rationale. Old Testament types cannot be applied willy-nilly to fundamentally different situations.

The fondness of Word of Faith teachers for this defence of the Lord's anointed is a strong indication of how indebted the movement is to Old Testament modes of spirituality. Paul's deference towards the person of the high priest after unwittingly insulting him is essentially a Jewish reaction: "I did not realize, brothers, that he was high priest; for it is written, 'You shall not speak evil of a leader of your people'" (Acts 23:5). That the Word of Faith teachers demand a similar immunity from criticism is indicative of a backward-looking theology that is more comfortable in the world of the old covenant than in that of the new.[58]

Faith and reason

As with other fundamentalist[59] arguments, the sharp distinction between revelation knowledge and sense knowledge has its origins in an earlier conflict with theological liberalism. It developed as a reaction to the extreme erosion of confidence in Christian truth both inside and outside the church. But the conflict no longer exists in the same form; the church no longer needs to be so suspicious of the power of critical reasoning or quite so anxious to defend the supernaturalist dimension of Christian experience.

In any case, there is a distinction to be made between the sort of reason that precludes as a matter of principle or prejudice any affirmation of the existence or faithfulness of God and the sort of reason that intelligently interprets Scripture or wisely decides how to act in difficult circumstances – or, for that matter, which discerns whether it is appropriate in a given situation to believe that God will act. The danger with the uncompromising insistence on faith is that it may easily preempt reasonable judgment about whether it is right to believe something. As a Christian I cannot allow 'reason' – rationality, logic, probability, past experience – to determine what I expect God to do: he may choose to transcend the rules and limitations of human reason. But there are other questions that I *should* ask. Does the Bible give me any ground for thinking that God will do this or that? Am I reading these texts correctly? Is my hope or expectation consistent with what I know of the character of God? Does the Holy Spirit confirm my faith?

The denigration of reason, moreover, does not allow for the possibility that the mind of the believer will have been *renewed* through the work of the Spirit. There is a certain irony here: first, because the Word of Faith movement places some emphasis on the renewal of the mind in order to grasp the functioning of faith;[60] and secondly, because there is the Word of Faith argument that the *mind's* capacity to imagine or 'visualize' a desired outcome does not have to be occult but may be redeemed and used in a godly manner. If the imagination can be renewed, why not the rational mind?

The Word of Faith movement pushes faith firmly beyond the boundaries of reason and common sense. Faith is understood essentially to be a supramundane capacity, quite distinct from other human faculties such as feeling or rational thought. It is the means by which a person gains access to the perfect mind and power of God and anything that impedes that access must be strenuously resisted. The Christian life, however, is a web of interacting, interdependent commitments, instincts and activities. The fundamentalist strategy isolates one or other of those elements, disconnects it from the vital whole, and absolutizes it: it is no longer one component cooperating organically and dynamically with other concerns and instincts but a dominant and repressive idea. There is a fundamentalism of ecclesial authority, a fundamentalism of reason, a fundamentalism of self-denial, a fundamentalism of the Word, a fundamentalism of Spirit. These all have their embodiment in the denominational and ideological structures of the church – we recognize them very easily. The Word of Faith movement embodies a fundamentalism of faith, in which faith is no longer an integrated part of a whole but an autonomous spiritual principle – another mental idol within the pantheon of fundamentalist convictions, with its own mythology and rituals, setting its own rules and practices. It is also inherently perfectionist: having become acutely aware of the lack of faith in the church, the Word of Faith movement aims to achieve a *perfect* life of faith.

Heresy or hyperbole?

Although there are significant flaws in Word of Faith teaching, we should not overlook the fact that much of the oddness may be attributed to the distinctive rhetoric employed by its proponents. Protestant evangelicals can be at times rather too fastidious and prosaic in their manner of expression and may have difficulty appreciating the more vivid and histrionic language that has always characterized Pentecostalism and its offshoots. From this point of view, the Word of Faith movement is in some ways better classified as folk religion than cultic. The rhetoric is notably populist. There is a heavy dependence on oral teaching and on a vigorously colloquial style of written teaching. Published material has often been transcribed from sermons. A high proportion of the more controversial statements have been excerpted by the critics from audiotapes and transcripts. The movement lacks formal intellectual reinforcement: it is articulated instead through the sort of 'irregular' forms of theology that Frank Macchia argues have been characteristic of Pentecostalism.[61] Copeland boasts: 'I don't preach doctrine, I preach faith.'[62]

As an example of how the language of the Word of Faith movement may be misconstrued, Hanegraaff takes issue with statements that deny God's 'legal right' to intervene directly in the world once Adam had ceded authority to Satan or that make God accountable to a 'Supreme Court of the Universe'.[63] If taken literally, of course, these assertions are ridiculous. But are they meant to be taken literally? Or are they simply dramatic metaphors for whatever theological necessity it was that kept God from directly overruling Adam's decision – functionally equivalent, perhaps, to the more familiar evangelistic illustration of sin as a ravine that separates God from mankind and which must be bridged by the cross of Christ? Read in this way they may be found to have real instructive value. The elaborate mythologizing of the atonement and the careful descriptions of the mechanics of faith function as a sort of verbal iconography, filling that vast space in the popular religious imagination between the finite mind of the believer and an invisible, transcendent God.

Similarly, Hanegraaff objects strongly to Copeland's 'blasphemous' pronouncement that God is the greatest failure of all time and that 'Satan *conquered* Jesus on the Cross'.[64] But are these statements the formulations of a careful systematic theology? Or are they merely instances of a flamboyant and somewhat reckless rhetoric? Is Copeland simply overstating his case? Is this not merely hype and provocation? Hanegraaff admits that Copeland says elsewhere that God 'is not a failure'.[65] But in any case, in context the statement is not so unreasonable.

> The biggest [failure] in the whole Bible is God, huh?! What, don't you turn that set off, I told you, you sit still a minute, you know me well enough to know that I wouldn't tell something that I couldn't prove from the Bible. But you just stop and think about it for a minute. I mean, He lost his top ranking most anointed angel, the first man He ever created, first woman He

> created, the whole earth and all the fullness therein, a third of the angels at least – that's a big loss man. I mean, you figure that out, that's a lot of real estate, brother, gone down the drain.
>
> Well since I'm God, I know how this thing works, the cardinal law is the law of giving and I so love the world, giving is the way out of this. Giving is the most powerful thing that I have at My command, and I'm going to give My way out of this problem. I have lost the earth, I have lost a third of the angels, and I have lost the Director of Praise. Then the Bible says, we give, and it causes a thanksgiving to God. He said, I lost the Director of Praise, I am going to give and get it all back.
>
> I'm going to have to give something that'll cost me, to get these laws into motion. I'm going to have to give something that'll cost me. Cause until it cost Me, I haven't kicked my faith out anywhere's (and He's got a faith).
>
> There was a moment when Jesus was separated from God. Jesus had gone into the place of the damned, the answer for Adam's treason. There was a moment there that the only thing God had to give had been released, and there was no guarantee of ever getting Him back, except the law of giving and receiving.[66]

Copeland uses the language and imagery of human production and commerce to say something quite profound about the atonement. While it may sound crude and overfamiliar to many Christians, the question remains whether the colourful anthropomorphizing is not merely figurative – a teaching device, an elaborate parabolic style appropriate to a particular religious culture. Hagin's chummy familiarity with Jesus is for many a very inadequate and inappropriate representation of the believer's relation to the Lord; others, however, perceive in it an expression of the winsome and unaffected intimacy of Hagin's relationship with God.

* * * *

If the rules by which a movement interprets Scripture are seriously flawed, it is inevitable that the belief system which that movement constructs for itself will also be flawed. The extent to which this is true for the Word of Faith movement will become apparent in the following chapters. However, two other general observations have been made.

The first, is that in highlighting the shortcomings of Word of Faith thinking, we should acknowledge the fact that similar hermeneutical and exegetical errors appear in mainstream evangelical teaching. To give just one example, if Word of Faith teaching typically misappropriates the Old Testament promises of material prosperity, a similar distortion commonly appears in standard evangelical analyses of biblical attitudes towards poverty, which are frequently blind to the significance of covenantal context for the interpretation of statements that express a divine preference for the poor or for the state of poverty. At best we should say that the argument has been short-circuited: a global socio-economic analysis cannot be derived directly from texts which address the problem of poverty *within Israel or within the household of God*. For example, Ron Sider's discussion of the significance of poverty in the Bible in *Rich Christians in an Age of Hunger*, barely acknowledges the question of how we move from statements that relate to the situation within Israel or the church to global political and economic engagement.[67] Word of Faith teachers would at least have a case for saying that their 'prosperity' interpretation is no less tendentious than the prevailing 'poverty' interpretation.

The second observation is that we should be careful not to mistake the genre of the Word of Faith teachings that we are evaluating. The writings on which we must base our analysis are not, for the most part, the product of detached theological reflection. They are works of popular, pragmatic exhortation and instruction, strongly coloured by the language and ethos of Pentecostalism. In order to understand this rhetoric we must enquire not only into the *meaning* of these writings but also into their *purpose*. We must ask not only whether what is said is an accurate representation of the teaching of Scripture, but also how these ideas and conceits *operate* within the distinctive culture of the Word of Faith movement.

7

Salvation and prosperity

The Word of Faith movement, on the whole, is much more interested in the effects of salvation than in the theory. The validity and extent of these effects, however, is naturally determined by a soteriology – an understanding of salvation. There is always a danger of inhibiting the grace of God by means of the doctrines that we construct for ourselves. But at the same time an authentic understanding of grace and blessing must be underpinned by an authentic understanding of what God has done through Christ. We do not intend to provide a comprehensive account of traditional evangelical opinion on these matters. Our limited purpose in this chapter is to assess those aspects of Word of Faith teaching that have generally been thought to be at odds with orthodoxy: the teaching about the nature of Christ, the doctrine of his spiritual death, and the belief that health and prosperity are guaranteed in the atonement.

The theory of a double atonement

Satan's sovereignty over the earth

We may begin by noting that there is no basis for the belief that at the fall absolute sovereignty over the earth was transferred from God to Satan. Satan may be described as the 'ruler of this world' (Jn. 12:31; 16:11) or as the 'god of this world' (2 Cor. 4:4), but this is not to the *exclusion* of Yahweh, who remains sovereign over his creation (cf. Ps. 24:1; 50:1-12). Although Satan may exercise a power over the nations (cf. Lk. 4:5-6)[1] which manifests itself in ungodliness and hostility towards Israel, God is judge of the earth (Gen. 18:25; Ps. 67:4; 82:8), not for a remote otherworldly future but within history. Babylon and Tyre experience divine judgment. Nineveh is threatened with destruction (Jon. 3:4). The nations may function as instruments of divine purpose. Cyrus is depicted as an anointed servant, obedient to the will of God (Is. 45:1, 13).[2] There is, moreover, a strong suggestion in New Testament eschatology that whatever power Satan may have had has been significantly curtailed by Jesus' death. The strongman has been bound (Mt. 12:29; Mk. 3:27); Jesus told his disciples, 'Now is the judgment of this world; now the ruler of this world will be driven out' (Jn. 12:31); the 'rulers and authorities' have been disarmed (Col. 2:15).

The eagerness of Word of Faith teachers to attribute sickness and poverty to demons is a natural corollary of the belief that Satan holds sovereignty over the fallen world. Probably the most significant argument against the preoccupation with demons is that it appears to stem from a fascination with the supernatural that is closer to animism or superstition than to biblical spirituality. The difference between the modern practice and the biblical encounter with demons appears most clearly in the fact that adverse circumstances are often attributed to demonic influence without the demon clearly manifesting itself. Whereas New Testament demonology is empirical, Word of Faith demonology is speculative.[3]

The question of Jesus' divinity

There are two distinct parts to the Word of Faith understanding of the incarnation. The first is that Christ became fully human by abandoning all the privileges of godhead. The second is that he became a second Adam, man in his unfallen state. Only at the end of his life did he die 'spiritually', as

Adam had died, in order to take upon himself the full depravity of mankind. Jesus, therefore, was not so much God incarnate, in the classic sense of the doctrine, as 'a god' – just as Adam had been formed as a replica of God, capable of relating to God through perfect faith.

Christ's 'self-emptying'

It is worth reminding ourselves that what we have come to think of as the 'incarnation' of God in the person of Jesus is not a single coherent thought in the New Testament. Rather, various concepts and images are used to articulate and define a developing awareness that his relation to the Father was unique and of critical theological significance: he was the Word made flesh, the one in whom God was reconciling the world to himself, in whom the fulness of deity dwelt, and so on. The formal binary christologies of the later church were an inevitable, and no doubt necessary, development, but they do not constitute an exhaustive representation of the complexity and fluidity of the New Testament understanding of the person of Christ.

What this means is that there is certainly room within New Testament christology to ascribe a thoroughgoing humanity to Christ. It is possible to argue that his experience of God, his relation to the Father, was qualitatively different from that of his disciples but not functionally different – that whatever divine attributes he possessed prior to the incarnation were relinquished so that he might take on the full limitations of created humanity. The crucial text here is Philippians 2:6-7. Interpretation of this passage is fraught with difficulties, but at its heart is the statement that Christ in some manner – as it is usually translated – 'emptied himself' in order to take on human form. The Greek verb in this phrase is *kenoō*, and the theory has therefore been labelled 'kenoticism'.

There have been numerous forms of kenotic christology. The idea is linked especially with the mid-nineteenth century German Lutheran theologian Gottfried Thomasius, who argued that Christ gave up all the privileges of divinity, becoming fully and only human. More moderate versions of the theory have placed less stress on the metaphysical implications and have endeavoured instead to affirm, in opposition to the persistent inclination of dogmatic tradition towards docetism, that the Gospel accounts of the crises in Jesus' life reveal a limited and authentically human consciousness.[4]

Evangelicalism appears ambivalent about the value of a kenotic christology. On the one hand, evangelical theology has gone a long way towards accepting the positive arguments about the humanity of Jesus. On the other, there remains scepticism about the metaphysical implications. At the theoretical level kenoticism has been felt to contradict the doctrine of the immutability of God and potentially the Chalcedonian Definition of AD 451, which asserted that Christ is 'truly God and truly man', having two natures in one person.[5] Biblically, it runs up against the widely expressed belief that God was in this man in a *unique* way – a belief that elicited statements which radically altered the shape of traditional Jewish monotheism.

It may be, however, that the image in Philippians 2:7 of Christ supposedly *emptying* himself has been mined for a metaphysical content that is not there. Paul's basic argument in this passage is that the Philippians should not act out of selfishness but should count others better than themselves; they should look not to their own interests only but also to the interests of others (2:3-4). It is an attitude, a state of mind, which is seen in Christ Jesus. This is a rather straightforward ethical matter, having to do only with the way the Philippians think about themselves and about others, and might lead us to consider that what is then said about Christ, by way of illustration, likewise has merely ethical implications. Although in the 'form (*morphēi*) of God', he chose not to put himself on a level of equality with God, but rather 'made himself of no value' and took instead the 'form (*morphēn*) of a servant'. This is the usual meaning of *kenoō* in Paul: to make something of no value, worthless, vain (Rom. 4:14; 1 Cor. 1:17; 1 Cor. 9:15; 2 Cor. 9:3; cf. also *kenos*).[6] If it is the meaning here, we should probably not try to make the passage answer the highly speculative questions that we have concerning whether Christ retained the attributes or power of deity.

Kenneth Copeland's argument that it had to be a man who paid the price for our redemption is too quickly dismissed. It is possible to conceive of a Jesus who was fully in accord with the Father with regard to his messianic purpose, one with the Father (cf. Jn. 10:30), but *really* divested of the infinite dimension of divine consciousness. Nothing in the Gospel narratives unequivocally points to a transcendent mind: Jesus appears to think and feel as a man thinks and feels. Even the high christology of John's Gospel does not so clearly contradict the Word of Faith position. Whitacre comments on Jesus' claim that 'I and the Father are one' (Jn. 10:30 RSV): 'Such a claim to oneness with God is not a claim to deity, since the same unity with God is true of Christians, who share in God's very life and are participants in his will, love, activity and power.'[7] Beasley-Murray makes the point that the neuter form of 'one' (*hen*) in this verse indicates a unity of purpose rather than of person.[8] He also argues that Jesus' deeply shocking statement in John 8:58, 'before Abraham was, I am', though certainly implying pre-existence, has to do primarily with salvation rather than with ontology – just as the original statement in Exodus 3:14 was a revelation not of God's metaphysical nature but of his 'steadfastness and faithfulness and his promise to help his people'.[9] Not everyone will agree with this more reductionist reading, but it suggests at least that Copeland may not have struck his ball quite so far off the fairway as at first appears.

The argument that Jesus 'did not use one tool in His earthly ministry that was not available to every Israelite through their covenant with God' is also not as preposterous as it may appear at first sight.[10] There is the characteristic failure to recognize the extent to which Jesus' ministry constituted a break from the past: the activity of the Spirit in the ministry of Jesus and the coming of the kingdom of God in power mean that he cannot be regarded simply as 'a prophet under the Abrahamic covenant'.[11] But Copeland is surely right to affirm an essential continuity between Jesus' ministry and our own.[12] If Jesus possessed an authentic human consciousness, his dependence on the Father for his ministry (cf. Jn. 10:37-38; 14:10) cannot have been so different from our own experience of faith. Paul says that because we are 'sons', God has 'sent the Spirit of his Son into our hearts' (Gal. 4:6) – the same Spirit by which Jesus cast out demons (cf. Mt. 12:28) and by which 'miracles' are worked among us (Gal. 3:5).

The issues here are too complex to allow us to make definitive judgments in a study of this nature, but too complex also for us simply to endorse Hank Hanegraaff's outraged accusation of 'blasphemy'.[13] Robert Bowman draws attention to statements made by Walter Martin, former head of the Christian Research Institute, that are strikingly similar to Copeland's position. He suggests that critics of the Word of Faith movement, including Martin, were perhaps 'too quick to accuse Copeland of denying the deity of Christ'.[14] At times Hanegraaff's argument is simply incorrect. Jesus' presentation of himself as the 'Son of man', for example, is of enormous importance for our understanding of his messianic role but certainly does not mean that he was 'claiming to be God'.[15] On the contrary, in view of the use of the term in Daniel 7 it would be more accurate to think that Jesus meant to identify himself with the 'holy ones of the Most High' who, having suffered intense persecution, would receive the kingdom *from* God (Dan. 7:18, 27) than to see in this self-designation a claim to divinity.

Christ as 'second Adam'

Paul certainly regarded Jesus as being in some sense a 'second man' or a 'second Adam'. The point of the argument, however, is not that Christ was of the same *nature* as Adam but that they are *functionally* equivalent, especially with regard to their descendants or successors: the effect of Christ's obedience is like the effect of Adam's disobedience in that it has profound implications *for the many* (Rom. 5:15-19); likewise, those who are of heaven bear the image of the man of heaven *just as* those who are of dust bear the image of the man of dust (1 Cor. 15:47-49). Apart from this it is the *contrast* between the two figures that emerges most sharply in Paul's argument: the first Adam became a 'living being', the second Adam a 'life-giving spirit' through the power of the resurrection.[16] The eschatological Spirit fundamentally differentiates Christ from Adam. There is no basis here for the Word of Faith view that salvation entails a reversion to a prelapsarian condition.

The doctrine of Christ's spiritual death

If Christ is a replica of the first Adam in his unfallen state, then in order to die for our sins he must die not only physically but also spiritually – he must take on the full extent of our sinful nature and become subject to Satan and death. That is the logic underlying the Word of Faith teaching that Christ died twice, and at first sight there is some point to it. If death is a consequence of sin, how could the sinless Jesus actually die? And if I am spiritually dead, must not Christ also die spiritually in order to redeem me? A similar line of argument appears in Calvin: 'Nothing had been done if Christ had only endured corporeal death.... And certainly had not his soul shared in the punishment, he would have been a Redeemer of bodies only' (*Institutes* 2.16.10, 12).

These particular theological puzzles, however, are not of apparent interest to the writers of the New Testament. In fact, the questions are probably misconceived. We should ask instead: how could this man who died on the cross be counted as righteous, obedient to God? The unique 'sinlessness' of Jesus is not presented in ontological terms in the New Testament: it is not seen as a consequence of the incarnation or of his conception by the Holy Spirit. It has to do rather with his unswerving commitment to fulfil the role of a messiah who would suffer and die for the sake of his people (cf. Heb. 4:15). Moreover, the argument that Christ became inherently sinful or even satanic at the time of his death is contradicted by those passages which describe the crucified Christ as the 'Lord of glory' (1 Cor. 2:8), as being like 'a lamb without defect or blemish' (1 Pet. 1:19), suffering as 'the righteous for the unrighteous' (3:18).[17]

The doctrine of a two-stage death has been built around a number of biblical texts, the most important being the prophecy in Isaiah 53:9 that 'he made his grave with the wicked, and with the rich in his death' (KJV), where the Hebrew word translated 'death' is plural (*mōṯāyw*). Critics have usually argued that the idiom has an intensive function, signifying perhaps an especially violent death.[18] It is also found in Ezekiel 28:8, 10, where it is said that the King of Tyre will die 'the deaths (*mᵉmôṯê*) of the wounded or violently slain (singular)' and 'the deaths (*môṯê*) of the uncircumcised (plural)'.[19]

The correspondence between the lifting up of the Son of man and the lifting up of the bronze serpent by Moses (Jn. 3:14) has to do with the removal of divine judgment from a sinful people. Once when the Israelites complained about the conditions in the wilderness, God sent poisonous snakes among them as judgment for their rebelliousness (Num. 21:4-9). Moses was instructed to make an image of a snake and set it on a pole. If a person was bitten, he had only to look upon the image and he would live. Word of Faith teaching maintains that by the analogy Jesus directly identifies himself with an image of Satan. But the point of the statement is rather that contemporary Israel, being no less rebellious, might likewise escape judgment and 'have eternal life' (3:15) by looking upon the Son of man lifted up on the cross (cf. Jn. 12:32). In the Old Testament story the snake is neither sin nor Satan but the instrument of divine judgment. There is no reason to think that Jesus draws on the wider symbolic significance of the image: the incident is merely a type of judgment and salvation for Israel.

It is always going to be difficult to understand Jesus' cry of dereliction from the cross: 'My God, my God, why have you forsaken me?' (Mt. 27:46).[20] This quotation from Psalm 22:1 can, of course, be made to fit a theory of two deaths: being now dead spiritually Jesus encounters the pain of separation from his Father, parallel to the expulsion of Adam from the garden. But it certainly does not make such a theory inevitable. If Jesus' utterance signifies a real sense of having been abandoned by God, it is also an allusion to the whole of Psalm 22, which is ultimately an expression of trust and of the expectation of salvation. Arguably, it is by reference to this complete 'narrative' of personal and national deliverance that we should interpret Jesus' cry. Although these words have often been interpreted soteriologically, as expressing the separation caused by Jesus' taking upon himself the sin of the world, nothing in Psalm 22 suggests that the abandonment has an atoning significance. We are certainly not compelled to think that it is the consequence of Jesus having become an object of sin.

Paul's statement that Christ 'became sin' (2 Cor. 5:21) does not describe the sort of macabre transformation of Christ's nature into something intrinsically sinful or satanic taught by the Word of Faith movement. Two general approaches have suggested themselves to interpreters.[21] The first is that Christ suffered *as though* he were a sinner. The second takes 'sin' to be an abbreviation for 'sin offering'. The word *hamartia*, meaning 'sin', is sometimes used in the Greek Old Testament for the Hebrew *ḥaṭṭā'ṯ* ('sin offering'). The idiom may have been used for the sake of the antithesis with 'we might become the righteousness of God'. Behind it, however, is undoubtedly the more specific image of the servant of the Lord, whose life is made 'an offering for sin', and who 'shall make many righteous, and... bear their iniquities' (Is. 53:10-11).

Finally, the argument from 1 Timothy 3:16 is mistaken. Copeland takes 'justified in the Spirit' to mean that Christ was 'made righteous' and therefore must previously have become 'unrighteous'. The phrase, however, is more properly translated 'vindicated in the Spirit' and is a reference to the resurrection.

The descent into hell and rebirth of Christ

The usual argument against the doctrine that Jesus died both physically and spiritually has been that the New Testament consistently makes his death on the cross *alone* the means by which sin is atoned for and men and women are reconciled to

God. It was through the cross that God 'disarmed the rulers and authorities and made a public example of them' (Col. 2:13-15). Peter's affirmation that Christ was 'put to death in the flesh, but made alive in the spirit' (1 Pet. 3:18) would appear to contradict the view that he also died spiritually. As Paul argues in 1 Corinthians 15:42-50, what is sown as a physical body, flesh and blood, is raised as a spiritual body. No statement is made to the effect that Christ's death was only a partial fulfilment of the work of redemption. The Old Testament typology of sacrifice requires no aftermath: it is through the death of the animal and the shedding of blood that atonement is effected (cf. Lev. 1:4-5).[22]

None of the creedal and summary statements in the New Testament speak of events of redemptive significance that occurred between Christ's death and his resurrection. The Son of man would suffer, Jesus said, be killed, and would rise again after three days (Mk. 8:31). On the day of Pentecost Peter told the people that although they had had Jesus killed, 'God raised him up, having freed him from death, because it was impossible for him to be held in its power' (Acts 2:23-24; cf. 3:14-15; 4:10; 5:30; 10:39-40). The tradition that Paul handed on stated simply that Christ died for our sins, was buried, and on the third day was raised (1 Cor. 15:3-4). The gospel he proclaimed had at its heart the reality of 'Christ crucified' (1 Cor. 1:23; 2:2). He boasted only in the 'cross of our Lord Jesus Christ' (Gal. 6:14).

According to Word of Faith teaching, however, having died not only physically but also spiritually, Christ fell into the hands of Satan, who dragged him down into hell to be tormented by the hosts of Satan. Various passages have been cited in support of this teaching, but although a doctrine of Christ's descent into hell has bobbed to the surface of Christian thinking from time to time, there is little really that one can make of it. The phrase 'descended into hell' in the traditional form of the Apostles' Creed translates the Latin *descendit ad inferna* and is better rendered, as in modern versions, 'descended to the dead'.[23]

The basic thought in the New Testament, in keeping with Jewish tradition, is simply that Christ descended to Hades, the place of the dead – that is, he died in the same way that anyone else would die. Acts 2:27 expresses the assurance that God would not leave his anointed in the grave to experience the decay of the body. Romans 10:7 uses the word 'abyss' to describe the place of the dead from which Christ has been raised (cf. Ps. 70:20 LXX). Ephesians 4:9 speaks only of the 'lower parts of the earth' and may not allude to Christ's death at all but to the incarnation or even, given Paul's argument here, to the coming of the Spirit.[24] In any case, none of these passages implies anything more than that Christ was dead for the period between Good Friday and Easter Sunday.

1 Peter 3:18-20 appears to describe a more complex scenario, but the basic confession is the same: Christ was put to death in the flesh and 'made alive in the spirit' – in other words, raised from the dead (cf. especially 1 Pet. 4:6; and Rom. 8:11; 1 Cor. 15:21-22). Nothing is said about him being tormented in hell. Whatever is meant by the proclamation to the spirits in prison, it appears to take place between the resurrection and the ascension (cf. 3:22) and therefore has no relevance for the Word of Faith argument.[25] We have seen already that the description of Christ as 'firstborn from the dead' in Colossians 1:18, like the 'firstfruits' image of 1 Corinthians 15:20, refers only to the resurrection, not to a *rebirth* in hell.[26]

The peculiar atonement mythology of the Word of Faith movement appears to have derived principally from E.W. Kenyon: the two deaths, the transformation of Christ into sin, becoming 'one with Satan', the descent of Christ into hell for three days and nights 'until the claims of Justice were fully met', the celebration of the demonic hordes, his being made alive again in hell as the 'firstborn out of death'.[27] Kenyon himself appears to have developed the argument almost as a hunch: 'I knew this for many years, but I had no scriptural evidence of it. One day I discovered Isaiah 53:9, the answer to my long search.... Jesus died two deaths on the cross: He died spiritually before He died physically.'[28] Kenyon believed the teaching to be true but had no scriptural evidence until he discovered the plural form of 'deaths' in Isaiah 53:9.

William DeArteaga suggests that Kenyon's account of Christ's descent into hell is a development of the ransom theory of atonement and is prefigured to varying degrees in Calvin's descriptions of Christ wrestling mentally with the powers of hell as he endured the full weight of divine vengeance, and in the writings of John Darby and Henry C. Mabie.[29] The doctrine is flawed, DeArteaga admits, but should not be condemned as heretical. Arguably, it is merely a picturesque and somewhat medieval embellishment of the basic belief that Christ died for our sins. Although many would regard this sort of mythologization as an absurd and unnecessary intellectual encumbrance on the gospel in the modern world, it is in tune with the more extreme Pentecostal instinct for spiritual vaudeville. It is a far cry from the sober and exact formulations of evangelical scholasticism, but then its purpose is also very different.

The return to Eden

The attempt to bolt a prosperity gospel on to a dispensationalist eschatology has led to some peculiar distortions.[30] First, the optimistic materialism of the Word of Faith movement is at odds with the expectation of an end-time tribulation and the rapture of the church out of the material world. Copeland appears, in fact, to have reinterpreted the seven years of 'tribulation' that is supposed to precede the coming of Christ, seeing it not as a manifestation of wrath but as an outpouring of God's glory. The 'blood, and fire, and vapour of smoke' of Acts 2:19 are not signs of judgment and disaster, he argues, but represent the blood of Jesus, the fire of the Holy Spirit, and the smoke of the glory of God – 'the physical manifestation of the very presence of God among us'.[31] For some forms of prosperity-oriented Christianity end-time expectations are muted. Paul Gifford comments on Kingsway International Christian Centre: 'The world is not ending: for these Christians it is just beginning.'[32] John Avanzini argues that the end-time church needs 'vast sums of money' in order to build thousands of new churches and pay off the debts of existing churches.[33] But why, if the end is about to come upon us?

Secondly, Word of Faith teaching defines salvation not primarily in eschatological terms but as the recovery of mankind's lost Edenic nature. Although this could be construed as a *realized* eschatology, there is an important distinction to be maintained between the anticipation of a future glory and the recovery of a lost perfection. The eschatological dimension is not entirely absent: it appears, for example, in Kenneth Hagin's use of Paul's statement that believers have been raised with Christ and seated with him 'in the heavenly places' (Eph. 2:6).[34] But motifs such as this have been reorganized around the central myth of regaining control over the earth and its resources.

Thirdly, although the Spirit features prominently in Word of Faith teaching, the centrality of the Edenic model of restoration makes Pentecost something of a non-event. Word of Faith spirituality operates more by means of the authority recovered from Satan than by the indwelling and gifts of the Spirit. Although the idea of the 'anointing' of God on the believer is prominent in Word of Faith teaching, it is understood in distinctly authoritarian terms.

Salvation and material prosperity

In addition to the usual benefits of salvation – forgiveness, the indwelling of the Spirit, the hope of eternal life – Word of Faith teaching insists that the believer now has the right both to immunity from adverse circumstances and to health and prosperity. These arguments need to be examined. Evangelicalism has usually assumed that 'fulness of life' is only imperfectly, and for the most part spiritually, realized in this age. Have we perhaps underestimated the seriousness with which the New Testament speaks of our being a 'new creation' in Christ (cf. 2 Cor. 5:17)?

Little gods?

The image of God

The belief that man was originally created as an 'exact duplicate' of God is based on Genesis 1:26-27.[35] If this is meant in anything like a literal sense, it is easily contradicted. There are several statements in the Old Testament which say that God is not like man (cf. Ex. 9:14; Num. 23:19; 1 Sam. 15:29; Hos. 11:9). The context of Genesis 1:26-27 suggests that the creation of man in the 'image' and 'likeness' of God relates principally to the dominion which he is given over the earth and its creatures (26-29). The thought here may only be that in order to exercise such a function man could not be *less* than the image and likeness of God, but neither this passage nor those dependent upon it offers any ground for interpreting the motif in ontological rather than functional or ethical terms.[36]

However, we should be careful not to overreact to Hagin's claim that 'Adam was the god of this world'. On the one hand, there are a number of things that this sort of statement clearly does not mean. It does not mean, for example, that humans were not created or that they possess any of the infinite attributes of deity or that they are worthy of worship.[37] On the other, the statement is connected in Hagin's argument to the thought of Adam's dominion over the earth: 'Originally, God made the earth and the fullness thereof, giving Adam dominion over all the works of His hands. In other words, Adam was the god of this world.'[38] What Hagin appears to mean by the phrase, therefore, is that Adam's dominion over the earth was derived from and comparable to God's greater sovereignty as creator. This is made explicit by Earl Paulk: 'We are "little gods," whether we admit it or not. What are "little gods"? A god is someone who has sovereignty. Everyone is sovereign within certain parameters.... We are sovereign in many areas of life because we are "little gods."'[39] The real point of the phrase, however, is probably not so much that Adam was godlike but that he once possessed the authority that was subsequently ceded to Satan, the 'god of this world' (2 Cor. 4:4).

Other aspects of the 'little gods' theory also prove to be more closely connected to the creation narratives than has usually been assumed. Copeland's argument that we are spirit beings, for example, could be interpreted as a theological assertion of the believer's divinity or as a denial of our material nature.[40] But in context it has to do only with Adam's capacity for 'close fellowship and communion' with God. The terminology is wayward and potentially misleading, but still it is important that we consider what is actually being said. Similarly, Copeland's statement about being a spirit in a body is often taken as evidence of an unbiblical anthropological dualism that makes the body a disposable container for the spirit, but the argument is essentially a practical, ethical one. 'God did not create you a spiritual schizophrenic': the reborn spirit does not have to inhabit a *sinful* body. By meditating on the Word of God we renew our minds, and the body 'will just tag along and do what it is told'. This is no more evidence for an anthropological dualism than is Jesus' statement that 'the spirit indeed is willing, but the flesh is weak' (Mt. 26:41) or Paul's acutely painful awareness of the internal conflict between the mind and the flesh (Rom. 7:15-23).

The more fundamental problem with Word of Faith teaching may be the tendency to understand salvation as a recovery of Adam's unfallen condition. Although the person who is 'in Christ' has become a 'new creation', the New Testament does not develop this thought in terms of a restoration of Eden or of the material prosperity that Adam and Eve enjoyed.[41] Paul's argument in 1 Corinthians 15:42-50 moves from Adam's 'physical' (*psychikos*) being to Christ's 'spiritual' being. We shared Adam's perishable nature; we *shall* share Christ's imperishable spiritual nature. There is no room in this schema for a recovery of Adam's unfallen state.

You are gods

When the Jews accused Jesus of blasphemy, claiming that he was making himself God, he replied by quoting Psalm 82:6: 'I say, "You are gods, children of the Most High, all of you"'

(Jn. 10:34). If the people of Israel could be called 'gods', why should they have a problem with Jesus calling himself the Son of God? It has been suggested by critics of Word of Faith teaching that the language of Psalm 82:6 is ironic ('So you think you are gods, do you?')[42], or that these are 'false gods'.[43] These interpretive strategems, however, appear to have been devised for polemical reasons: the positive aspect of the statement must be taken seriously.

According to Jewish tradition it was at the giving of the Law that the people were addressed as 'gods'. If they had remained obedient, they would have lived forever, but they sinned in making the calf and so became subject to death: 'you shall die like mortals' (Ps. 82:7).[44] Since Jesus also says that it was those who received the 'word of God' who were called gods (Jn. 10:35), it seems likely that he uses the expression in a similar way: those who receive the word of God may be called 'gods', but if they sin, if they fail to act justly (cf. Ps. 82:2-4), they will 'die like mortals'. Jesus, by contrast, who was sanctified by the Father and who is doing the works of the Father (Jn. 10:36-37), has a legitimate claim to the title 'Son of God' – in this context, one who will live forever. It must at least be arguable that those who now receive the living Word of God, who are no longer under condemnation, who will live forever, may also be called 'gods'. It is unlikely, however, that either Jesus or the psalmist meant the designation literally: in Psalm 82:6 'gods' is a figurative description of the righteous who will live forever, *in contrast* to the unrighteous whose end will be death.[45] Morever, Jesus does not apply the idiom directly to his followers, and it does not appear elsewhere in the New Testament. There is no basis for making it a normative description of the believer.

Partakers of divine nature

The other passage that has been thought to support the argument that believers are 'little gods' is 2 Peter 1:4, which states that believers have escaped from the corruption that is in the world and become 'participants of the divine nature'.

The context suggests two directions in which the phrase 'divine nature' may be explicated. First, it is contrasted with the 'corruption that is in the world because of lust', from which the believer has escaped. This should probably be understood in physical terms as a reference to human mortality and the corruptibility of the flesh (cf. Rom. 8:21; 1 Cor. 15:42, 50, 52-54; Gal. 6:8), though there is a close link in the New Testament between physical corruption and moral corruption as the attached phrase 'because of lust' indicates. In this case, to share in the 'divine nature' is to share in the incorruptible life of God.[46] It is important to note that the adjective 'divine' is not used to attribute an intrinsic divinity to the believer. It describes something which belongs essentially to God, but which has become accessible to those who have been called 'by his own glory and goodness'. Secondly, having received 'everything needed for life and godliness' (3), we should ensure that our character and behaviour are consistent with the nature of God. To partake of the divine nature is to act *like* God, to exhibit the qualities described in verses 5-7 (goodness, knowledge, self-control, etc.).

Incarnations of God

Christians are like Christ in a number of respects: we receive the same Spirit at baptism, we may be called 'sons of God', we may look to God as Father with the same trust, we will do the same works that Jesus did, and eventually we will reign with Christ. These similarities certainly blur the distinction between Christ and those in him and provide some basis for the idea that we share a common identity.

Christian orthodoxy, of course, has come to regard the person of Jesus as the unique, perfectly balanced conjunction of two natures, divine and human. This is a post-biblical rationalization of the fragmented insights that emerge in the New Testament writings. But even allowing for this, it is clear that there are aspects of the relationship between Jesus and the Father that are not reproduced in the believer. Those who believed in Jesus' name are given power to become 'children of God', but Jesus is the 'only-begotten' Son (*monogonēs*: Jn. 1:18; cf. 3:16, 18; 1 Jn. 4:9); and it is never said of the believer that he is an 'incarnation' of the Word of God through which all things were made, or that any disciple may also be the 'true light, which enlightens everyone' (Jn. 1:9). Language normally reserved for God is transferred to Jesus but not to the believer. The believer is never addressed as *kyrios* ('Lord') or described in the language of Old Testament theophany.

The teaching that we are little gods or incarnations of God, however, can be interpreted in different ways. Is it meant to be taken literally, as an expression of some sort of pantheism or polytheism? Or is it really only a metaphor for something that is more recognizably biblical? When Morris Cerullo tells his audience that they are not looking at him but at God, at Jesus, is this hubris or hyperbole? Does he mean that Morris Cerullo is really God or, as the passage which Hanegraaff quotes appears to suggest, only that he, like any believer, is a 'son of God', a 'manifestation of the expression of all that God is and all that God has'?[47] As instinctively critical outsiders we do not always grasp this function of religious language. Arguably the rhetoric is meant to startle the audience, to jolt people out of a spiritual complacency, to open eyes to the full potential of being in Christ. Bowman acknowledges the shock-tactics but attributes them to the general hostility of these teachers towards traditional Christianity.[48] He does not allow for the possibility that within its proper context the rhetoric may have a more constructive function. We still have to ask, of course, whether this is a *responsible* rhetoric – if it has the power to motivate, it also has the power to mislead. But this may be a more appropriate judgment than the customary accusations of blasphemy.[49]

There may also be an historical dimension to take into consideration. It is worth at least making note of the fact that similar statements can be found in the writings of the Church Fathers. Irenaus comments with respect to Psalm 82:6-7: 'we have not been made gods from the beginning, but at first merely men, then at length gods' (*Adversus Haereses* 4.38.4). Athanasius writes that God 'was made man that we might be made God' (*De Incarnatione*, 54.3). More relevantly, Joe

McIntyre notes parallels in the works of the nineteenth century Holiness and Faith-Cure writers. A.J. Gordon, for example, spoke of the 'miracle of the incarnation' being repeated in the believer. A.B. Simpson described how the 'mystery of the incarnation is repeated every time a soul is created anew in Jesus Christ'. McIntyre suggests that the extravagance of the language reflects the excitement of the rediscovery of the reality and power of the Holy Spirit at this time. It is a response both to the pantheism of the metaphysical cults and to the reductionism of secular materialism. 'In studying the literature of the day,' he writes, 'it seems that the dramatic realization that the Holy Spirit, who is God, had condescended to indwell human nature, to "incarnate" Himself in man, was so striking that many in this period of evangelical history… used the language of *the* incarnation to describe the wonder of the Holy Spirit's indwelling redeemed man.'[50]

The 'devastating implications' that Hanegraaff thinks will ensue from this 'doctrine of demons' now begin to appear somewhat overstated.[51] On the one hand, to describe believers as 'little gods' does not necessarily contradict the fundamental belief in one God. On the other, the serpent was arguably correct in telling Eve, 'you will be like God (or gods)' (Gen. 3:5). But there are problems, nevertheless, perhaps the most important being that this sort of language tends to diminish the presence and function of the Spirit in the life of the believer. This is a persistent failing of Word of Faith teaching. Too much emphasis is placed on the intrinsic status of the believer, too little on the active indwelling of God.

Already kings?

Hagin quotes the Amplified version of Romans 5:17 (we will 'reign as kings in life through the One Jesus Christ') and makes it the basis for a stirring affirmation of the believer's right not to be oppressed by adverse circumstances:

> We are to reign as kings in life. That means that we have dominion over our lives. We are to dominate, not be dominated.

> Circumstances are not to dominate us. We are to dominate circumstances. Poverty is not to rule and reign over us. We are to rule and reign over poverty. Disease and sickness are not to rule and reign over us. We are to rule and reign over sickness. We are to reign as kings in life by Christ Jesus, in whom we have redemption.[52]

Paul's statement, however, has a future reference (*basileusousin*).[53] Believers do not yet reign (cf. 1 Cor. 4:8). What they have already received is 'the abundance of grace and the free gift of righteousness', as a result of which they will not be ruled by sin. Instead grace will prevail in their lives 'through justification leading to eternal life' (Rom. 5:21). It is grace rather than the believer which reigns in the present. Hagin also cites 1 John 4:4 KJV. John assures his readers that 'Ye are of God... and have overcome them', which Hagin takes to mean that they *have* (not *will*) overcome the forces of evil.[54] What 'them' refers to, however, is not the forces of evil that make our lives painful and difficult but the false prophets which do not confess that Jesus is the Christ and which deceive the world (1 Jn. 4:1-5). John means no more than that his readers (not *all* Christians) have not succumbed to false teaching about Christ. This is very different from saying that they reign as kings in the present life beyond the reach of evil circumstances. As so often, a contingent statement has been improperly taken out of context and universalized.

One also misses in Word of Faith teaching in this regard adequate appreciation of the fact that to whatever extent believers have been set free from the dominion of Satan, raised with Christ, and blessed 'with every spiritual blessing in the heavenly places' (Eph. 1:3), it is for the purpose of being witnesses to the power of God and instruments of compassion in the world. Too often the intense motivational rhetoric of Word of Faith preaching stops short of spelling out what the believer is to do with the abundance of life that she has received in Christ, other than defend her prosperity against Satan's incursions and fund Word of Faith ministries.

The curse of the law

The argument is often put forward by Word of Faith teachers that sickness and poverty are included in the 'curse of the law' from which believers have been redeemed (Gal. 3:10).[55] There is, at first sight, some point to this. As the Jews crossed over into the land which God had promised to their forebears, they were presented with a stark choice: obedience to the law would bring blessing; disobedience and idolatry would bring a curse (Deut. 30:18-20; cf. Josh. 8:34). The horrors of the curse, including poverty and sickness, are listed in graphic detail in Deuteronomy 28:15-68 (cf. Deut. 11:26-28; 27:15-26). Moreover, Paul clearly has this context in mind in Galatians 3:10-14. In verse 10 he quotes, somewhat loosely, Deuteronomy 27:26: 'Cursed is everyone who does not observe and obey all the things written in the book of the law.'

The argument must be addressed on two levels. It is important to see, in the first place, that these curses constitute not a general human condition – not a consequence of the fall – but a *particular* judgment upon a disobedient nation determined by a covenant to which all the people had said 'Amen' (Deut. 27:26): 'The LORD will send upon you disaster, panic, and frustration in everything you attempt to do, until you are destroyed and perish quickly, on account of the evil of your deeds, because you have forsaken me' (Deut. 28:20). The point is that the nation will be destroyed, principally through military defeat, subjugation and exile (25, 36, 48-52, 64, 68). Destitution and disease are only *secondary* consequences of this judgment. All we can say, then, is that when poverty and disease are part of a particular divine judgment, they may clearly be regarded as a curse. But that is very different from the view that poverty and disease are *normally* a curse. When Paul says that 'Christ redeemed us from the curse of the law' (Gal. 3:13), he means only that we are no longer liable to judgment or to the suffering that comes *as a consequence of judgment*, not that we should never experience poverty or sickness.[56]

Secondly, we must take into account the fact that Paul has broadened and generalized the scope of the Old Testament argument. What concerns him is not the historical judgment that hangs over Israel but the principle of the thing: those who rely on works of the law must inevitably fall under the curse – on the one hand, because no one can 'observe and obey all the things written in the book of the law' (Gal. 3:10), and on the other, because the 'one who is righteous will live by faith' (11). But if they are under the curse, naturally they cannot receive the blessing of Abraham. If in the experience of the believer the blessing is the reception of the Spirit through faith, the curse from which we have been redeemed is realized in the failure to find life, in the finality of death. As Paul wrote in Romans 8:2: 'the law of the Spirit of life in Christ Jesus has set you free from the law of sin and of death'. Sickness and poverty do not enter into the argument.

The blessing of Abraham

The positive counterpart to the 'curse of the law' is the 'blessing of Abraham' (Gal. 3:14). Prosperity teaching maintains that the blessing of Abraham inherited by Israel was material as well as spiritual, a reversal of the curses described in Deuteronomy 28.[57] But although it is correct to say that Abraham was *blessed* materially (Gen. 24:1, 35), Paul's argument does not allow us to transfer the expectation of material abundance to the person who has become a descendant of Abraham through faith. His interest is only in that aspect of the 'blessing of Abraham' which has a bearing on the fate of the nations (3:8; cf. Gen. 12:2-3; 17:4-5; 18:18). What he is concerned to demonstrate is that this blessing, understood principally as the reception of the Spirit (Gal. 3:14; cf. 3:1-5),[58] comes to the Gentiles on the basis of faith rather than through their inclusion in the covenant with Moses. Abraham's personal prosperity is irrelevant to this argument:[59] it is neither through his wealth nor through the land that the nations of the world will be blessed but through his *descendants*, and specifically through the one 'offspring', which is Christ (3:16). We are not blessed *in the same manner* that Abraham was blessed; we are blessed in receiving the Spirit because God promised Abraham that through his offspring 'shall all the nations of the earth gain blessing for themselves' (Gen. 22:18; cf. 26:4; 28:14).

The poverty of Christ and the wealth of the church

The argument about wealth being entailed in the atonement appears less frequently than the corresponding argument about health. Paul's statement that Christ became poor so that we might become rich (2 Cor. 8:9) is sometimes reckoned to support the view, but the contention cannot be sustained. The wealth of the Corinthians must be measured in spiritual terms, just as the wealth which Christ renounced was the glory which he shared with the Father, and the poverty by which he made them rich was the spiritual weakness of the cross.[60] The immediate interpretive context is provided by verse 7: they are rich in that they abound in everything, 'in faith, in speech, in knowledge, in utmost eagerness, and in our love for you'. We find the same argument in 1 Corinthians 1:5-7, where the Corinthians are said to have been 'enriched in him, in speech and knowledge of every kind' – a reference to the 'gifts' of the Spirit that they have received as they 'wait for the revealing of our Lord Jesus Christ'. This is the 'wealth' that has become theirs through Christ's death. There is more to be said, however, for the view that material generosity on the part of the church will result in material generosity on the part of God (2 Cor. 9:10-11). We will return to this point later.

By his stripes we are healed?

There is, of course, disagreement among evangelicals as to whether we should expect God to heal supernaturally today. There is no need to adjudicate between the conflicting views here. We will restrict ourselves to addressing two basic questions raised by Word of Faith teaching about physical healing. First, has healing been guaranteed in the atonement? Secondly, is it right to believe that God wishes to heal every sick believer?

The more general question of whether sickness is spiritual in origin can be dealt with quite briefly. It is certainly correct to say that all suffering ultimately has its origin in the Fall. It is also undoubtedly the case that mental and spiritual dysfunctionality may have an adverse affect a person's physical well-being. But to draw a tight causal link between spiritual and physical reality, to the extent that the presence of any sickness in the body is determined by the balance of faith and fear, is neither theologically nor empirically defensible.[61] Such a view diminishes our participation in the created world by disconnecting us from material reality: the health of the body is believed to be governed not by its material nature but by an immaterial, spiritual state of affairs – the believer's faith or lack of it. This appears to run counter to Paul's argument that even believers 'groan inwardly' along with the whole of creation 'while we wait for adoption, the redemption of our bodies' (Rom. 8:23). Biblical anthropology remains fundamentally monistic and holistic. Sickness, therefore, must be regarded as a consequence of the fallenness and corruptibility of our physical nature. Paul makes it clear that we will not escape the perishability of the flesh until we die (cf. 1 Cor. 15:42, 50-54).

Is healing guaranteed in the atonement?

The usual response to the Word of Faith argument has been that while forgiveness of sins is immediately valid for all who confess faith in Christ's atoning sacrifice, healing is at best an imperfect and unpredictable sign of the presence of the kingdom of God and assurance of a final state of affairs in which 'Death will be no more; mourning and crying and pain will be no more' (Rev. 21:4). Robert Jackson summarizes the ambiguity of the situation in a *Themelios* article on 'Prosperity theology and the faith movement':

> When healing does take place, it is a reminder that Christians are a part of the new kingdom, it is a sign that God is supreme, and it is a portent of things to come. When healing does not

> take place, it shows that the new kingdom will not finally arrive until the second coming, and that until then, even Christians must face having to live in the domain of the evil one.[62]

The belief that Christ bore not only our sins but also our physical illnesses on the cross is based principally on Isaiah 53:4-5: 'Surely he has borne our infirmities and carried our diseases; yet we accounted him stricken, struck down by God, and afflicted. But he was wounded for our transgressions, crushed for our iniquities; upon him was the punishment that made us whole, and by his bruises we are healed.'

Perhaps the most important point to make about this difficult passage is that the sickness borne by the 'suffering servant', like the wounds inflicted upon him, was the direct consequence of judgment on a sinful and lawless people. As with the curse of the law, it is not disease in general that mars the life of the servant but the physical signs of God's anger against a people that had gone astray like sheep (cf. Deut. 28:58-61).[63] It is probably only within the rather narrow context of the Mosaic covenant, with its specific penalties for disobedience, that a connection can safely be made between atonement for sin and healing of sickness. Even then, the poetic character of this passage at least raises the possibility that Isaiah meant the healing of Israel's diseases to function as a *metaphor* for a more broadly conceived salvation.[64]

Matthew found a direct fulfilment of Isaiah's description of a servant who 'took our infirmities and bore our diseases' in the healing ministry of Jesus: 'That evening they brought to him many who were possessed with demons; and he cast out the spirits with a word, and cured all who were sick. This was to fulfill what had been spoken through the prophet Isaiah, "He took our infirmities and bore our diseases"' (Mt. 8:17). The Word of Faith movement naturally takes this as evidence for an intimate connection between the atonement and Jesus' healing ministry: the suffering by which he 'bore the sin of many' (Is. 53:12) is also the suffering by which 'we are healed' (Is. 53:5). But the conclusions we may legitimately draw from this verse are somewhat limited. Matthew uses the prophecy only to confirm that Jesus' ministry fulfilled the redemptive function of the suffering servant. If the healing of Israel's sickness in Isaiah 53:4-5, whether literal or metaphorical, signified the forgiveness of sin and the lifting of divine judgment, this is likely also to be the point of Matthew's comment: Jesus' healing of the sick was a *sign* that salvation had come to the people.[65] This is why such an emphatic connection is made between the authority to forgive sins and the power to heal (Mk. 2:10-11; Lk. 5:24). It does not mean that the forgiveness of sins necessarily entails the healing of sickness or that healing through the ministry of the church is universally guaranteed.[66]

The verse is also quoted in 1 Peter 2:24: 'He himself bore our sins in his body on the cross, so that, free from sins, we might live for righteousness; by his wounds you have been healed.' Peter's intention here is quite explicit: he sets out Christ's response to suffering as an example for Christian servants who suffer unjustly at the hands of their masters (1 Pet. 2:21). In order to develop and reinforce the analogy he draws upon the account of the 'suffering servant' in Isaiah 53:4-12. Christ had done nothing wrong, but he did not threaten or revile his persecutors; instead he 'entrusted himself to the one who judges justly' (1 Pet. 2:23).

The allusion to Isaiah's prophecy, however, takes us beyond the argument about patiently suffering unjust treatment, for Christ's sufferings were not only exemplary, they were redemptive (24). At this point Peter adds a statement drawn from Isaiah 53:5: 'by his wounds you have been healed'. It seems unlikely that he means the reader to take this reference to healing literally. The affirmation of healing runs parallel both to the preceding thought about living for righteousness and to the explanatory comments in verse 25 that the sheep which went astray have now 'returned to the shepherd and guardian of your souls' (cf. Is. 53:6). Healing becomes a metaphor for this reconciliation and perhaps, more specifically, for the freedom from judgment brought about by the vicarious suffering of God's servant. The emphasis, in any case, is presumably on the *wounding* of Christ because this is what makes him a fitting model for the 'suffering servants' whom Peter addresses.

Two other texts merit consideration. Psalm 103 is a wonderful celebration of the faithfulness and compassion of God towards Israel. Verse 3 describes the Lord as one who 'forgives all your iniquity, who heals all your diseases', and this has naturally been taken as an argument for the link between atonement and healing. It is difficult to draw hard and fast theological conclusions from a text of this nature, but some comments can be made. The statement presupposes the covenant with both its promise of blessing to those who are obedient and its warning of judgment for those who are disobedient (cf. 17-18). For reasons that we have already considered this arrangement cannot simply be transferred to the situation of the church. We should also note the personal and contingent aspect of David's affirmations in these opening verses. The psalm is addressed in the first place to the writer's own 'soul': 'your iniquity' and 'your diseases' have a singular referent. Whether or not a particular incident or sickness is in view, it is certainly unwarranted to generalize from David's personal experience. He blesses the Lord because he has received forgiveness and healing, but this does not amount to a theological statement about the universal availability of healing.[67]

The second text is Proverbs 4:20-22: 'My child, be attentive to my words; incline your ear to my sayings.... For they are life to those who find them, and healing to all their flesh.'[68] This would appear to vindicate the Word of Faith teaching that if we are obedient to the Word of God, we may expect to receive physical healing. The word for healing (*marᵉpē'*), however, is mostly used metaphorically (eg. 2 Chron. 36:16; Prov. 6:15; 12:18; 13:17; 29:1; Jer. 8:15; 14:19; 33:6; Mal. 4:2), and given the emphasis on 'life' in verses 22-23 this may be the more appropriate interpretation here.[69] Proverbs 16:24 reads literally: 'Pleasant words are a honeycomb, sweet to the soul and healing to the bone.' The same idiom is found in Psalms 6:3; 38:4; Proverbs 3:8. The healing of the bones is simply a metaphor for a more general state of well-being.

The atonement removes from us the liability to judgment as a consequence of our sins and of our innate sinfulness. For the

Jews who trusted in Jesus this meant in the first place redemption from the covenantal judgment that was about to come upon Israel; the healing of diseases was a concrete indication, on the one hand, that Jesus fulfilled the role of the suffering servant and, on the other, that those who believed in him were no longer under the curse of the law. On a universal level, Jews and Gentiles are redeemed from the judgment of death that resulted from Adam's sin. The direct consequence of the atonement, therefore, is the forgiveness of sins and of sinfulness: we are no longer *under judgment* because of sin, but the fundamental *condition* of sinfulness, which is the ultimate cause of sickness, remains.

Forgiveness, however, makes it possible for the believer to live in the presence of God and initiates the process of transformation or sanctification which we associate with the indwelling of the Holy Spirit. This has certain consequences, one of which *may* be the healing of sickness.[70] Healing is not only an extrinsic sign of something else – of Jesus' messianic authority, for example, of the validity of the disciples' mandate, of the imminence of the kingdom of God, or of a new move of God's Spirit. It is also, both in the life of Jesus and, if we accept it, in the ministry of the church today, an actual demonstration of the renewing presence of the Spirit, a victory over evil, a step towards the wholeness and well-being that are the hallmarks of eternal life.[71] But the process of recreation or sanctification in real terms remains imperfect, incomplete, progressive: we continue to sin, we do not enjoy unimpaired fellowship with God, and we must still face death, which is the ultimate demonstration of our fallen condition.

Healing, therefore, is a direct consequence not of the atonement but of the presence of the Spirit in the individual and especially in the church: it is effected in a corporate context through the exercise of the gift of healing or through collective prayer (Jas. 5:14-15). We do not find statements in the New Testament to the effect: 'once you were sick but now you are all healed in the Lord'. Jesus did not say to the woman who was healed when she touched the hem of his garment, 'Go in peace and be sick no more.' Divine healing remains the exception rather than the rule for the believer, not an automatic benefit but a manifestation of the active and spontaneous grace of God.[72]

Is it ever not God's will to heal?

The Word of Faith movement is unequivocal in its rejection of the view that sickness may have positive spiritual value:

> One notion that the enemy has used to brainwash Christians into being dominated has been what the Church has taught about "suffering."... There are some people who think they are supposed to suffer.... They think that through suffering, they will merit or actually earn the right to be in the Kingdom of God.
>
> This idea about "suffering" has proven to be one of the biggest stumbling blocks in all Christianity. It is really a satanic doctrine. The enemy infiltrated it into the Church through the pulpit to make Christians feel a sense of guilt if they did not go through some sort of deprivation. Basically, it follows the idea that surely God is not going to just give Christians all the things He talks about in the Bible; we have to pay something for it. So people have thought of the suffering they have gone through as a way of "balancing the scales" or "evening the score" between themselves and God.[73]

We agree in principle that suffering is contrary to the will of God, that ultimately the susceptibility of the body to illness is a consequence of the fall. We may recognize the temptation to exploit suffering as a means of gaining God's attention or favour or mercy. But still, we must question the absolute argument that it is always God's intention to heal immediately and never God's intention to use sickness for our benefit or for his purposes.

In the first place, allowance must be made for the physical and mental suffering that comes from persecution or from the physical hazards of missionary activity (eg. 2 Cor. 4:8-12; 11:23-28; Heb. 11:35-38; Rev. 2:9-10). The Word of Faith movement generally recognizes these as being for the Christian the only legitimate forms of suffering.[74] Opponents of prosperity teaching do not always see the distinction.

In fact, the Word of Faith argument that it is only suffering for or with or because of Christ that is regarded positively in the New Testament carries some weight.[75] Certainly the exceptions proposed by Douglas Moo are doubtful.[76] The expression 'the sufferings of this present time' (Rom. 8:18) must be understood eschatologically, as a reference to the sufferings that Christians face because they have become 'joint heirs with Christ' (17). The hardships listed in verse 35 are ones which threaten to separate the believer from the love of Christ: if they are not directly the result of persecution, they certainly reflect the difficult circumstances of apostolic ministry. Similarly, whatever the precise nature of Paul's afflictions in Asia (Moo suggests an illness rather than persecution), it is nevertheless clear that he regarded them as a by-product of his ministry and as a means of sharing in the 'sufferings of Christ' (2 Cor. 1:3-10; cf. Phil. 3:10; Col. 1:24). The argument that 'tribulations' (Rom. 5:3-4) and 'trials' (Jas. 1:24) cannot be restricted to persecution is also unconvincing. The link between suffering and glory in Romans 5:2-5 (cf. 8:17) and between the enduring of a 'trial' and receiving the 'crown of life' is in both cases meant to recall the model of Christ's suffering. This is the suffering for the sake of Christ that will be rewarded with glorious life beyond death.

Secondly, illness may sometimes be interpreted as a sign of judgment: 'For all who eat and drink without discerning the body, eat and drink judgment against themselves. For this reason many of you are weak and ill, and some have died' (1 Cor. 11:29-30). This is not a problem for Word of Faith teaching because health is only assured for those who obey the Word of God.

Thirdly, there is the possibility that God means to use an illness in order to correct or redirect a person. Even Hagin has admitted (after a revelation from Jesus) that God allowed Satan to injure him on one occasion because he had slipped out of God's 'perfect will' into his 'permissive will', putting his teaching ministry before his prophetic ministry.[77] Paul originally proclaimed the gospel in Galatia 'because of a physical infirmity' (Gal. 4:13), and was forced to endure his 'thorn in the flesh', a 'messenger of Satan', as a curb on his spiritual pride (2 Cor. 12:7-9).[78] The nature of these afflictions has, of course, been the subject of much scholarly debate. There is a case for thinking that the thorn was something external to Paul, perhaps his Judaizing opponents.[79] This is how the Word of Faith movement has tended to interpret the statement. However, the singular form of the affliction makes this unlikely; and more importantly, the fact that Paul regards this as a matter of 'weakness' (9, 10) strongly suggests that he is thinking of something that affected him directly in his own person.[80] There is no indication either here or in the scathing polemic against the Judaizers in Galatians and Philippians that he regarded this harrassment either as a means by which God was glorified or as an instrument for his own sanctification.

Finally, there are a few examples of persistent illnesses suffered by believers which are incompatible with the Word of Faith paradigm. The 'weakness of the flesh' that gave Paul the opportunity to preach in Galatia was serious enough and lasted long enough to be a trial to the Galatians and potentially a reason for them to despise him (Gal. 4:13-15). Epaphroditus' illness (Phil. 2:26-27) appears to have been both serious and protracted. The phrase 'God had mercy on him' may suggest that he recovered naturally rather than through more overtly miraculous intervention,[81] though we should also note that Paul regarded Epaphroditus' suffering as being for the sake of Christ (30). Paul encouraged Timothy to take a little wine 'for the sake of your stomach and your frequent ailments' (1 Tim. 5:23). John Thomas remarks: 'The writer both refuses to suggest that this illness was a sign of some flaw in Timothy's spirituality and refrains from attributing its origin to any specific cause.'[82] Trophimus was left ill in Miletus (2 Tim. 4:20). There is no indication that any of these men ought simply to have confessed their healing by faith.

These examples have no explicit theological significance, but we must ask whether it is legitimate to find positive spiritual value in the way in which a person deals with sickness. Commenting on 1 Corinthians 6:19-20 Hagin asks, 'Could God get any glory out of the body, the temple of the Holy Spirit, which is deformed or defaced with sickness?'[83] This is not a valid inference from the passage: in Paul's argument the temple of the body is defiled by immorality, not by illness. But even if we grant the general principle, that a sick body does not bring glory to God, we cannot exclude the possibility that God is glorified more through a person's endurance of suffering than through the wholeness of his body. Job would be an obvious example, but Job was too much of a test case. Other instances are difficult to find. But if we do not have good grounds otherwise for expecting every believer always to be healed, we must surely allow that God may choose to manifest himself through the faithfulness of a sick person.

* * * *

If the Word of Faith movement errs on the side of triumphalism, we should recognize that this is essentially an overreaction to the reductionism and defeatism – the 'poverty' gospel – that have characterized much Christian spirituality.[84] Hagin undoubtedly pushes the argument too far at times, but the intention is to help believers break out of a negative and limiting mind-set and begin to realize the spiritual potential that is theirs in Christ. The Faith movement may promise people too much, but there is at least the defence that it is better to aim too high and fall short than to aim at mediocrity and hit it. Copeland's impassioned exhortation on the basis of 2 Corinthians 4:6-7 to experience and express more of the glory of God provides a similar example:

> You are as big on the inside as all of heaven! The Glory of God is in you. The faith of God is in you. The love of God is in you. The mind of Christ, the Anointed One, is in you. All the fruit of the spirit is in you. Healing is in you. Deliverance is in you. All the wealth of heaven itself is in you.

> Those things were born in you when you were born again and they ought to be flowing out of that mortal, subject-to-death, meat-and-blood-and-bone body you're living in right now! The Glory of God should be pouring out of that earthen vessel![85]

The biblical argument is overstated, the eschatology over-realized, the idealism overblown. But this is the rhetoric of motivation – what we would call exhortation. It aims to engender among ordinary believers, often in the context of intense worship, an excitement and confidence in the powerful reality of God. It drives us too far up the mountain of faith – to the point where the air becomes too thin and most of us struggle to breathe; but as inevitably we slip and tumble back down, we may yet find ourselves coming to rest further up than we were before.

8

The word of faith

The law of faith

As with most human activities, the degree to which faith may be regulated and disciplined varies considerably. At one end of the scale it may manifest itself as a highly intuitive and spontaneous response to the presence of God, at the other as a structured set of principles and procedures, rules, by which the believer's relationship with God is governed.

The understanding of faith that lies at the heart of the Word of Faith movement belongs well to the structured end of the spectrum. The premise is that Christian spirituality is reducible to the operation of a set of spiritual laws, of which the law of faith is the most important. In place of the rather fluid, undeveloped and haphazard notions of faith with which we normally work, we are offered a simple but rigorous formula: believe it, claim it, receive it. What has been largely factored out in the process, however, is the element of personality – that measure of unpredictability that we associate with the hiddenness of the mind of the other and the operation of free-will. What remains is a narrowly defined, highly objectified conception of faith that is more a mechanism or 'hypostasis' than a quality of interpersonal relations.

Indeed, much is made of the statement in Hebrews 11:1 (KJV) that 'faith is the substance (*hypostasis*) of things hoped for', as though this means that faith is the raw material from which everything is made. But even the rather misleading KJV translation does not mean that faith is the mystical stuff out of which our hopes are fulfilled. The point is that it is through faith that 'things hoped for' become real to us – substantial – just as faith also provides an assurance or conviction (*elenchos*) of 'things not seen'. In the particular context of the argument in Hebrews, faith gives believers the 'confidence' not to shrink back in the face of persecution but to persevere until the coming of the Lord and in that way attain the 'things hoped for' (cf. 10:35-39).

In constructing spiritual laws we take what is intrinsic to the character and mind and purpose of God and externalize it. We take such essential qualities as faithfulness and compassion and translate them into a legal apparatus that may in principle be operated without dealing directly with God – a religious system which, like the Jewish law, inevitably comes to constitute an intermediate structure between people and God. As such, a reliance on spiritual laws is likely to diminish the personality and autonomy of God and restrict the life in the Spirit. In effect it produces a form of deism, differing from classical deism only in that it incorporates the miraculous into the system; but the *God* of the system is pushed into the background. Although in principle it is God who answers the prayer of faith, in practice the success of the prayer lies in the operation of the law of faith, not in the goodness or compassion of God. Faith is understood by the Word of Faith movement to operate rather in the manner of a lever moving behind the surface of visible reality. The action of a lever is not arbitrary: if you move one end, you will bring about a predictable and regular effect at the other end, depending on how the mechanism has been designed. Similarly, if you activate one end of the lever of faith by means of positive confession, you will necessarily achieve the desired result at the other end.

In the end, it is not so much God who is glorified as the system of spiritual laws, which guarantees that certain actions (such as giving) produce certain effects (such as receiving in abundance). There is less of an incentive to rejoice in the goodness and love of God, but more reason to elevate the role of the faith-teacher who knows how to operate the system. Whether this amounts to 'faith in faith' rather than faith in God, as critics often charge is debatable.[1] Faith still operates within a covenantal framework: the laws are underwritten by God and express the will of God, which means that it is inappropriate to regard such a conception of faith as a form of magic.[2] The real problem lies in the complex epistemological apparatus that has been installed between the believer and the God of the covenant.

The 'faith' which the Word of Faith movement seeks to restore is not fundamentally an attitude of eschatologically-oriented trust in the context of a fallen world. It is rather a return to the 'faith' of Adam, to the condition of an unfallen humanity. This has created confusion. Adam's relation to God was not governed by faith, for there was no separation: God walked in the garden (Gen. 3:8). But Word of Faith teaching has superimposed this prelapsarian model, in which there is no margin of error or unpredictability, on the New Testament description of faith.

The faith of God

The argument that the expression *echete pistin theou* in Mark 11:22 means 'have the faith *of* God', rather than 'have faith *in* God' as it is usually translated, is difficult to keep airborne, for at least three reasons.

First, although genitive constructions of this type – not least with *pistis* – are often ambiguous,[3] there appears to be no compelling reason why the phrase should *not* mean 'have faith in God'. The expression occurs only here in the Greek Bible,[4] but there is the analogous expression *elpidi theou* in Psalms of Solomon 17:34, which means 'through hope in God', not 'through the hope of God', and *pistei alētheias* in 2 Thessalonians 2:13 clearly means 'faith in the truth'.[5] There has been some debate over whether *pistis Iēsou* in Romans 3:22, 26, Galatians 2:16; 3:22, and Philippians 3:9 means 'faith in Jesus' or the 'faith or faithfulness of Jesus'.[6] Morna Hooker suggests that the use of the unusual expression in Mark 11:22 reminds us that 'the exhortation to have faith in God is in fact based on God's own faithfulness'.[7] If then 'have faith *in* God' is at least an acceptable translation, those who wish to interpret the phrase otherwise must give contextual reasons for their view.

Secondly, there is the general objection that the Bible does not otherwise attribute faith to God.[8] Faith is consistently a human stance with regard to what is unseen or uncertain; it implies both some measure of ignorance or weakness or insecurity on the part of the one who has faith and a dependence on a greater power.[9] For God to create by a *word of faith*, rather than by a word of intrinsic authority, would make him dependent on prior laws of the cosmos. Hebrews 11:3 is sometimes cited as evidence that God has faith: 'By faith we understand that the worlds were prepared by the word of God, so that what is seen was made from things that are not visible.' But the verse clearly speaks of the faith by which *we* attribute the existence of the physical world to an invisible, non-empirical origin – that is, the word of God in creation.[10]

Thirdly, a reference to the faith *of* God makes no sense in the context. Most importantly, Jesus explains what he means by having faith: "...if anyone says to this mountain, 'Go, throw yourself into the sea,' and does not doubt in his heart but believes that what he says will happen, it will be done for him" (23). Such faith clearly carries with it the possibility of doubt, of a failure of faith. It is also a faith which expects *God* to do something. This is at least implicit in the statement in the following verse 'whatever you ask for in prayer, believe that you have received it' (24); it is explicit in such related texts as Matthew 7:7-11; 18:19, John 16:23, and 1 John 5:14. It is clearly nonsensical to suppose that God likewise exercises a faith that must be sustained in the face of doubt and which asks for something from a power greater than itself.

DeArteaga's defence of spiritual laws

The argument has been made that spiritual laws simply reflect the order that God has built into creation or that they are an expression of the consistency and trustworthiness of God.[11] William DeArteaga makes the case:

> The understanding of the reliability of God's promises is an element of evangelical theology of long standing. We agree with it completely. But notice, if God's promises are reliable because of His character, they will always be executed when humans meet their conditions. If this is the case, then there is only a semantic difference between God's promises and spiritual laws. In fact one might be defined in terms of the other: The key element is that God's character is so righteous, and His power so awesome, that His promises behave as laws.[12]

But this is not entirely convincing. First, the argument makes no reference to the historical, covenantal or personal contexts in which the promises of God are made. Not every promise of God can be rewritten as a spiritual law. Secondly, it is an elementary category mistake to suppose that spiritual laws can be understood by analogy with, or as an extension of, physical laws. Physical laws are descriptions of observed regularities in nature: they help us to deal efficiently with the physical world. Spiritual laws, however, purport to define how we experience *God*. Spiritual and physical laws differ, therefore, to the extent that God and material reality differ: one is personal, the other impersonal, one is creator, the other created, and so on. There is more than just a 'semantic' difference between the logic of personal reliability and the logic that determines the operation of an objective law.

The laws that govern human relationships are far more complex than the laws that determine in which direction an apple will travel when it leaves the twig – so complex that we do not usually attempt to describe personal relationships in such terms. We speak instead of probabilities, fears, desires, hopes, disappointments, surprises. While we do not wish to attribute to God the fickleness and frailty that characterize human personality, we must be careful at the same time not to reduce our conception of God to something *sub*-personal. We might suggest, in fact, that it is the degree of *uncertainty* in faith that safeguards for us the authentic personhood of God. But this is a general condition: it is important that we are able to attribute the failure of faith to our continued entanglement in a fallen creation without necessarily having to pin the blame on an individual. The failure to trust God is not a personal failure alone: underlying it is the fact that every believer remains epistemologically alienated from God: 'we know only in part, and we prophesy only in part; but when the complete comes, the partial will come to an end' (1 Cor. 13:9-10).

Most evangelicals would probably feel, therefore, that the Word of Faith movement has achieved consistency at the expense of our humanity and to the exclusion of the grace of God. This, at least, is the perennial danger with any spiritual idealism. This is not to say that there are no 'spiritual laws' in the Bible. Kenneth Copeland mentions Jesus' statement, 'If you do not forgive, then the Father cannot forgive you' (cf. Mt. 6:14-15; 18:35; Mk. 11:25).[13] This could reasonably be described, albeit perhaps metaphorically, as a 'spiritual law' – a regular connection between cause and effect in the spiritual domain.[14] It would certainly be possible to restate the idea in more acceptable terms. Joe McIntyre, for example, quotes Spurgeon's argument that God's 'truth and honor bind Him to do as He said' and that this does not in any way limit his liberty: 'for the promise is always the declaration of His sovereign will and good pleasure, and it is ever His delight to act according to His word'.[15] The idea becomes problematic when the perception and implementation of these laws distorts or displaces the relationship with God through the Spirit that lies at the heart of Christian spirituality. Spiritual laws, in the end, are statements about God, not adequate rules for the successful Christian life.

It is also important to recognize the pragmatic purpose behind the Word of Faith rhetoric. The point has already been made that much of Word of Faith argumentation is aimed at helping people to grasp the power and immediacy of faith, in reaction to the natural tendency to doubt and defer. It has something of the extravagance and hyperbole that we find in Jesus' parables. It is meant to open eyes. It is an attempt to drum into the minds of obtuse and faithless Christians the fact that the kingdom of God opens up new and extravagant possibilities for their lives.

The idea that faith is a substantive force or spiritual law, therefore, may be a departure from the orthodox relational understanding, but it can also be seen as a rhetorical strategy – a means of making a rather abstract and elusive notion more comprehensible. It helps people to make practical and consistent use of faith in their daily lives. Copeland does the same thing when he describes the love of God *in quite realistic terms* as an 'invisible shield', an 'unseen power that goes into operation when a person is developed in the love of God and knows how to walk in it'.[16] It seems fair to say that either despite or because of the elaborate methodology of faith, the Word of Faith movement, both in its teaching and in its praxis, exhibits a real desire to demonstrate the power of the redeemed life. We may regard the theory as misleading and unnecessary, but we might hesitate to condemn the practice outright. All believers rely on some sort of mental furniture in order to give shape to the life of faith, and there is some reason to think that a significant correlation exists between spiritual enthusiasm and rhetorical enthusiasm.

The power of thoughts and words

Two aspects in particular of the Word of Faith doctrine of faith have provoked the charge that it borders on the occult. One is the emphasis on visualization; the other is the insistence that the prayer of faith must be spoken aloud or confessed. In a sense these are the inside and outside of the same phenomenon – the process of enhancing and intensifying the act of exercising faith so that it becomes a more tangible, manageable and focused part of a person's spirituality. But critics have argued that visualization is a common occult technique and that positive confession runs dangerously close to the magical belief that certain words, certain utterances, have the power directly to affect reality.

Visualization

The practice of actively and deliberately visualizing desired outcomes in the mind is alien to evangelical spirituality but a common New Age and occult technique. For most critics this has been adequate reason to condemn the practice,[17] but an interesting defence has been mounted on the grounds that visualization may be a function of the *renewed* Christian mind. Copeland is fully aware of the objections to visualization but argues simply that the devil has stolen a spiritual method, a means of engaging the force of faith, that should be used for godly purposes.[18] The imagination is God-given and when used in conjunction with the Word of God can be 'a tremendous thing': it is a way of 'building real Bible hope'.[19] DeArteaga has taken the defence of visualization further, arguing that there is a legitimate place in Christian spirituality for the creative use of the redeemed imagination. He quotes Jonathan Edwards to this effect:

> As God has given us such a faculty as the imagination and so made us that we cannot think of things spiritual and invisible, without some exercise of this faculty; so, it appears to me, that such is our state and nature, that this faculty is really subservient and helpful to the other faculties of the mind, when proper use is made of it.... It appears to me manifest, in many instances with which I have been acquainted, that God has really made use of this faculty to truly divine purposes....[20]

The important question is what do we do with the images that our imaginations are able to fashion. DeArteaga approves of the advice given by Brooks Alexander: 'Use images in prayer as a means of communication *to* God. Do not use your own created images as a source of communication *from* God. Use images as you use words – to express your worship and your petition. Do not use images as instruments of control, having power in themselves because of their nature.'[21] If anything, the advice may be over-cautious. There is some confusion here between the use of images in communication from God and the use of images to control reality or influence the course of events. If God speaks through the Spirit to the church today, there seems no reason why he should not make use of the 'fallen imagination' as a medium of communication. In fact, given the invisible nature of God, it is difficult to see how we may conceive of him and his purposes at all *without* making some use of our imaginations. There are no doubt pitfalls to be avoided in the prophetic use of the imagination, but this is rather different to the idea that by inducing images in our minds we may 'manipulate reality'.

The controlling influence of mental images is no doubt a construct of modern psychology. Although imagery features prominently in the Bible in prophetic discourse, there is no explicit appreciation of the power of the imagination to shape our expectations and behaviour.[22] This does not necessarily mean, however, that we cannot use the language and paradigms of modern psychology to describe either a false or an authentic spirituality. Copeland appears to recognize this when he says: 'Instead of the phrase "building an inner image with the promises of God" I could have just said "building real Bible hope with the promises of God" because that's what it is.'[23] It is obviously important to ask whether in the process of translation from biblical to modern categories anything important has been lost or distorted. But there is also a pragmatic test to apply: is the Spirit of God evident in the spirituality that is shaped by these concepts or only the human spirit?

Positive confession

The fundamental problem with the doctrine of positive confession is that it appears to attribute to speech a function that extends beyond the normal processes of interpersonal communication. A confession, either positive or negative in intention, activates a spiritual law which has certain inevitable effects. The theory is at least *analogous* to the magical notion that a person can affect reality by reciting particular 'spells'.[24] Stephen Hunt puts the case against the doctrine: 'Positive confession, put succinctly, seems to embrace a law of metaphysical causation in that what is spoken by the believer in faith operates the spiritual law of faith itself and brings what is "confessed" into material reality.'[25]

Clearly any prayer needs to be articulated in some way. As Copeland says, 'The force of faith is released by words.'[26] The force of any idea or feeling is released by words. We could go on to describe this effect as a 'law', as Copeland does: 'Faith-filled words put the law of the Spirit of life into operation.' But the real reason for the efficacy of faith-filled words is that they *communicate*. In prayer we *express* trust in God, we ask for something from God; we do not speak it into existence. Prayer still allows God the freedom to act, the freedom to determine what is best, the freedom to bless or withhold blessing. There is a fine line between the 'positive confession' which is an expression of trust in God or the activation of an authority given by God and the 'positive confession' which is somehow believed to be the effective *means* by which a desired goal is achieved. Anything that suggests that spiritual power has been brought into the sphere of *human* control amounts in principle to a form of idolatry or occult manipulation.[27]

If we understand prayer as being fundamentally a matter of communication between people and God, it is difficult to see why a prayer articulated silently should be any less effective than one spoken out loud. The most incoherent groans of our hearts are interpreted by the Spirit, who 'intercedes with sighs too deep for words' (Rom. 8:26). There is, no doubt, a greater psychological commitment involved in speaking out; there is also an important corporate dimension as Christians agree with one another in prayer. But these functions do not amount to an absolute requirement that the prayer of faith be spoken aloud. The force of faith may also be released by actions, without words – many were healed simply by touching the edge of

Jesus' garment (Mt. 9:20-21; 14:36; Mk. 3:10; 5:27-28; 6:56; Lk. 6:19; 8:44). It is not the confession but the expectation that characterizes such faith.

Negative speech is likely to have negative results, positive speech is likely to have positive results. But this is not because words activate spiritual laws. The idealist or metaphysical explanation is redundant. Words are powerful because speech is powerful: the tongue is a fire that can set a whole forest burning (Jas. 3:5). Words disclose the thoughts and emotions that are in a person: as Jesus told the Pharisees, 'out of the abundance of the heart the mouth speaks' (Mt. 12:34). Words communicate and by communicating they change minds or reinforce attitudes or open up new opportunities; they persuade, they inform, they provoke anger; they may promote a healthy spiritual environment or they may poison the atmosphere. Creflo Dollar writes: 'I make confessions because I'm trying to get my heart to line up with the Word of God.'[28] But this is a very *realistic*, psychologically intelligible explanation of positive confession. Moreover, because this is a matter of communication, the social and psychological context of speech must also be taken into account. Positive speech can have negative effects: it may appear over-sentimental or cloying or insincere or unrealistic.

Proverbs 6:2 is a popular proof-text for the view that our words may affect our circumstances for better or for worse: '...you are snared by the utterance of your lips, caught by the words of your mouth.' The crude Word of Faith interpretation is hardly worth refuting: the meaning of the verse is the entirely straightforward one that if you make a pledge to someone (6:1), no matter how unwisely, you are bound by your words.[29] Similarly, there is no basis for the argument that according to Romans 4:17 KJV both God and Abraham exercised a faith that called 'things which be not as though they were'.[30] On the one hand, this is not a definition of faith, and on the other, it is not attributed to Abraham. Rather, Paul's point is that Abraham had faith in the God who is powerful enough to give life to the dead and create out of nothing.

Romans 10:9-10 is often taken as justification for the insistence on spoken confession: 'if you confess with your lips that Jesus is Lord and believe in your heart that God raised him from the dead, you will be saved.' Dollar summarizes: 'Basically, confession brings salvation into being.'[31] Paul has adapted Deuteronomy 30:14 to his argument about faith: 'the word is very near to you; it is in your mouth and in your heart for you to observe.' His point is not so much that faith must be confessed but that the possibility of faith, and the righteousness that accompanies it, is very near. It is undoubtedly important that faith in Christ is confessed publicly, but this is incidental to his purpose here and does not, in any case, constitute a paradigm for every prayer of faith.

Speaking to a problem

There are occasions when Jesus directly addresses inanimate objects or encourages his disciples to do so. For example, he 'rebuked the wind, and said to the sea, "Peace! Be still!"' (Mk. 4:39; cf. Lk. 8:24); he 'rebuked' a fever (Lk. 4:39); he cursed the fig tree (Mt. 21:19; Mk. 11:14); and he told the disciples: "Truly I tell you, if you say to this mountain, 'Be taken up and thrown into the sea...'" (Mk. 11:23; cf. Mt. 21:21). Do these texts suggest that such words have the power directly to affect material reality? Copeland makes the distinction explicit with reference to this passage: 'Your fourth step of faith is: *Speak to the problem*. Notice, I didn't say talk to God about the problem, I said speak to the problem itself.'[32] There is no place for uncertainty: God is bound by his Word. 'As a believer, you have a right to make commands in the Name of Jesus.'[33] Kenneth Hagin says that 'Faith will work by *saying* without *praying*.'[34]

There is good reason to doubt whether those instances where Jesus spoke directly to inanimate objects are meant to be paradigmatic for the ministry of the believer. The stilling of the storm and the cursing of the fig tree are both highly symbolic and prophetic actions. The language of 'rebuking' natural objects or conditions recalls certain statements in the

Old Testament about God rebuking the sea (eg. 2 Sam. 22:16; Ps. 18:16; Ps. 105.9; Is. 50:2) or wild animals (Ps. 67:31). They are likely, therefore, to be implicit claims to fulfil the function of divinity, and we may judge it inappropriate for believers to imitate Jesus in this respect.

Although the saying about the mountain in Mark 11:23 is couched in rather impersonal terms, the general rule in verse 24 is stated in the form of prayer to God (cf. Mt. 21:22; Jn. 16:23-24). The relational aspect is underlined further in verse 25 by the emphasis on forgiveness. It seems likely, moreover, that the saying has a particular symbolic and eschatological reference. It forms part of Jesus' explanation of the withering of the fig-tree and for that reason must be more than a statement about the power of faith. Lane, for example, thinks that it may be an allusion to the prophecy in Zechariah 14 that the Lord would stand upon the Mount of Olives, the mountain would be split in two, and the whole land would be turned into a plain (4, 10; cf. Is. 40:4; Lk. 3:5). 'The prayer in question is then specifically a Passover prayer for God to establish his reign.'[35] Alternatively it may be the destruction of the temple mount that is intended.[36] However, the allusion is imprecise and 11:24 appears to be a much more general statement about the effectiveness of the prayer of faith.[37]

The prayer of faith

Any critique of the Word of Faith movement, however, must take very seriously those passages in the New Testament which teach a quite radical trust in God. At the centre of this teaching there is a simple and seemingly unequivocal promise, repeated in all four gospels in one form or another and echoed in James and 1 John: 'ask for whatever you wish, and it will be done for you' (Jn. 15:7; cf. Mk. 11:24 = Mt. 21:22; Mt. 7:7 = Lk. 11:9; Mt. 18:19; Jn. 14:13-14; 16:23-24; Jas. 1:6-7; cf. 5:15; 1 Jn. 3:21-22; 5:14-15). Word of Faith spirituality is driven by the conviction that these affirmations should be taken quite literally and very seriously. Both the theoretical description of faith in terms of the operation of spiritual laws and the practical emphasis on the power of thoughts and words to facilitate or obstruct the working of faith are the product of this determination: they constitute the overdeveloped methodology by which faith is to be implemented. While we need to avoid this sort of deformation of the life of faith, we should give some thought to the general preconditions for effective prayer, not least because it is important to acknowledge the intention behind the Word of Faith teaching.

1. **Communion with Christ**. Many of the statements about receiving whatever we ask for are set in the context of teaching about the continuing relation of the disciples to Jesus after his death and resurrection: 'If you abide in me, and my words abide in you, ask for whatever you wish, and it will be done for you' (Jn. 15:7). To ask the Father for something 'in Jesus' name' invokes the authority of the risen Lord (Jn. 14:12-14; 16:24). Similarly, if two or three are gathered in Jesus' name, he will be there with them, and whatever they ask for, 'it will be done for you by my Father in heaven' (Mt. 18:19-20).

   These promises are important because Jesus knows that he will not always be physically present with the disciples (see especially Jn. 16:16-24). They are an assurance that the kingdom of God will not grind to a halt after his death: if Jesus caused the fig-tree to wither, the disciples would do no less. But these statements also make it clear that prayer will only be effective if Jesus remains a living and authoritative presence among them – as two or three gather in his name, as they remain in him and he in them, as they pray to the Father in his name. The effectiveness of the prayer of faith, therefore, is dependent principally on whether the person and ministry of Jesus find a continuation in the lives and activity of the disciples.

2. **Being right with God**. There is a requirement of righteousness and obedience: 'if our hearts do not condemn us, we have boldness before God; and we receive from him

whatever we ask, because we obey his commandments and do what pleases him' (1 Jn. 3:21-22). James reminds his readers that the 'prayer of the righteous is powerful and effective' (Jas. 5:16).

3. **Believing right**. The one who prays should not doubt but should believe 'that what you say will come to pass' (Mk. 11:24; cf. Mt. 14:31). James may have had Jesus' teaching in mind when he wrote that a person who doubts is like 'a wave of the sea, driven and tossed by the wind' and should not expect to receive anything from the Lord (Jas. 1:6-7). Healings in the Gospels are generally attributed to the faith either of the sick person (eg. Mk. 5:34; Lk. 18:42) or of those who brought the sick person to Jesus (eg. Mt. 8:13). Where that faith was lacking, Jesus was unable heal (Mk. 6:5-6a; cf. Heb. 11:6). According to James 5:15 the 'prayer of faith (*hē euchē tēs pisteōs*) will save the sick'.

The insistence that a person should believe and not doubt raises the question of what mental state is required by such faith. To what extent does faith depend on the conscious and sustained exclusion of doubt from our minds in order to be effective? Of course, this is a very modern concern: the New Testament has little interest in the psychology of faith. The closest we get to a definition of doubt is James 1:7-8. James characterizes the doubter as one who is 'double-minded' (*dipsuchos*) and 'unstable (*akatastatos*) in every way', easily distracted from his purpose as a wave is blown this way and that by the wind. Although it would be natural to take this description of single-minded and concentrated belief as a model for all prayer, a word of caution needs to be inserted. The asking in faith which James describes appears in the context of an exhortation to persevere in the face of persecution. He urges his readers to reap the spiritual benefits that may result from such a period of testing: 'let endurance have its full effect, so that you may be mature and complete, lacking in nothing' (1:4). This context at least intensifies the need for unwavering, single-minded faith in order to receive from God that which is essentially a product of endurance – in the particular instance, wisdom (5). We cannot categorically say that such intensely focused, persistent faith belongs only to crisis situations, but it could be argued that James is less interested in the mental condition of belief than in the general determination of the believer to remain faithful to Christ during a period of severe testing. We may recall at this point that the context of Mark 11:23-24, and perhaps the reference to 'this mountain', strongly suggest a situation of eschatological crisis.

The distinction becomes important in view of the enormous mental and emotional effort required by Word of Faith teaching in order to sustain a radical faith in the face of doubt and empirical evidence to the contrary. There comes a point where faith ceases to be a matter of trust in God and becomes instead merely a difficult mental exercise – one that is as contrary to grace as any ascetic discipline. This is where the analogy with positive thinking becomes relevant. The Word of Faith movement has crawled so far along the branch of faith that it has had to resort to the levitational powers of positive thinking in order to keep the branch from breaking.

A more appropriate description of the life of faith would probably differentiate between an underlying and persistent attitude of trust in God as Father and the sporadic moments of more radical faith that arise as we discover and act upon the will of God in particular situations. But such faith is experienced more as a gift of grace than as the predictable outworking of a spiritual law. Jesus' response to the disciples' request that he should 'Increase our faith' suggests that the efficacy of faith is determined not by our mental capacity to believe – or to suspend disbelief – but by the power of God: "If you had faith the size of a mustard seed, you could say to this mulberry tree, 'Be uprooted and planted in the sea,' and it would obey you" (Lk. 17:5-6; cf. Mt. 17:20). In the end, it is the act of discernment that rescues us from presumption and from the burden of generating and sustaining within ourselves a sufficiently intense and intransigent attitude of faith.

4. **The work of the Spirit**. Although we act in faith partly in response to the consistent principles that we find in Scripture, faith should also be a response to the more direct and personal witness of the Spirit in the life of the believer. There are at least two aspects to this, both having to do with the way in which faith is contextualized.

   First, the more rigorously systematic or legalistic our approach to faith, the less likely we are to hear what God is saying to us in the here and now. Faith must take into account certain general and universal conditions; but it must also deal with the unique opportunities and constraints of the actual situation. God speaks not only in general and universal terms but also in particular and contingent terms. Charles Farah and others have made a distinction (not an absolute one – Farah calls it a 'theological construct') between *rhēma*, denoting a contingent word spoken under particular circumstances, and *logos*, denoting God's universal Word to mankind.[38] A literal translation of Acts 10:44 illustrates the distinction: 'While Peter was still speaking these words (*ta rhēmata tauta*), the Holy Spirit fell upon all who heard the word (*ton logon*)'. Here again we encounter the tendency of Word of Faith teaching to promote a deistic spirituality in which the rules of faith have been absolutely and universally determined, making the direct involvement of God in our lives more or less superfluous.

   Secondly, there must be doubts about the Word of Faith assumption that the faith to move mountains is given to every believer. Hagin finds support for this position in Romans 12:3, but the verse, in fact, has no direct relevance to this argument – if anything, the phrase 'according to the measure of faith that God has assigned' suggests that not everyone has the same measure of faith. 1 Corinthians 12:9 lists 'faith' as one of the gifts of the Spirit which is given to some but not all in the body of Christ. We will consider in the final chapter whether perhaps this insight offers a way of assimilating the radical Word of Faith perspective into a more comprehensive and diversified understanding of how different individuals exercise trust in God.

5. **Persevering in prayer**. We may ask, finally, whether there is any biblical basis for the view that the genuine prayer of faith has had effect even though the symptoms of illness persist. Much is made of the fact that Jesus uses an aorist in Mark 11:24: 'whatever you ask for in prayer, believe that you have received (*elabete*) it'. New Testament scholarship usually explains this as a Semitic prophetic idiom expressing the certainty of some future event.[39] The final clause, 'and it will be yours', suggests a future fulfilment of the request. All that can really be said about the ten lepers (Lk. 17:12-14) is that they acted on the assumption that by the time they reached the priests, they would have been healed. There is nothing in the story to suggest that they were *spiritually* or otherwise healed before they noticed that they had been made clean.

There is also a more general question to ask: Does the principle work in other situations? For example, if a person is unemployed and prays for a job, could we say that she has received that job even though the symptoms of unemployment persist? Is she to go out to work in the morning even though she has nowhere to go? If this is absurd, what makes the prayer for healing different, other than the fact that health is a more mysterious thing than employment?

If there is any justification for this sort of argument, it can only be the pragmatic one that it encourages people to take their prayer of faith more seriously – a mental discipline, a trick of the mind almost, that helps prevent faith from dissolving into doubt and forgetfulness. It could be regarded as an extension of the more normal argument that we must persevere in prayer until we receive an answer: by believing that we have already received, we lock ourselves into the expectation that God will eventually give us what we ask for. But such a rationale has reduced the doctrine to an unnecessary psychological device. It certainly cannot be argued that this constitutes a higher form of faith. It is no less a matter of faith to believe that God *will* heal or that he *will* provide financial resources than to believe that he has already done so only the tangible evidence is not yet there. Such a defiance of the evidence is unrealistic – if not actually dishonest – and potentially dangerous. There is a fundamental philosophical difference between the belief that God will act in the future and the denial of present reality that is entailed in Word of Faith teaching. As Robert Bowman writes, 'faith does not ignore physical facts. Rather, faith refuses to allow facts or circumstances to shake our confidence in God's ability to do what he promised.'[40] The problem is that there is no room in Word of Faith theology for the possibility that God may not want to heal or make prosperous, therefore these might as well be present realities as future. There is no need to defer fulfilment. Inevitably, though, this shifts the practice of faith away from a persistent and active trust in the God who will act towards a blinkered preoccupation with the symptoms as we look for the supposed reality to manifest itself.

* * * *

Faith can never be a perfect ability or state of mind. It remains a human faculty and therefore remains subject to the psychological and epistemological limitations of our fallenness. The Word of Faith movement seeks to transcend the fallibility of faith. In many instances this no doubt amounts to dangerous spiritual presumption; in other cases, it may be no more than faith overreaching itself. But we cannot ignore the fact that the New Testament sets the bar very high. We may have got used to flopping underneath it in lackadaisical fashion; but should we berate those who are reckless enough to attempt to jump over it? Are we sure that our perspective on faith is so much superior? Are we sure we understand the rhetoric of 'spiritual laws' and 'positive confession'? To speak of faith as a force or law or to invest spoken words with a quasi-material power may be a matter less of metaphysics than of metaphor. Implicit in the rhetoric is perhaps the thought that faith *may* be seen as something more mechanical, and therefore more *reliable*, than our customary, ill-defined notions permit. We may wish to argue that faith is much more than this, that the functional metaphors devalue faith; but then we must be sure that we do not make the affirmation of the sovereignty of God an excuse for fatalism and inaction.

9

Poverty and wealth in the Old Testament

The central tenet of prosperity teaching is that believers will prosper, especially in financial terms, if they are obedient to the word of God. The natural corollary to this assumption is that for a believer to be in a state of poverty is contrary to the will of God. In fact, reflections upon wealth and poverty in the Bible are complex and ambivalent. The Bible does not consist fundamentally of a set of abstract, universally applicable precepts. As we work through the different passages and arguments, it will become apparent that teaching about wealth and poverty is not centred on the well-being of the individual but is controlled by two related *historical* principles. The first is the covenant with Israel; the second is the historical crisis precipitated by the failure of the covenant.

The creation narratives

The universal basis for material prosperity is to be found, in the first place, in the creation narratives. The material world, at least in so far as it satisfied mankind's requirements for food, was declared to be good. The garden needed some care and cultivation, but the implication is that the work would not have been arduous; and, with one notable exception, Adam and Eve could eat freely of the trees of the garden (Gen. 2:15-17; cf. 1:29). No conclusions can be drawn from these texts, however, regarding the value of manufactured goods. The nakedness of

Adam and Eve represents an innocence and natural sufficiency that, one imagines, had little need for artefacts.

Although there is no explicit statement to the effect, poverty and suffering are naturally seen to derive from the exclusion of the couple from Eden. The man will struggle to make a livelihood from a cursed ground that produces thorns and thistles. He will eat bread by the sweat of his brow; the woman will suffer pain in childbirth. Dominion over the natural world is not forfeited at the fall (Ps. 8:6-8; cf. Gen. 1:28-30), but the earth does not belong to him to use just as he wishes (Ps. 24:1; cf. Ex. 19:5; Deut. 26:10; 1 Chron. 29:12; Job 41:11; Ps. 50:12). Work may still be a means of blessing (Ps. 128:1-2), however; and nothing in the Old Testament suggests that the production and trading of goods are regarded as inherently sinful activities (cf. Prov. 31:14, 16, 18, 20, 30), though again we might hesitate to draw any firm conclusions from this about the value of modern industrialized consumer culture. A certain critique of materialism emerges in the prophetic denunciation of idolatry and the proclamation of judgment against the nations, but the primary motivation for this is theological rather than ethical.

The covenant with Abram

The covenant with Abram entailed in the first place the abandonment of his own country and family. By leaving these things behind and accepting the uncertainties of migration he made himself eligible to receive a new land in which he would become the father of a great nation and a blessing to all the families of the earth. These are the dominant elements in the promises given by God to Abram (Gen. 12:2-3, 7; 15:18; 17:8; 22:17). The material prosperity of the patriarchs is highlighted (cf. 20:14-16; 24:35; 26:13; 30:43; 47:27) but remains throughout the narratives a secondary theme. It is only at a later stage that the natural wealth of the 'promised land' becomes thematically significant: for the Jews of the Exodus and the conquest Canaan was 'a good and broad land, a land flowing with milk and honey' (Ex. 3:8; cf. 3:17; 13:5; Lev. 20:24; Num. 13:27). The expectation of agricultural abundance and financial prosperity is elaborated upon in Deuteronomy 8:7-16.

Prosperity and the law of Moses

The covenant with Moses was intended to regulate the life of a people inhabiting a naturally bountiful land. The basic rule was very simple: if the people kept the law of God, they would enjoy a comprehensive prosperity that included both health and wealth:

> If you heed these ordinances, by diligently observing them, the LORD your God will maintain with you the covenant loyalty that he swore to your ancestors; he will love you, bless you, and multiply you; he will bless the fruit of your womb and the fruit of your ground, your grain and your wine and your oil, the increase of your cattle and the issue of your flock, in the land that he swore to your ancestors to give you. You shall be the most blessed of peoples, with neither sterility nor barrenness among you or your livestock. The LORD will turn away from you every illness; all the dread diseases of Egypt that you experienced, he will not inflict on you, but he will lay them on all who hate you. (Deut. 7:12-15; cf. Ex. 23:25-26; Deut. 6:1-3; 15:4-6; 28:1-14)

This is not a prosperity to be *claimed* by faith. The focus is quite different: it is bestowed upon the people in response to their obedience to the law. The basic formula is: keep the law, please God, do justice, and you will be blessed. Prosperity is not so much a goal as a by-product. Jesus' argument about seeking first the kingdom of God (Mt. 6:33; Lk. 12:31) is a natural development of this principle.

Statements about prosperity clearly relate in the first place to the nation as a whole, and the argument is sometimes made that these promises should not be applied at the individual level. The question arises, however, as to how this national prosperity was to come about if not through the prosperity of individuals. The law enjoins various forms of giving and an assiduous concern for the well-being of the poor, but it does not enforce economic equality or the redistribution of wealth within the community.[1] On the contrary, private property is protected. Given this, the hope of national prosperity was bound to entail disparities of wealth within the nation. The ideal, however, was that wealth would come to the righteous individual and his family (cf. Ps. 37:25-26). It is against this background that we must understand the sanctified hedonism that is encouraged in the Wisdom literature: 'Go, eat your bread with enjoyment, and drink your wine with a merry heart; for God has long ago approved what you do' (Eccl. 9:7; cf. 3:12-13; 8:15).[2] The promise of divine blessing is especially reinforced in instances where an Israelite might suffer financially as a result of keeping the law and observing the demands of justice (eg. Deut. 15:10, 18; 24:19). This element of redress is largely missing from Word of Faith teaching, where the assumption is rather that obedience leads directly to prosperity, not by way of injustice and deprivation.

Poverty, on the other hand, can be seen both as a source of wretchedness ('The wealth of the rich is their fortress; the poverty of the poor is their ruin', Prov. 10:15), and as a manifestation of judgment. The latter is arguably the case in 1 Samuel 2:7-8. Taken out of context Hannah's assertion that 'the Lord makes poor and makes rich' appears to suggest that poverty and wealth are of equal spiritual value. But 'the Lord makes poor' forms part of a pronouncement of judgment on the unrighteous – the rich and powerful enemies of God – while wealth from the Lord is virtually an eschatological blessing on the poor (cf. Lk. 1:46-55).[3]

The right use of prosperity

A large part of the law of Moses consists of rules governing the economic life of the nation. The conditions for material prosperity, therefore, include justice and generosity in the use of money and goods.

On entry into the promised land property was to be distributed fairly, according to the size of the group (Num. 26:54).[4] Prohibitions against theft and covetousness were incorporated into the decalogue (Ex. 20:15, 17; cf. 22:1-15). There were laws against the theft of property (Deut. 19:14; 27:17), against bribery (Ex. 23:8; Deut. 16:19), against unjust commercial dealings (Lev. 19:35-36), laws protecting the right of the first born to inherit (Deut. 21:15-17). The requirement of judicial impartiality with regard both to the poor and the rich (Ex. 23:2-3; Lev. 19:15) weakens the argument that God is biased towards the poor.[5]

Property rights, however, were not considered absolute. Ownership of land was qualified by the recognition that the people were in the final analysis only 'aliens and tenants' in a land leased to them by God. For that reason the land could not be sold in perpetuity (Lev. 25:23; cf. Ex. 19:5). Gleaning rights were also indicative of the fact that the land was reckoned to belong to God (Lev. 19:9-10; Deut. 24:19-22) – they were the means by which the poor were enabled to share in the prosperity of the land.[6]

The law of Jubilee, the sabbath year, and the sabbath itself imposed further constraints on the acquisition and accumulation of wealth and built into the economic system a significant requirement of trust in God as provider.[7] Every seventh year was to be a sabbath, when the land would lie fallow, and all the people and animals who worked it were to rest (Ex. 23:10-11; Lev. 25:2-7, 20-22). During this year the poor were allowed to eat from the land. For the rest God promised adequate provision: 'I will order my blessing for you in the sixth year, so that it will yield a crop for three years' (Lev. 25:21). Debts were also to be remitted because 'the Lord's remission has been proclaimed' (Deut. 15:1-2) and Hebrew slaves released (Ex. 21:2) every seventh year.[8] After 49 years the year of Jubilee would be proclaimed throughout the land (Lev. 25). In theory at least, land that had been leased to avert poverty was returned to its original owners and indentured Israelite servants were set free in recognition of the fact that they were first of all God's servants (Lev. 25:42).

Taxation in one form or another constituted a final constraint on the personal use of wealth.[9] A tenth of the produce of the land and every tenth animal from a herd or flock was reckoned to belong to the Lord (Lev. 27:30-33). It was given to the Levites (Num. 18:21-24), who had no land of their own, and they in turn gave a tenth to the priests (Num. 18:25-29). Deuteronomy 14:22-27 prescribes a second tithe of agricul-tural produce which was either to be eaten by the household 'in the place that he will choose as a dwelling for his name' or, if distance was prohibitive, sold and the money used to buy food to be eaten at the place of worship. The reason given was that 'you may learn to fear the Lord your God always' (23). Every third year the tithe was stored not only for the use of the Levites but also to feed those on the margins of the economy – the resident aliens, the orphans, and the widows – 'so that the Lord your God may bless you in all the work that you undertake' (Deut. 14:29).[10] In addition to the tithes the Jews also paid a flat rate annual 'temple' tax of a half shekel, which was originally given as a ransom or atonement for their lives 'so that no plague may come upon them for being registered' (Ex. 30:12). The terms of the tax (especially v.15) clearly presuppose a significant disparity between the rich and the poor in Israel.

The continued presence of the poor in Israel

That prosperity was promised to the *nation* primarily is evidenced by the fact that no contradiction was perceived between this expectation and the presence of destitute individuals within the community. Deuteronomy 15 deals first with the remission of debts between Israelites in the seventh year. To remove the obvious anxiety that this stipulation might have produced, there follows the assurance that there would be 'no one in need among you, because the Lord is sure to bless you in the land that the LORD your God is giving you as a possession to occupy' (4). As long as they observed the commandments, they could expect to lend to many nations and not borrow (5-6). The possibility that a needy person might appear among the people ('a member of your community') is not attributed to a failure of obedience. Rather, it is treated as an opportunity for open-handed generosity, even if the seventh year is approaching (7-11). In this way the wealth of an obedient nation was shared with the individual in need.[11]

The existence of a range of laws aimed at mitigating economic hardship is also indicative of the fact that poverty was recognized as an inevitable structural feature of Jewish economic life, despite the covenantal promise.[12] Protection was guaranteed for aliens on the grounds that the Jews had also been aliens in Egypt (Ex. 22:21; 23:9; Lev. 19:33-34). For the same reason relatives who fell into difficulty were not to be exploited (Lev. 25:35-43). Gleaning rights guaranteed food for the landless and impoverished (Lev. 19:9-10; Deut. 24:19-22). A sliding scale for offerings and sacrifices and for various penalties allowed the poor to fulfil their obligations under the law (Lev. 5:7, 11; 12:8; 14:21-22). It was forbidden to take a person's means of livelihood as collateral in a court of law (Deut. 24:6). The laws against taking interest on loans also appear to apply only within the covenant community (Ex. 22:25-27; Lev. 25:35-38; Deut. 23:19-20). The distinction is made explicit in Deuteronomy 23:20: 'On loans to a foreigner you may charge interest, but on loans to another Israelite you may not charge interest.' The laws were intended as a means by which the rich might act righteously towards the poor. They appear to presuppose a situation in which most loans were charitable rather than commercial.[13]

The Jews were expected to care for the needy out of the abundance that God would give them if they were faithful in keeping the law (Deut. 15:7-11; 23:20). The wealthy and powerful were under obligation to ensure that the poor and defenceless were not denied justice or turned away from the table of Israel's prosperity (Ps. 82:3-4; cf. Job 31:16-23). The fulfilment of these responsibilities was a significant mark of righteousness (Prov. 29:7). An authentic piety expressed itself in, among other things, sharing bread with the hungry, providing shelter for the 'homeless poor', and covering the naked (Is. 58:7).[14]

The law of Moses was meant to regulate the communal and economic life of a redeemed people. No attempt is made to recommend it to or impose it upon other societies. Deuteronomy 4:6 suggests that other peoples – perhaps especially the people of the land which the Israelites were about to occupy – might acknowledge the wisdom of Israel's 'statutes and ordinances', provided that they were properly observed. Prophetic critique and condemnation of the nations sometimes had a strong socio-economic dimension to it (Is. 14; Ezek. 26-28). But it is probably too much to claim that God 'intended Israel's Law to enlighten the nations'.[15] The economic principles articulated in the Law, though not without universal value, were too closely bound up with the covenantal relationship. Micah 4:1-2 looks forward to a time when the nations will come to 'the mountain of the Lord's house' to learn his ways and be instructed in *Torah*, but this belongs to an eschatological future.

The failure of economic justice in Israel

The problem, of course, was that Israel did not keep the commandments, and the wealthy did not, for the most part, look after the interests of the poor. It is generally accepted that the introduction of the monarchy had a number of undesirable, and not entirely unforeseen (cf. 1 Sam. 8:10-18), consequences which contributed to the breakdown of economic justice and exacerbated the disparity between rich and poor.[16] In particular, the emergence of patrician and business classes led to a demand for cheap labour and the unrestrained exploitation of the poor. Ancestral properties, the mainstay of the earlier tribal economy, were acquired by wealthy landowners, creating dependency (cf. Is. 5:8). The affluence that came with national and urban expansion generated a love of luxury and ostentation that could hardly be reconciled with the ethos of the Mosaic covenant.

The response to economic injustice comes in a number of forms. There are general warnings in the Wisdom literature about the moral and spiritual dangers of wealth. The prosperity of the wicked presents a persistent moral problem

(Ps. 73:12). Wealth is frequently shown to be a transient and ultimately worthless commodity (Job 1:21; Ps. 39:4-6; 49:16-17; Prov. 11:28; 23:4-5; Eccl. 5:8-17; 6:1-12). The vanity of a self-centred and loveless pursuit of wealth is condemned (Eccl. 4:7-8; cf. Ps. 52:6-7; Prov. 28:20). The virtues of moderation and sufficiency are extolled.[17] Righteous poverty is regarded as preferable to the 'abundance of many wicked' (Ps. 37:16). Wisdom and honour are to be sought instead of silver and gold (Prov. 8:10-11; cf. 3:13-16; 16:16; 22:1).

In all of this, however, the covenantal link between obedience and prosperity does not entirely fall into abeyance (cf. Hezekiah, Josiah, Daniel).[18] A careful distinction is maintained between the righteous and the unrighteous wealthy, between those who are rewarded for their faithfulness and those who trust in their wealth rather than in God. 'Those who trust in their riches will wither' (Prov. 11:28; cf. Job 31:24-28); but for those who fear the Lord 'wealth and riches are in their houses' (Ps. 112:3; cf. Ps. 128), wisdom holds 'riches and honor' in her left hand (Prov. 3:16; cf. 22:4), 'prosperity rewards the righteous' (Prov. 13:21), the 'reward for humility and fear of the LORD is riches and honor and life' (Prov. 22:4). Idleness is condemned; industry is encouraged and the wealth it produces counted as a good thing (Prov. 10:4; 28:19; Eccl. 5:12; but note Prov. 23:4).

The more substantial critique of economic injustice comes from the prophets. After idolatry the failure to deal fairly and generously with the poor and oppressed is the most significant factor in the judgment that came upon both Israel and Judah.[19] Craig Blomberg identifies five general categories of religious and ethical failure in relation to wealth and material possessions condemned by the prophets: the worship of idols made from expensive materials (cf. Is. 2:20; Hos. 2:8); the substitution of religious ritual for compassion and justice (Jer. 7:4-7); the direct exploitation of the poor (Is. 1:21-23; 3:14-15; Amos 2:6; 5:11-12; 8:4-6); the arrogance of the rich who boast of their wealth and think themselves immune to judgment (Amos 4:1; 6:4-6); and the greed and venality of Israel's political and religious leaders, who profit from their positions of authority and influence: 'Its rulers give judgment for a bribe, its priests teach for a price, its prophets give oracles for money; yet they lean upon the LORD and say, "Surely the LORD is with us! No harm shall come upon us"' (Mic. 3:11).[20]

Judgment and salvation

If there is poverty in Israel, it is not because the poor have lacked faith or have failed to fulfil the word of God or have not given to the Lord's work.[21] At the individual level poverty may be attributed to idleness or moral failure, but systemic poverty is usually understood to be the result of injustice on the part of the rich, and the solution lies in their hands: to act righteously and to provide for those in need.[22] Even the command to 'bring the full tithe into the storehouse' to see whether God will 'not open the windows of heaven for you and pour down for you an overflowing blessing' (Mal. 3:10) is essentially a matter of fulfilling the law (7). It is directed not at those who lack wealth but at the nation as a whole (9), which means in effect those who 'oppress the hired workers in their wages, the widow and the orphan, against those who thrust aside the alien, and do not fear me' (5).

The unrighteous wealthy, who deny justice to the needy and oppress the poor, will suffer eschatological judgment on a 'day of punishment' (Is. 10:3),[23] but this is to be interpreted in historical terms: they will lose everything when God sends the Assyrians 'against the people of my wrath' (5-6). Jeremiah reproaches the people of Jerusalem because 'on your skirts is found the lifeblood of the innocent poor', and warns them of impending judgment (Jer. 2:34-35; cf. Zech. 7:8-12). The riches of the unrighteous will be of no use on the day of wrath (Prov. 11:4; cf. Ps. 49:7). Proverbs 13:22 suggests that the wealth of the wicked will be given to the righteous.

Conversely, the poor are beneficiaries of divine favour *insofar* as they are victims of injustice. He is 'a refuge to the poor, a refuge to the needy in their distress' (Is. 25:4). It is probably inappropriate to speak of the special favour of God towards the poor apart from the polemic against injustice. Poverty is not a naturally blessed state, but the unethical behaviour that sustains and exacerbates poverty is a breach of the covenant and the assurance is that God will act both to judge the unrighteous and to restore the oppressed. But the poor are also, inevitably, more likely to look to the Lord for help (cf. Ps. 9:9-10; 69:32-33) and be found in the company of the righteous (Ps. 14:5-6). At times a more direct equation between poverty and righteousness appears (Ps. 37:12-16; Is. 3:15).[24] But the point may be less that the poor are especially righteous than that they are *part of* God's people.

There is, finally, the eschatological motif of the nations bringing their wealth into the restored Jerusalem (eg. Is. 60:5-7, 9, 11; 61:6; Hag. 2:7-8; Zech. 14:14). Such wealth is a sign of the ultimate defeat of Israel's enemies, of the honour that Israel shall receive among the nations, and of the glory of the rebuilt house of the Lord in Jerusalem. How we should regard the fulfilment of these prophecies, however, is a difficult question. Perhaps we must fall back on the notion of a cumulative and sporadic fulfilment in the rebuilding of the city and temple under Ezra and Nehemiah, in the replacement of Herod's temple with the living 'temple' of the church (cf. 1 Cor. 3:16; 1 Pet. 2:5), and in John's vision of a new Jerusalem into which 'the kings of the earth will bring their glory' (Rev. 21:24). This sequence, however, does not allow for the view, promoted by Word of Faith teachers, that the wealth of the nations will be used to finance the mission of the church. The image of pagan wealth being brought into the city belongs to the final overthrow of the enemies of the people of God and to the consummation of God's reign, not to the intermediate period of the church's mission.

* * * *

It is probably not possible to extract from all this a single right attitude in the Old Testament towards material prosperity. Under certain circumstances the poor may be seen to be on safer ground spiritually than the rich. But the promises of prosperity according to the terms of the covenant remain. They are not rescinded on the grounds that Israel's economy has developed far beyond the conditions originally envisaged in the Law of Moses or because exploitation and oppression became the order of the day. There is no doubt validity in the argument that the ideal lifestyle consists in an avoidance of both extremes and their concomitant dangers: 'Remove far from me falsehood and lying; give me neither poverty nor riches; feed me with the food that I need, or I shall be full, and deny you, and say, "Who is the LORD?" or I shall be poor, and steal, and profane the name of my God.' (Prov. 30:8-9).[25] But the more powerful ideal is probably that of the righteous individual who, with his family, is blessed by the Lord with abundance and security and who gives generously to the poor (cf. Ps. 37:25-26; Ps. 112).

10

Poverty and wealth in the Gospels

Broadly speaking Jewish society in the first century can be divided into three economic groups. Among the very wealthy were the high-priestly families, the Herodians, the older aristocracy, and prosperous merchants. A small middle class was made up of skilled artisans, small-scale farmers, and merchants. Then there was the mass of the poor – mostly rural peasants, the people of the land (*'am hā-'āreṣ*): small landowners, tenant farmers, and the landless (hired labourers and beggars). In the context of first century Judaism the poor were marginalized not only economically but also religiously on account of their imperfect observance of the Law.

In general terms the Old Testament understanding of prosperity as a mark of divine favour still had force.[1] The equation, however, was qualified in two respects. First, it was apparent that most wealth was acquired unjustly, which meant that the truly righteous were likely to be poor. This was essentially an empirical observation. It was generally believed that material goods were limited in quantity so that the excessive accumulation of wealth by some was inevitably at the expense of others. Secondly, the wealthy were expected to demonstrate their supposed righteousness by giving generously, either directly or through religious institutions. Governing institutions rarely intervened to help the poor.

Jesus' critique of wealth

The Gospels present a more pessimistic perspective on wealth than the Old Testament because what Jesus anticipated was not a simple consolidation or regeneration of a Torah-based community but a traumatic upheaval and a transition to a new type of community based on a new covenant. Within this transitional perspective there is no assurance that the righteous will be prosperous. Jesus did not bring prosperity to the poor in the way that he brought healing to the sick. But we should keep in mind the fact that Jesus foresaw no prosperity for Israel. The nation faced ruin, and in view of the coming crisis the acquisition of wealth was more or less irrelevant. This was not a time for the sort of prosperity that had been vouchsafed for the righteous under the covenant – a circumstance which must be taken into account as we consider the various texts in which Jesus expresses a strongly negative attitude towards wealth.

'Woe to you who are rich...'

In the sermon on the plain recorded in Luke 6:17-49 Jesus pronounced blessings upon the poor and woes upon the rich. Both the blessings and the woes presuppose a future reversal of circumstances (20-26). The poor will receive the kingdom of God, the hungry will be fed, those who weep will laugh. The rich can expect no further consolation, those who are full will be hungry, those who laugh will mourn and weep. The nature of the rhetoric does not oblige us to treat this as an absolute distinction, but it is clear that Jesus foresaw a broad division within Israel between those who were destitute and disenfranchised, particularly those who would be made outcasts 'on account of the Son of Man' (22), and those who enjoyed wealth and recognition in their lifetime.

The wealthy young ruler and the kingdom of God

When the rich young ruler went away grieving because 'he had many possessions', Jesus warned the disciples, 'Truly I tell you, it will be hard for a rich person to enter the kingdom of heaven. Again I tell you, it is easier for a camel to go through the eye of a needle than for someone who is rich to enter the kingdom of God' (Mt. 19:23-24).[2] The incident provides a concrete illustration of the nature and depth of the division between the poor and the rich. How could a young man like this align himself with the Son of man, who was to be rejected and killed by the political-religious establishment? In the first place, it is just this dilemma which makes the salvation of the rich so difficult. In the context, entering the kingdom of God or being saved entailed a very real abandonment of one's old life and following of Jesus (cf. Lk. 18:22, 28).

Word of Faith teachers have dealt with the challenge of this incident in various ways. Kenneth Copeland is concerned to demonstrate that the man was not at fault for having great wealth, and that it is not God's way to break us spiritually by making us poor. He argues that the man went away unhappy because although God had prospered him, he had not understood the significance of Proverbs 19:17: 'Whoever is kind to the poor lends to the Lord, and will be repaid in full.' The young man had missed an opportunity to receive even more from God by giving to the poor.[3]

F.K.C. Price goes as far as to suggest that the statement 'he had great possessions' is a misinterpretation ('I plan definitely to ask the Lord about this when I see Him') and should read: 'great possessions had him' – ie. that his wealth had an unbreakable hold over his life.[4] The rather cavalier approach to Scripture may be tongue in cheek – in any case, the play on words is probably not too wide of the mark. But still, we cannot get round the fact that the wealth of this 'righteous' man constituted a serious obstacle between him and the kingdom of God and that Jesus instructed him to get rid of it. We have seen already that Price's argument that the man kept most of the proceeds from the sale of his possessions is specious.[5]

An abomination in the sight of God?

Luke 16:15 poses an interesting question. Jesus had warned the disciples that they could not serve both God and wealth. Some Pharisees overheard this and scoffed at the sentiment. But Jesus retorted: 'You are those who justify yourselves in the sight of others; but God knows your hearts; for what is prized by human beings is an abomination in the sight of God.' In view of the general context and Luke's description of the Pharisees as 'lovers of money' (14), it has been suggested that it is wealth that Jesus condemns as an 'abomination', and that this is 'arguably the strongest statement about wealth in the Bible'.[6] What probably determines Jesus' meaning here, however, is the parallel between the self-justification of the Pharisees '*in the sight of others*' and the 'abomination *in the sight of God*'. The Pharisees believed that their wealth gave them religious status, perhaps because prosperity was viewed as a mark of divine favour. It is this reliance on wealth as the basis for justification, rather than on the state of the heart, that is an abomination to God. In effect, it repeats the earlier point that the *love* of wealth, *devotion* to mammon, inevitably precludes love of God, in which case there is no absolute condemnation of wealth here.

The rich man and Lazarus

The argument about the rewards of the wealthy is applied to the rich man tormented in the fires of Hades (Lk. 16:19-31), who is told by Abraham: 'Child, remember that during your lifetime you received your good things...' (Lk. 16:25). Added to this is the failure to show compassion towards the diseased beggar. The description of the man suggests a more ostentatious and self-indulgent lifestyle (perhaps emulating the Roman upper-classes)[7] than that of the rich young ruler. The story also conveys a greater pessimism about the likelihood of the rich changing their ways (31). The literary character of the parable strongly suggests that the rich man and Lazarus are symbolic figures: they represent in an extreme form the unrighteous wealthy and the religiously unacceptable poor in Israel, whose fortunes are destined to be reversed in the age to come.

The rich fool

Jesus told the parable of the rich fool as a warning against greed and materialism: 'for one's life does not consist in the abundance of possessions' (Lk. 12:15). The point of the parable is quite conventional: wealth accumulated on earth will count for nothing at death; it is a fool who values treasure on earth more highly than treasure in heaven (Lk. 12:21, cf. 33; Mt. 6:19). The danger of wealth is that it preoccupies the heart and mind to the exclusion of God (Mt. 6:21). The argument is made most succinctly in the image of a slave's divided loyalties: 'No one can serve two masters; for a slave will either hate the one and love the other, or be devoted to the one and despise the other. You cannot serve God and wealth' (Mt. 6:24).

Copeland has cleverly argued that Jesus' teaching about storing up treasure for ourselves in heaven is to be taken quite literally. By giving we deposit money in the vaults of heaven, where it earns up to a hundredfold increase and is safe from the depradations of rust and thieves, inflation and depression. When we need the money, we have simply to draw it from our heavenly account – indeed, this is the mechanism by which the heavenly Father provides for the needs of those who seek the kingdom of God first (6:33).[8] The idea that we will not have access to this treasure until we get to heaven is something that the poverty-minded church has added.

The interpretation is an intriguing one, but is it what Jesus meant in this passage? He adds to the teaching the aphorism 'where your treasure is, there your heart will be also' (Mt. 6:21; Lk. 12:34). It hardly seems likely that he meant the disciples to set their hearts on their bank balances, even if the money were kept in heaven. It is the 'kingdom of God and his righteousness' that should be their primary objective (Mt. 6:33; cf. Lk. 12:31). There is the further problem that the argument again diminishes the direct personal involvement of God in our lives. We receive because we have already put the money in, not because God knows that we need material things and cares for us. Perhaps the best way to interpret the image of treasure in heaven would be to regard it as the grace of God towards the disciple which may be expressed in terms of material provision in the present age but is not limited to that.

A bias towards the poor?

There is no 'critique' of poverty in Jesus' teaching to match his often quite virulent condemnation of the rich. Poverty does not stand between a person and the kingdom of God in the way that wealth might – just as the sick are healed and their sins forgiven, but are never reproached by Jesus, either specifically or in general terms, for not claiming the health to which they are entitled. What is very difficult for the rich is much easier for the poor. Jesus' central concern is how these two groups, which are defined not only by their relative wealth but also by their presumed religious status, respond to the proclamation and manifestation of the coming kingdom of God.

A crucial aspect of what the kingdom of God meant, however, was the enactment of judgment upon the unrighteous wealthy and the corresponding 'salvation' of the poor and oppressed. There is a profound socio-political dimension to the coming of the kingdom of God. In the synagogue in Nazareth Jesus interpreted his mission in terms of Isaiah 61:1-2: 'The Spirit of the Lord is upon me, because he has anointed me to bring good news to the poor. He has sent me to proclaim release to the captives and recovery of sight to the blind, to let the oppressed go free, to proclaim the year of the Lord's favour' (Lk. 4:18-19; cf. 7:22; Mt. 11:5).[9] But it is important to note that the proclamation of hope in Isaiah 61 is not universal; it concerns the restoration of Israel.

There is undoubtedly here a 'bias' towards the poor, but it belongs in the first place to the particular context of the judgment and salvation of Israel – a point that is often missed in evangelical studies that are anxious to establish a biblical case for a political agenda, albeit a worthy one.[10] The bias emerges precisely because the kingdom of God was rejected by those who should have known better. The man who had prepared a great dinner sent his servant out into the streets to 'bring in the poor, the crippled, the blind, and the lame' because those who had originally been invited refused to come (Lk. 14:15-24). The blessing pronounced upon the poor (Mt. 5:3; Lk. 6:20) pertains to the historical and eschatological crisis of the coming of the kingdom of God. It is part of the polemic against a corrupt religious-political establishment, whose failing was to horde wealth and exploit the poor. But more importantly, by quoting from Isaiah 61 Jesus affirms that salvation for Israel would come about through the restoration of those who were suffering and oppressed. There is certainly a physical dimension to this restoration: 'the blind receive their sight, the lame walk, the lepers are cleansed, the deaf hear, the dead are raised' (Lk. 7:22). But the poor have 'good news brought to them' (*euangelizontai*: cf. Lk. 4:18): Jesus does not say that they shall be made rich.[11]

This makes it more difficult to decide whether Jesus' hostility to wealth and commitment to the poor should be read as normative – a 'fundamental religious-ethical tenet', as Thomas Schmidt terms it.[12] Are the rich condemned because they are rich? Are the poor blessed because they are poor? Or are these secondary factors? Jesus says, 'Woe to you who are rich, for you have received your consolation' (Lk. 6:24), but he also says, 'Woe to you who are laughing now, for you will mourn and weep' (25). Does that mean that hostility to laughter is also a 'fundamental religious-ethical tenet' in the gospels? No, the context is critical. Jesus pronounces judgment on a group of people who have failed to live up to the standards of righteousness required by the covenant, who have profited from injustice, and who exhibit an obdurate complacency about their standing before God. In the context of this particular judgment wealth is condemned because it is bound up with the moral and religious failure of the group. But the general inference that God no longer blesses by means of wealth is probably not warranted.

The lifestyle of discipleship

Equally, we must understand the manner and lifestyle of discipleship described in the Gospels as being determined by both the social and the salvation-historical circumstances of Jesus' ministry. Discipleship was defined, in very real terms, by the long walk to the cross and then the long walk from the cross.

Were Jesus and the disciples wealthy?

The Word of Faith movement has sometimes maintained that Jesus and his disciples were comparatively affluent. John Avanzini has argued, for example, that the group had sufficient funds to justify the luxury of a dishonest treasurer, that they bought their own food (cf. Jn. 4:8), that the comment about the Son of man having nowhere to lay his head (Lk. 9:58) related only to the emergency situation in Samaria, that Jesus in fact had a 'nice house' of his own (Jn. 1:38-39), that he had received substantial funding from the magi, and that he 'wore designer clothes' – a reference to the supposedly expensive 'seamless' tunic described in John 19:23.[13] Jesus, in other words, was the prototype of the modern, well-dressed, immaculately groomed, lavishly funded, preacher of prosperity. The argument is overstated and falls down in several of its details – Jesus was certainly not staying in his own home while in Judea at the time of his baptism; Matthew sets the saying about the Son of man having nowhere to lay his head in a different context (Mt. 8:20); and according to Beasley-Murray the seamless garment was 'not particularly unusual in Palestine' and could have been made by his mother.[14] But as a corrective to any popular misconceptions about the extreme poverty of Jesus there may be some point to the argument.[15]

The disciples were not drawn from the destitute. James and John, with their father, had a prosperous fishing business (Mk. 1:20). Peter's house in Capernaum was large enough, and the family presumably wealthy enough, to accommodate the twelve and provide a base for their activities (Mk. 1:29-31 and pars.; cf. 2:1; 9:33; Mt. 4:13; 17:24-25). Matthew the tax-collector was a low-ranking civil-servant. The insecurity that came with the itinerant nature of Jesus' ministry was freely chosen.[16] The disciples deserved to receive board and lodging (Lk. 10:17; cf. Mt. 10:10). They also received material support as they travelled from 'some women who had been cured of evil spirits and infirmities' (Lk. 8:1-3). Some from the wider group of disciples had quite considerable wealth and social status: Joseph of Arimathea, for example, and perhaps Nicodemus.

'We have left everything to follow you'

Much of Jesus' teaching about discipleship presupposes either the immediate circumstances of his ministry or the extreme insecurity that those who confessed his name would face in the years following his death. When Peter protests, 'Look, we have left everything and followed you' (Mk. 10:28), he means it quite literally, not in the way that believers today might profess to have turned their backs on the world to follow Jesus.

The simple fact of the matter was that Jesus did not stand still: he had first to preach the gospel and heal the sick in the towns and villages of Galilee and Judea, then he had to make that fateful journey to Jerusalem. He had no official sanction or support for his mission. Although he would happily eat with the wealthy, to a large extent his ministry led him to those who had least to give. Any serious disciple of Jesus had to accept the same conditions: as Jesus said, 'No one who puts a hand to the plough and looks back is fit for the kingdom of God' (Lk. 9:62). Although it is natural for us to spiritualize this sort of statement, it appears that Jesus was thinking in quite concrete and realistic terms. To be his disciple, to be part of the kingdom of God, was to be part of an uprooted eschatological community that would both precipitate, and suffer as a result of, the radical realignment that was taking place in Israel.

Jesus warned the crowds that followed him that a disciple must first 'hate father and mother, wife and children, brothers and sisters, yes, and even life itself' (Lk. 14:26) – because what was coming upon Israel would cause terrible social upheaval (Lk. 12:49-53; cf. Mt. 10:34) and bring with it the likelihood that they would lose their possessions (cf. Heb. 10:32-34) and even their lives for his sake. Under those circumstances a disciple must first count the cost (Lk. 14:28-32). Jesus insisted that a person who was not prepared to 'carry the cross' should not seek to follow him (Lk. 14:27; cf. 9:23; Mt. 16:24; Mk. 8:34); and he added emphatically, 'none of you can become my disciple if you do not give up all your possessions' (Lk. 14:33; cf. 12:33). The twelve were sent out to the lost sheep of Israel to tell people that the kingdom of God had come near and to heal the sick. They were to receive no payment. They travelled empty-handed: 'no bread, no bag, no money in their belts' (Mk. 6:8; cf. Mt. 10:5-10; Lk. 9:2-3).

It is against the background of this sort of commitment that we must – in the first place – understand the promises of material provision (Mt. 6:30-33; Lk. 12:22-34). The prayer 'Give us this day our daily bread' (Mt. 6:11; cf. Lk. 11:3) may have eschatological overtones,[17] but it is also the prayer of a disciple who has left behind or sold his possessions and means of livelihood.

This was not simply radical discipleship. It was the only form of discipleship likely to have any success in the eschatological crisis which Jesus foresaw would soon engulf Israel. But it was also a form of discipleship that would be abundantly rewarded. Jesus encouraged the 'little flock' to sell their possessions and give alms because 'it is your Father's good pleasure to give you the kingdom' (Lk. 12:32-33). And he promised Peter: 'Truly I tell you, there is no one who has left house or brothers or sisters or mother or father or children or fields, for my sake and for the sake of the good news, who will not receive a hundredfold now in this age – houses, brothers and sisters, mothers and children, and fields with persecutions – and in the age to come eternal life' (Mk. 10:29-30).

This hundredfold return is certainly to be understood in material terms, but any attempt to make this statement the basis for a 'prosperity gospel' must take certain things into account. First, the promise is made to those who *leave everything* in order to be with Jesus and participate in the work of preaching the good news of the kingdom. It cannot be applied to those who choose to *keep* a good part of what they have. Secondly, whereas what are left behind are *private* possessions and biological family, what are gained in abundance are *communal* possessions and spiritual family. Thirdly, Jesus does not say that his disciples should give up everything *in order to* obtain greater material prosperity, whether private or communal. The purpose is made quite clear: 'for my sake and for the sake of the good news' (Mk. 10:29; cf. Jn. 6:68). Finally, in Mark's version, though not in Matthew's, Jesus adds the disturbing, but entirely apposite, qualification 'with persecutions' (Mk. 10:30; Mt. 19:29). Prosperity teaching has the habit of playing down the potential suffering and hardship involved in discipleship. Copeland, for example, has interpreted Jesus' statements about his disciples needing to 'take up their cross' (Mt. 10:38; 16:24; Mk. 8:34; Lk. 9:23; 14:27) to mean that they must put up with 'selfish, unlovely people'.[18] This is fatuous, as is Kenneth Hagin's argument from Mark 10:30 that followers of Jesus can expect to be persecuted because they are prosperous.[19]

Giving to the poor

The practice of giving to the poor featured prominently in Jewish piety but within the unique community that formed around Jesus it seems to have become much more a way of life. Judas wanted to know, albeit insincerely, why the perfume with which Mary anointed Jesus' feet was not sold and the money given to the poor (Jn. 12:4-6). The comment about him stealing from the purse seems to indicate that money was regularly given to the poor from communal funds (cf. Jn. 13:29). Without being prompted Zacchaeus offered to give half of his possessions to the poor (Lk. 19:8). Jesus taught his followers to give alms without ostentation (Mt. 6:2-4), and expected them to continue giving to the poor after his death (Mt. 26:11; Mk. 14:7). The leading motivation, presumably, was that the disciple would be set free to follow Jesus. At the extreme the disciples were also expected to give to their enemies: 'Give to everyone who begs from you; and if anyone takes away your goods, do not ask for them again' (Lk. 6:30). The exemplary function of such an action is made clear: it is a way of demonstrating the extraordinary nature of God's love (35-36). But the act of giving was not without intrinsic value as an expression of compassion.[20]

Jesus also articulated a principle of giving and receiving from God: 'give, and it will be given to you. A good measure, pressed down, shaken together, running over, will be put into your lap; for the measure you give will be the measure you get back' (Lk. 6:38). A similar argument is found in the Old Testament with regard to tithing (cf. Prov. 3:9-10; Mal. 3:9-11). Jesus, however, has made it a more general rule. The text gives us no reason to think that what is received is of a different kind to what is given. The verse would seem to confirm a key Word of Faith dictum that if we give financially, God will give money back to us. It should probably be understood, however, against the background of the more narrowly focused promise in Mark 10:29-30, which makes the reward in this age a communal one, not a guaranteed individual return.

A rather different principle is formulated by Jesus during a meal at the house of a leader of the Pharisees (Lk. 14:12-14). He warns his host not to invite to dinner those whom he knows will return the favour but rather to invite 'the poor, the crippled, the lame, and the blind', who cannot repay him, because then he can expect to be 'repaid at the resurrection of the righteous'. The difference is explained by the circumstances. Luke 6:38 is addressed to the disciples: Jesus assures them that God will provide for them abundantly as they give to others. For the Pharisee to hold a banquet for the poor would be an act not of faith in the generosity of God but of righteousness: by means of acts such as these he might hope to escape judgment.

* * * *

Just as in the Old Testament the theme of wealth and poverty must be understood in relation to the story of the people of God, so the many statements in the Gospels that address these issues cannot be disconnected from the story of Jesus and his disciples. If we lose sight of this narrative, which is a salvation-historical narrative, and more precisely an eschatological narrative, we are likely to skew the significance of both wealth and poverty for the kingdom of God. Some care must be taken if we are to make Jesus' critique of wealth and the economic life of the disciples paradigmatic for the ministry of the church. These issues take us beyond the scope of this report, but something more will need to be said on this subject in the final chapter.

11

Poverty and wealth in the New Testament church

We may expect that the situation of the New Testament church will bring us closer to a normative state of affairs. But we must still be careful in drawing conclusions for our own circumstances from early Christian praxis. James 5:1-12, in particular, keeps us in the context of first century Jewish Christianity.[1] Paul's teaching also presupposes some sort of impending crisis (1 Cor. 7:26), and there is the possibilty that this circumstance has resulted in a certain deviation from what we might think of as an ethical or kingdom 'norm'.

The communal life of the early church

Jesus' insistence that his followers should sell their possessions (Lk. 12:33; 14:33) was directly implemented in the communal life of the early church in Jerusalem. Those who had land and property sold what they owned and brought the money to the apostles, who distributed it to those among the believers who had need (Acts 2:44-45; 4:32-35). A Levite called Joseph, who was later given the name Barnabas by the apostles, exemplified the practice (Acts 4:36-37). The fate of Ananias and Sapphira served as a warning to any who might be tempted to act with less than full integrity (Acts 5:1-11). The daily distribution of food to widows (Acts 6:1) was one practical example of how the sharing of wealth worked.

The common ownership of property, however, was not absolute. It appears that people retained possession of their property but regarded it as being held for the benefit of the group. It is likely that goods were sold to meet needs as they arose over time: there was no enforced, one-off redistribution of wealth.[2] Ananias and Sapphira were given the option of keeping part of the proceeds from their land: their sin was to lie to the apostles and to the Holy Spirit (Acts 5:3, 9). The description of Tabitha as having been 'devoted to good works and acts of charity' rather suggests that she acted independently, giving from her own resources (Acts 9:36). On his escape from prison Peter went to 'the house of Mary, the mother of John whose other name was Mark' (Acts 12:12): the house was used by the church but was recognized as belonging to Mary. Mnason was an 'early disciple' who had his own house in Jerusalem (Acts 21:16).[3] This continuation of private ownership probably means that basic socio-economic distinctions remained in evidence in the Jerusalem church.

There is no evidence that churches outside Palestine adopted quite the same model. Although there was undoubtedly a high level of mutual support within the communities, the evidence suggests that there was no systematic abandonment of private property. There were wealthy patrons (Rom. 16:1-2); groups met in private homes (Rom. 16:5; 1 Cor. 16:19; Col. 4:15; Phlm. 1:2); people continued to hold public office (Acts 13:6-12; Rom. 16:23) or to run businesses (Acts 16:14; 18:2-3); masters and slaves continued in their respective positions (1 Cor. 7:21-24; Eph. 6:5-9; Col. 3:22-4:1; 1 Tim. 6:2); disparities between poor and wealthy believers were evident in the churches and the cause of some tension (1 Cor. 11:20-22). When Agabus came from Jerusalem to Antioch with his prophecy of impending famine, the disciples there appear to have responded on an individual basis, 'according to their ability' (Acts 11:29), though this does not exclude the possibility that they also had a communal fund for local requirements.

It is natural, therefore, to see the early communalism as a pragmatic response, inspired by Jesus' own teaching and the practice of his immediate disciples, to the unique circumstances faced in Jerusalem.[4] It is likely that many of the poorest of Jerusalem – the beggar at the Beautiful Gate, for example – would have responded to the preaching of the apostles. Converts from among the diaspora pilgrims on the day of Pentecost would have had no means of support if they had stayed on in the city. Moreover, association with a discredited messiah may have disqualified the needy from receiving the usual forms of public charity.[5] More importantly, Jesus had left the disciples with a strong belief that they would experience considerable hardship and dislocation in the period leading up to God's judgment upon the city. The sharing of wealth and possessions offered security and some hope of economic stability in times of distress.

The detrimental effect of wealth on a person's spiritual life

Despite the presence of wealthy people in the church, apostolic teaching is predominantly critical of wealth.

James

James' extensive teaching about wealth presupposes the conditions of early Jewish Christianity.[6] The lowly believer is encouraged to boast in his 'being raised up'; the wealthy person (presumably the wealthy believer, though this is not certain)[7] should boast in 'being brought low' (Jas. 1:9-10). While 'lowliness' would normally be a spiritual and moral quality, the antithesis here indicates that James primarily has in mind the lowliness that accompanies poverty. The reason why the rich person should rejoice in having been brought low may be no more than conventional reflection on the transience of wealth, but the image of the flower of the field withering in the heat of the sun may have more to it than that. James warns the rich later that miseries are coming upon them, that their accumulated wealth is the fruit of corruption and exploitation and will only serve as evidence against them in the last days

(5:1-6), that a crisis of divine judgment is imminent (5:9). His point may be that the only hope that the wealthy have in the face of the very real socio-economic devastation that will come upon them is to be abased.[8]

The argument against wealth is developed further in James 2:1-7. The chief complaint is against the expression of favouritism towards the rich in the assemblies (1-4).[9] The manner in which James points up the irony and injustice of their behaviour, however, is striking. The 'poor in the world', whom they so readily humiliate, have been chosen by God 'to be rich in faith and to be heirs of the kingdom that he has promised to those who love him' (2:5); but the rich, to whom they show such deference, oppress them and drag them to court and blaspheme the name of Christ (2:6-7). Quite why James casts the oppression of the church in such stark economic terms is not clear, but the argument must reflect the actual circumstances of the struggling diaspora Jewish-Christian communities: there is no need to draw universal conclusions about divine favouritism towards the poor or the wickedness of the rich. The eschatological horizon is important. The 'poor' are those believers who suffer at the hands of the rich and powerful for the sake of the 'excellent name' that was invoked over them (2:7). If they stand the test, they will 'receive the crown of life that the Lord has promised to those who love him' (1:12). But for now they must be patient as they wait for the Lord, by whose coming they will be vindicated (5:7-9).

Paul

Although it is probable that Paul came from a rather well-to-do family, he appears mostly suspicious of wealth and generally expresses a quite clear preference for moderation and contentment. He rebukes the wealthy in Corinth for their disregard for 'those who have nothing' (1 Cor. 11:22). Writing to Timothy, he speaks at some length about the damaging effects of wealth on the life of faith, warning him that unscrupulous people will exploit the gospel for personal gain

(1 Tim. 6:3-10, 17-19). He uses the word *porismos* in 1 Timothy 6:6 polemically and probably metaphorically: whereas the false teacher imagines that godliness is a means of *financial* gain (5), Paul argues that the only 'profit' worth having is acquired through 'godliness with self-sufficiency (*autarkeias*)'.[10] He makes use of the commonplace argument against acquisitiveness, that we brought nothing into the world and will take nothing out of it (7).[11] It is enough to have food and clothing (8). Paul speaks only in general terms about the 'many senseless and harmful desires that plunge people into ruin and destruction'; there are those who 'in their eagerness to be rich… have wandered away from the faith and pierced themselves with many pains' (9-10).

We should keep in mind that the argument against wealth in these verses is directed specifically at those who teach something other than 'the sound words of our Lord Jesus Christ and the teaching that is in accordance with godliness' (1 Tim. 6:3). Presumably Paul has seen Christian leaders and teachers fall into just this trap. Timothy is encouraged to shun the pursuit of wealth and to seek instead 'righteousness, godliness, faith, love, endurance, gentleness' (1 Tim. 6:11). The rich should not 'set their hopes on the uncertainty of riches, but rather on God who richly provides us with everything for our enjoyment' (1 Tim. 6:17).

The world is passing away

The eschatological context is particularly prominent in 1 John 2:15-17. John warns his readers not to love the things that are in the world – 'the desire of the flesh, the desire of the eyes, the pride in riches' – because 'the world and its desire are passing away'. The imminence of the eschatological moment is underlined in verse 18: 'Children, it is the last hour!' The things of the world will be of no value to them at this time of crisis, they will not save them: only those 'who do the will of God' will live forever (17). The church has tended to take this as a universal principle, but while we would obviously want to insist that doing the will of God is always more important than having material things, the question arises whether *in the absence of a real and immediate eschatological crisis* the same absolute distinction applies. True, many would claim that we are indeed in the last days and that John's argument is fully relevant to the situation of the church today. But it is surely self-deluding to think that we currently face the sort of upheaval and transition described by New Testament apocalyptic. If this is not a time of eschatological crisis, then there may be scope for a more positive evaluation of wealth.

The practice of giving

The obligation of the rich

Those who 'in the present age are rich' are to be taught to 'do good, to be rich in good works, generous, and ready to share' (1 Tim. 6:17-18). This is a natural extension of the Old Testament principle of charitable giving. As F.K.C. Price points out, the rich are not instructed to sell their possessions and give the money to the poor, whether directly or through the church.[12] The assumption is merely that socially derived inequalities of wealth will be offset somewhat by the generosity and good works of the rich (1 Cor. 11:18-22; 2 Cor. 8:13-15; Eph. 4:28; cf. Jas.1:27; 2:14-17). Priority is given to the household of God (Gal. 6:10; 1 Tim. 5:8; cf. Acts 11:27-30), though this no doubt reflects the disadvantaged situation of the church at the time. The statement that God 'richly provides us with everything for our enjoyment' could be taken to mean that, having given generously to the poor and having put their trust unequivocally in God, the rich were free to enjoy the wealth with which God had blessed them.

Paul's argument that by doing good the rich will store up for themselves 'the treasure of a good foundation for the future, so that they may take hold of the life that really is life' (1 Tim. 6:19), may simply echo Jesus' teaching about gaining treasure in heaven (Mt. 19:21, and pars.; Lk. 12:20-21, 33). There is a consistent recognition in the Pastoral Epistles, however, that the practical dimension of faith may have an impact on a person's 'salvation'. So, for example, Paul says that the woman 'will be saved through childbearing, provided they continue in faith and love and holiness, with modesty' (1 Tim. 2:15). He does not mean that a woman is saved by procreation rather than by grace but that, given the cultural conditions of the early church and the particular susceptibility of women to false teaching, a lifestyle of faithful domesticity is more conducive to perseverance in the faith than gadding about town (1 Tim. 4:11-14) or entertaining false teachers in their homes (2 Tim. 3:6).[13] Likewise, then, Paul regards the right use of wealth not as a *means* of gaining eternal life but as a safeguard against the *loss* of faith – particularly the loss of faith that might come about through the influence of teachers who mistakenly think that 'godliness is a means of gain'.

Organized Christian care

Care for the needy was also an organized activity and a matter of church policy. The Jerusalem church asked Paul and Barnabas to 'remember the poor' (Gal. 2:10). The resulting collection for the churches in Judea was a unique undertaking but required considerable organization (Rom. 15:25-29; 1 Cor. 16:1-4; 2 Cor. 8-9). The collection was to be, fundamentally, an expression of the grace of God in the life of the giver (2 Cor. 8:1): the word charis ('grace') recurs a number of times throughout this section as a direct description of the offering and the attitude that motivated it (8:4, 6, 7, 19; 9:14). The gift should be evidence of the love of believers for one another (8:8, 24). Though an expression of 'obedience to the confession of the gospel of Christ' (2 Cor. 9:13), it should not be coerced but should flow from a genuine willingness to give (8:8, 11; 9:5, 7), for 'God loves a cheerful giver' (9:7). Giving should be proportionate to what one has rather than what one does not have (2 Cor. 8:12). The goal is not to impose an unreasonable burden on the giver but to establish a 'fair balance between your present abundance and their need' (8:13-14). By the time of the Pastoral Epistles a rather sophisticated system of registering destitute widows for support had been established (1 Tim. 5:3-16).

The gift of giving

The emphasis on grace in 2 Corinthians 8-9 underlines the fact that giving is, potentially at least, a gift of the Spirit, a *charisma* (cf. Rom. 12:8). This is what transforms routine or organized charity into something distinctly Christian or *Christlike*. It also accounts at least for some of the disparities in giving that we see in the church: giving may be a common obligation for Christians, but not all have the gift of giving. The contribution of the church in Macedonia to the collection provided the outstanding example of such grace (2 Cor. 8:1-5). Benny Hinn has stated that the 'very existence of the churches of Macedonia' is a 'standing reproach to the "blab it and grab it" gospel', because even in their extreme poverty and affliction they demonstrated a 'wealth of generosity'.[14] It was in this act of selfless liberality that the grace of God was manifested (8:1); nothing is said about them receiving even more in return.

Tithing in the church

Because tithing remains a difficult and controversial topic among evangelicals, we will attempt only a limited response to the Word of Faith argument here. The practice of tithing is justified by Kenneth Copeland on the grounds that the structures of the old covenant recur typologically in the new covenant.[15] There is a problem with this argument in that the inheritance received under the new covenant, though analogous to Israel's possession of the land, is of a fundamentally different kind. Israel tithed from the produce of the land which God had given them. According to the typology, we would have to tithe from the produce of the spiritual inheritance that we have in Christ, which hardly makes sense.

Copeland argues that tithing predates the law: Abraham gave a tenth of the spoil of battle to Melchizedek (Gen. 14:20).[16] Because today we bring our tithes to a High Priest who is greater than Melchizedek, we can expect greater blessings. Abraham's 'tithe' to Melchizedek, however, was a one-off, voluntary offering in recognition of the victory that God had given him in battle. There is no indication that he regularly tithed from his income.[17] Jacob's promise when he set up the stone at Bethel ('of all that you give me I will surely give one tenth to you') also relates to the particular expectation of success in his search for a wife (Gen. 28:22). Jacob left Paddan-aram a prosperous man (31:18), though it is not actually stated that he gave a tenth of this wealth to God.

Copeland also sees in Hebrews 7:8 a reference to Jesus as the one who receives tithes from the church.[18] However, the 'one of whom it is testified that he lives' is not Christ but Melchizedek, who 'resembling the Son of God, ... remains a priest forever' (3). Christ is a 'priest forever, according to the order of Melchizedek' (17), but nothing can be inferred from this regarding tithing: the point is only that Christ is superior to the Levitical priesthood. In fact, the implication may be that the law of tithing has been superseded in Christ (18-19) – Christ's priesthood is of such a nature that it does not have to be supported by means of tithes. But the argument is only about the means by which the priest enables access to God (18-27).

Sowing and reaping

As part of his exhortation to the Corinthians to give generously Paul argues that they will reap in proportion to the manner of their sowing (2 Cor. 9:6). The principle invoked here is found throughout the Bible (Prov. 3:9-10; Mal. 3:9-11; Lk. 6:38; 2 Cor. 9:6-11; Gal. 6:7-8). It also constitutes a major plank in the platform of prosperity teaching. The sowing that Paul has in mind is clearly of a financial nature. The question is whether the reaping envisaged is of the same kind. Were the Corinthians entitled to expect *material* abundance from God as a 'reward' for their generosity? Or were the benefits that Paul was confident would accrue to them of a more spiritual or even eschatological nature?

Paul speaks of what the Corinthians will receive in various ways. At a mundane level he explains the benefits of reciprocal support (8:13-14). More fundamentally, he stresses the ability of God to 'cause all grace to overflow' to the Corinthians (9:8, paraphrase). This grace is not the thing in itself but the prior theological basis for whatever may come. Whatever they receive will be a manifestation of the abundant grace of God. In more concrete terms Paul tells them that as recipients of such grace they can expect to have complete *autarkeia*.[19] This word, which comes trailing clouds of Stoic moralizing, orginally signified a state of financial independence or self-sufficiency but came to acquire by the New Testament period the weaker and more general sense of 'sufficiency' or 'contentment'.[20] This appears to be the meaning here and in 1 Timothy 6:6. The adjective *autarkēs* in Philippians 4:11 also suggests 'contentment' without the particular nuance of *self*-sufficiency, which hardly fits the circumstances of Paul's imprisonment.[21]

Some have argued that the sufficiency Paul has in mind is essentially of a spiritual nature.[22] This is unnecessary. The God-given *autarkeia* must at least provide the material basis for the Corinthians to 'share abundantly in every good work'; and any increase of their 'seed for sowing' that results from their giving (10) must also be understood in material terms. The quotation from Psalm 112 introduces the conventional paradigm of the righteous person who deals generously, who lends, who conducts his affairs with justice (5), who has 'distributed freely' and 'given to the poor' (9), and in whose house will be 'wealth and riches' (3). Paul's argument here certainly invokes the Old Testament paradigm of the righteous Jew who gives to the poor and is blessed by God.[23] The blessing, however, is not restricted to this economy of giving and receiving. Such a person is also rewarded with an enduring righteousness (Ps. 112:3, 9) and will receive the 'harvest of... righteousness' (2 Cor. 9:10; cf. Hos. 10:12).[24]

Paul assures the Philippians, who have given generously to him through Epaphroditus, that God 'will fully satisfy every need of yours' (Phil. 4:19), we can hardly say that this *excludes* material needs. But it would be absurd to suggest that when he says, 'I seek the profit that accumulates to your account' (17), he means this literally. What *Paul* seeks is the spiritual well-being of the churches. The argument is a little different in Galatians 6:7-10. The issue here is not the specific one of financial assistance but the more general principle: 'if you sow to the Spirit, you will reap eternal life from the Spirit' (8). While the sowing may be understood in quite practical terms as doing good, the reaping appears to be eschatological. In his address to the Ephesian elders Paul reminds them of Jesus' dictum that 'it is more blessed to give than to receive' (Acts 20:35). His argument here does not rule out receiving from God, but the underlying model is one of working hard in order to support the weak, and he presents his own practice as an example: 'You know for yourselves that I worked with my own hands to support myself and my companions' (34).

Money and ministry

Prosperity teachers justify costly ministries and lavish lifestyles on various grounds. If they have prospered, it is because they have learnt the lessons of faith and only exemplify the sort of prosperity that God wishes to bestow on all his children. A private jet helps an evangelist to cope with the stresses of an intense national and global ministry. Evangelism can be an expensive business.

The principle of Christian ministers being supported by those whom they serve is well-founded (1 Cor. 9:4-14; cf. Mt. 10:10; Lk. 10:7; 3 Jn. 5-8). Giving to Christian ministry is an important means of participating in the gospel (Phil. 4:15; 3 Jn. 8). But there is no suggestion that the minister should expect to enjoy significant financial prosperity. An apostle has a right to accommodation, food and drink, for himself and his wife. The analogies Paul uses argue for no more than a normal livelihood; they do not justify the expectation of financial abundance or profit. Paul's recommendation that 'the elders who rule well be considered worthy of double honour' (1 Tim. 5:17) must be understood in financial terms (cf. 18), but probably has in view an honorarium rather than a salary.[25] The significance of 'double' is less clear. The quotations in verse 18 suggest that his argument is that the elders should be paid, not that they should be paid more than they or others are already receiving. In this case, 'double' may only bring out the two-fold sense of 'honour' as both 'respect' and 'honorarium'.[26] There is no basis for John Avanzini's argument that a minister should receive '*at least* twice as much money as the average wage-earner in your community'.[27]

That Paul preferred *not* to be supported on a regular basis by the churches which he served cannot simply be dismissed. Although he makes it clear that this is a personal and somewhat exceptional decision, it nevertheless makes it much more difficult to accept the model of the Christian minister who seeks, or at least expects, to *prosper* from the financial support of the church. Although our own standards of sufficiency and prosperity are different to Paul's, we cannot help but be struck by the contrast between the ethos underlying his ministry and that of the Word of Faith teachers who regard the Rolex watch and the luxury car as signs of divine approval. We hear little from the Word of Faith teachers about how Paul wore himself out working as a tentmaker in order not to be a financial burden (Acts 20:33-34; 1 Cor. 4:12; 1 Thess. 2:9; 2 Thess. 3:7-10).

There is also no escaping the willingness of Paul and other apostles to endure hardship and deprivation for the sake of the gospel (1 Cor. 4:11-13; 2 Cor. 6:10). They are treated 'as poor, yet making many rich; as having nothing, yet possessing everything' (2 Cor. 6:10). Paul has learnt from experience how to be content (*autarkēs einai*) in all circumstances: he has been 'initiated into the mysteries' (*memuēmai*) of being well-fed and of being hungry, of having abundance and of being in want (Phil. 4:11-12).

The warnings against 'peddling' the word of God or exploiting piety for financial gain are especially severe

(2 Cor. 2:17; 1 Tim. 6:5). The insistence in the Pastorals that an elder or deacon should not be a lover of money (1 Tim. 3:3, 8; Tit.1:7) reflects the fact that Paul had seen believers wander from the faith because of greed (1 Tim. 6:10). His concern for transparency and integrity in financial matters is also evident in the arrangements made for conveying the collection to Jerusalem (2 Cor. 8:18-22). The unrelenting pressure on people to give that characterizes much Word of Faith ministry certainly has no precedent in the New Testament.

The potential for enjoying material prosperity is there but the church is under restraint – for two main reasons: first, there is the moral obligation to reduce inequality, especially amongst believers; and secondly, there are the moral and spiritual dangers inherent in the possession of wealth. If these two requirements are taken account of, the possibility of a righteous and godly prosperity would appear not to be excluded. But on the whole the apostles were rather pessimistic about the spiritual effects of wealth.

* * * *

The formal Old Testament equation of obedience and prosperity, already seriously underminded by the failure of Israel as a nation to keep the covenant, is not carried over into the New Testament. The reason is essentially two-fold. On the one hand, the teaching of the New Testament anticipates a period of massive upheaval (cf. 1 Cor. 7:26, 29-31). On the other, the church is thought of as a missionary organization at odds with the wider community in which it is immersed. There is the possibility, however, that the expansion and consolidation of the church over the last two thousand years has created a rather different situation. Whatever our expectations may be regarding the second coming, it is clear that the church is not caught up in an eschatological crisis or, for the most part, subject to the dangers and deprivations that result from persecution. Only a small proportion of Christians are engaged in the sort of ministry that might expose them to extreme financial insecurity. Is it possible that under such circumstances some sort of prosperity theology might re-emerge? Is there scope for the church, if less perfectly and less extensively than Word of Faith teachers would like, to experience the abundance of God's provision in response to faithfulness and obedience? We will return to this question in the final chapter.

12

Ministry and ethics

At the heart of Word of Faith spirituality is a fundamentalism, or an idealism, that manifests itself in two principal ways – as both Word and Faith. There is a fundamentalism of Scripture not so much as revealed truth but as promise or covenant; and there is a fundamentalism of faith as the means by which the promises of Scripture are activated in the life of the believer. The Word of God contains a set of rights and privileges that the believer should lay claim to by faith and fully expect to receive because the Word of God cannot be anything but one hundred per cent reliable. Faith opens the way to the attainment of an ideal state of being Christian in which victory over Satan and prosperity in all areas of life are guaranteed. In the previous chapters we examined in some detail the theoretical difficulties posed by the Word of Faith argument. Here we will consider rather more briefly the main pastoral and ethical implications of this body of teaching.

Evangelicalism obviously has no objection to the view that the Word of God is true and should be taken as the authoritative basis for the life of faith. Moreover, many would admit that the evangelical church frequently falls short of the ideals of discipleship and faith that appear in the Bible. We may, then, regard the Word of Faith movement's refusal to settle for mediocrity and compromise in response to the assurances of Scripture with some feelings of inadequacy. If we are able to listen to the message without great prejudice, it is difficult not to be impressed by the heroic and inspirational stance of this faith-idealism. Experience, however, suggests that this single-minded determination to take the promises of God seriously has resulted in the construction of a spiritual system that distorts the practice of biblical faith in a number of ways.

A fundamentalism of faith

In the first place, it would seem to make faith in principle an *infallible* means of getting spiritual results. In order to ensure the efficacy of faith in the life of the ordinary believer, the Word of Faith movement has developed a highly functional and formulaic spirituality. Success in the spiritual life is not a haphazard affair: we can be certain of achieving our spiritual objectives if we act in accordance with the various laws that were embedded by God in the universe at creation – rather as the Jews were guaranteed prosperity if they observed the rules prescribed in the Torah.

The analogy points to the obvious danger: the systematization of spiritual life has the inevitable effect of diminishing or marginalizing the believer's relationship with God. There is no suggestion that the believer is saved by activating a spiritual law, or even that such a 'legalistic' spirituality is meant to substitute for knowing and loving God as Father. Formally at least, Word of Faith teaching is able to give proper place to the work of grace in salvation and in the inauguration of new life. But Word of Faith spirituality is dominated by the determination to get results, to prosper, and this is where the legalism comes into play: the practical outworking of the spiritual life, whether as personal sanctification or as ministry, is governed by the operation of spiritual laws. Having been redeemed by Christ's death from the control of Satan and incorporated into the covenant of promise, we are in a position to activate those mechanisms by which we fulfil the purposes of God and bring about prosperity in our lives.

This fundamentalism of faith is merely a variation on the perfectionist argument of the Holiness movement and is flawed in the same way: at a certain point the struggle to do better spiritually, in whatever respect, begins to exclude the operation of grace.[1] It becomes apparent, for example, in the need to suppress negative thoughts. The point is made by Ken Sarles: 'Concern over the influence of doubt and negative thought on the believer's life... places an enormous burden on the believer to control his thoughts in order to achieve prosperity, a burden that is nowhere found in Scripture.'[2] Such a psychological burden is little different in effect to the burden of the law that Jesus sought to lift from the shoulders of his followers (cf. Mt. 11:29-30; 23:2-4).

We cannot afford to push faith beyond the reach of grace. Wealth, like sex and power, is a hazardous commodity. The more we pursue even a God-given prosperity, the greater the likelihood of being ruined by it. Aware of the dangers, we impose rules upon ourselves in order to ensure that this power is handled correctly; but the irony – indeed the tragedy – is that these rules will sooner or later become a new legalism. If we are *full of the Holy Spirit*, the power may be manageable. If we are not, it is certain that wealth will corrupt us in one way or another – either through greed or through the need to control that greed by means of the law.

It is also arguable – though the argument is beyond the scope of this book – that the extreme idealist commitment is less a mark of an authentic trust in God than of some form of psychological or social dysfunctionality. Not all believers are able or willing to take the step of intellectual abandonment, the suspension of critical judgment, required by the Word of Faith movement. Many would regard the enforced expulsion of doubt, the obstinate insistence on belief in the face of contrary symptoms, as manifestations of an unhealthy state of mind. Critics have sometimes suggested that prosperity teaching appeals to obsessive personalities.[3] Because faith is understood to a large extent as a mental capacity, rather than as an act of practical and existential trust, the success of faith is made overly dependent on the ability of the believer to sustain an unnatural psychological condition.

We would want to say, however, that the exercise of faith is not an end in itself but a response to the call of God. An authentic spirituality must be more than the struggle to make faith work. The process of being conformed to the image of Christ comes neither through the development of an expertise in applying a set of spiritual rules nor through a radical and obstinate suspension of judgment but through the transformation of the person – mind, emotions, personality. The development of spiritual habits may be a significant part of this process, but the relationship of love and servanthood which the believer has with the Father cannot be adequately worked out through the restrictive methodology of Word of Faith teaching. A utilitarian spirituality of this nature makes the indwelling of the Spirit superfluous: we have recovered the authority over the material world that Adam ceded to Satan and no longer need the working of the Spirit in us.

The failure of intregity

The fundamentalism of faith generates tensions and distortions: it stretches our humanity to the point where it is bound eventually to snap. Although it will often be necessary to attribute the moral and pastoral failings of the Word of Faith movement to the personal shortcomings of its proponents, we should not overlook the extent to which a fundamentalist or idealist theology creates a spiritual environment in which such failings are more likely to happen. Just as a rationalist biblical fundamentalism is likely to conceal or misrepresent the intellectual difficulties presented by Scripture, a fundamentalism of faith will always be tempted to conceal or misrepresent the *failure of faith*, to manipulate people and circumstances in order to maintain the appearance of effectiveness. Even the best of ideals has this capacity to corrupt. It may be done quite deliberately and cynically, but it is likely that the Word of Faith teacher is often unaware of how reality is being subtly reshaped and stage-managed to conform to the preached ideal.

If we find ourselves inclined to dismiss the claims for visions and miracles out of hand as so much hokum and humbug, we should be careful to ensure that the same criteria are applied within evangelicalism generally. Nevertheless, the Word of Faith movement undoubtedly faces a credibility problem.[4] What are we to make, for example, of Kenneth Hagin's claim to have healed a 72 year old woman of a large abdominal tumour by hitting her in the stomach as the Lord had instructed?[5] Or of Kenneth Copeland's report of mass levitation in a church in Africa as a result of a confrontation with a local witch-doctor?

> ...all of a sudden, everyone in that church building started rising off the floor and got about four feet in the air where they were suspended – that is, everyone except that witch doctor who just kept running across the front of the room, jumping as high as he could. But God's presence was so strong that no one paid any attention to that old boy.[6]

It must also be said that the Word of Faith teachers lay themselves open to the charge that, intentionally or otherwise, they have exploited 'religion' (*eusebeia*) for the purpose of financial gain (cf. 1 Tim. 6:5). They have been accused of raising large sums of money by 'leasing and selling their data banks'.[7] There are the perennial complaints that Word of Faith preachers manipulate their audiences through something akin to hypnotic suggestion or downright emotional blackmail and intimidation. At a crusade filmed as part of a documentary for British television on healing, Benny Hinn warned his audience that after the year 2000 many disasters would hit the world and told them that only those who gave to the Lord's work would be spared.[8] The impression is given at times that these ministries exist simply to raise money to perpetuate their existence, through a closed loop of faith and giving. In this regard they differ somewhat from the older faith ministries which raised funds through faith to maintain charitable institutions. There is perhaps a case for saying that global evangelism requires big money; but the Word of Faith movement must also answer for the way it has discredited the gospel in the eyes of the world. Whatever the intentions of the Word of Faith healers and fundraisers, they have for the most part failed to deal with the massive collateral damage that their campaigns have caused – the disillusionment and bitterness and heartache.

There is a fine line between bold leadership and megalomania. Many evangelicals find the egotism and self-promotion of prosperity teachers difficult to stomach. The reliance on revelation knowledge, even in its less extreme forms, generates an implicit impression of spiritual superiority that is bound to be divisive. The clubbiness of the fraternity of Word of Faith ministers is disquieting from the outside. We are not in a position to determine the extent to which accusations of this sort are justified, but it is worth quoting Paul's declared policy of transparency with regard to the preaching of the gospel: 'We have renounced the shameful things that one hides; we refuse to practise cunning or to falsify God's word; but by the open statement of the truth we commend ourselves to the conscience of everyone in the sight of God' (2 Cor. 4:2; cf. 2:17).

The failure of compassion

In the rush to be successful there will always be winners and losers. There is no reason to doubt that many people have 'prospered' by applying Word of Faith principles to their lives. But it is also true that many others have been trampled on in the stampede and left bruised and bleeding by the roadside. The disproportionate emphasis placed on prosperity and well-being in Word of Faith teaching has made it difficult for the movement to deal usefully and compassionately with those who fail to live up to the demands of an idealized faith. We see this in the numbers of people who have turned their backs on the movement because of the pain and disappointment it has caused them. We see it in the lack of pastoral insight and resources in Word of Faith teaching. Pastoral ministry is geared largely towards enabling prosperity in the lives of others. Mutuality exists at the level of giving and receiving but fails at the level of care. It is a movement dominated by propagandists – men and women who are hardly able to acknowledge any malfunction in the system, let alone respond with humility and pastoral sensitivity to those who, for whatever reason, have been seriously hurt by their 'ministry'. Charles Farah tells the story of a girl 'stricken with guilt and remorse' because her faith had been inadequate to heal her. She could only conclude that Jesus did not love her enough to heal her. Farah quotes the comments of a Lutheran minister: 'They have turned the ministry of healing into a ministry of condemnation.'[9]

There is no shortage of documented cases of people dying, or nearly dying, because medical help was withheld on account of a commitment of faith.[10] Hobart Freeman was indicted in 1984 on a charge of 'aiding and inducing reckless homicide' after he encouraged the parents of a 15 year old girl not to allow her medical treatment. She died of preventable kidney failure.[10] Enormous psychological and spiritual damage has also been done by the argument that a failure to be healed is attributable to a lack of faith or to sin. Farah writes:

> My concern is for the thousands of people for whom the faith message has not worked, who are now far from God and some even actually disbelieve because their expectations were dashed. They applied what they knew, but a loved one died. They exercised faith, but another lies crippled. They went to their leaders and were told, "It's your lack of faith. If you only had faith, this would not have happened."[12]

Christian debt counselling services are aware of the numbers of Christians who get into difficulties as a result of their adherence to prosperity teaching.[13]

In the end, Word of Faith teaching is too indiscriminate with regard to the operation of faith, too individualistic in its understanding of prosperity. On the one hand, the mechanical application of spiritual laws overrules the contextualized discernment and judgment of the individual. On the other, the attainment of prosperity is conceived too much as a private blessing, to the exclusion of God's commitment to maintain the community of disciples. Copeland's exhortation to trust the promises of God and expect abundance in this 'last little sliver of time' before Jesus returns is fine. But the effect is spoilt by the assurance that all our enemies – financial, physical, relational – will be made our footstool.[14] True, we have in some sense been raised up and made to sit in the heavenly places (Eph. 2:6), but it is *Christ's* enemies, not ours, who will be overcome. Paul's eschatology is *Christ*-centred. It is not that the believer does not in some sense benefit from Christ's victory, but the emphasis in Word of Faith teaching has drifted too far in the direction of a self-centred and uncaring triumphalism.

The validity of suffering

In its mission to recover Adam's unfallen state the Word of Faith movement has viewed suffering as an almost entirely negative experience, a sign of spiritual failure, an impediment to spiritual fulfilment. Evangelicalism has usually assumed that the final and complete escape from suffering belongs to the new heaven and new earth (Rev. 21:3-4). But the argument against the Word of Faith position is not simply that the denial of suffering is unrealistic. The New Testament takes suffering very seriously, and there are certain respects in which we would want to ascribe a much more positive value to suffering than Word of Faith teaching is willing to allow.

However much we may wish to stress the right of God's children to receive and enjoy the goodness and generosity of their heavenly Father, we must also affirm the right of the follower of Jesus Christ to deny himself or herself, become weak or destitute, for the sake of others. Word of Faith teaching makes the mistake of assuming that an enthusiasm for the good things in life and self-denial are mutually exclusive options for the believer.

Evangelicalism may at times have over-emphasized the *theologia crucis* and impaired the capacity of the believer to experience an innocent and godly hedonism. Hagin's complaint that the church has 'preached a "cross" religion, and we need to preach a "throne" religion' has some force to it.[15] But within the eschatological framework of New Testament spirituality it can hardly be denied that the cross constitutes a central paradigm and standard for Christian discipleship (Mt. 16:24; Mk. 8:34; Lk. 9:23; 14:27; Gal. 6:14; Phil. 2:4-8; 3:10; Heb. 12:1-3). Word of Faith theology has difficulty accommodating this idea. The motif of suffering for the sake of others is not absent entirely,[16] but it tends to be eclipsed by the determination to experience the blessings of God. We will make some attempt to resolve this conflict of interests in the final chapter.

The New Testament regards suffering for Christ as a fundamental means by which faith is strengthened and God glorified (cf. Rom. 5:3-5; 8:17; Heb. 5:8; 1 Pet. 1:6-7; 5:10). Hagin recognizes this: 'Suffering will make you grow spiritually in a hurry.'[17] But this sort of admission has the appearance of having been erected on the periphery of Word of Faith teaching in order to deflect some of the criticism aimed at it.

We do not wish to deny that poverty and sickness are contrary to the will of God for his people, but it is very often precisely these circumstances that give rise to the most profound expressions of faith and compassion. A theology that is unable to tolerate the continuation of suffering risks removing the deepest stimulus for love. We are bound to have misgivings about the capacity of the Word of Faith movement to respond to suffering with a genuine compassion. The instinct is not to love but to correct the deficiences in a person's understanding and faith and enable well-being and prosperity. This is not in itself wrong, but there is a real danger of callousness and an insensitivity to the psychological need that people may have to work through the pain of disappointment or bereavement.[18] In the worst cases we see an impersonal production-line processing of the sick and needy. Where the Word of Faith movement has demonstrated an authentic compassion,[19] we might question whether this is because of or inspite of the central dogmatic commitments.

In the end we are left with a question: Which is more Christlike? Which is more godly? To enjoy righteous prosperity or to show the character of Christ in the midst of suffering? Benny Hinn remarked, after encountering Christians in the Philippines:

'My feelings about prosperity began changing when I was in Manila earlier this year. Some of the most precious Christians live there amid such poverty, such need. Yet you see such satisfaction, such fulfilment with them. They are happier than many Christians I know in America who have everything.'[20]

The priority of the kingdom of God

The Word of Faith movement's fixation with the faith-prosperity equation inevitably has the effect of marginalizing other concerns, such as worship, justice, the immaterial dimensions of human relationships. It is rather like Christmas, when the children get so excited about the presents that they forget the people, forget the occasion, forget the reason for celebrating. Although in principle Word of Faith teaching recognizes the priority of the kingdom of God and his righteousness, the prosperity agenda tends to displace the higher objectives.[21] The gospel is too often packaged as a miracle plan for gaining financial security or as a programme for developing one's inner potential.[22] This may only be packaging, and it may have the merit of connecting the good news of the kingdom with people's real needs, but there is a very real danger of getting things back to front.

Material prosperity, in whatever form it comes, should be an addendum to the pursuit of righteousness – a manifestation of the Father's goodness towards those who seek to obey him. Psalm 1:1-3 describes a man who will 'prosper', but this is a man whose 'delight is in the law of the Lord' (2), not a man who deliberately seeks prosperity. The Word of Faith movement has reconfigured the logic: seeking the kingdom of God and his righteousness are made the *precondition* for blessing, a means to an end. The point of Jesus' teaching in Matthew 6:25-34 is not that the disciples will become prosperous if they put the kingdom of God first but that they will not be left destitute. The worry that Jesus addresses is not that they will not achieve great wealth because they have followed him but that they will have nothing at all.

The goal should be to seek the kingdom and righteousness of God, and the measure of success, and of whether God is faithful, must be whether these things are attained – not whether some material or social or personal blessing has been added to this endeavour. 'For the kingdom of God is not food and drink but righteousness and peace and joy in the Holy Spirit' (Rom. 14:17). But this should not preclude the possibility of blessing: faith is entitled to anticipate the concrete, worldly goodness of God. Faith is greatly diminished if it cannot recognise and celebrate the good things that the Father wishes to give his children.

Unclear message about materialism and economic injustice

For the most part the Word of Faith movement has not sought to address wealth and poverty as global political issues. The emphasis has been on the prosperity of the individual and the evangelistic ministry of the church. In some respects this restricted outlook is understandable, but it may also be regarded as irresponsible and naïve.[23] A movement that is so blatantly preoccupied with the acquisition of wealth cannot pretend that its teachings and actions have no wider moral implications – if only for the negative reason that one of the strongest arguments against current prosperity theology is that it serves the interests of an already wealthy Western church and is indifferent to the massive suffering of the world's poor.

A church obsessed with prosperity, even with godly prosperity, will find it difficult to speak out against economic and social injustice. Contrasting the rise of prosperity teaching in Africa with the predominance of liberation theology in South America, Paul Gifford comments: 'Inasmuch as it distracts attention from any economic system and merely fosters the intention to be among those who prosper within it, the Gospel of Prosperity is the polar opposite of liberation theology.'[24] John Stott argues that we are faced with a stark choice:

> In the light of these... biblical truths, and of the contemporary destitution of millions, it is not possible for affluent Christians to 'stay rich', in the sense of accepting no modification of economic lifestyle. We cannot maintain a 'good life' (of extravagance) and a 'good conscience' simultaneously. One or other has to be sacrificed. Either we keep our conscience and reduce our affluence, or we keep our affluence and smother our conscience. We have to choose between God and mammon.[25]

Of course, this polarization of the options – between a theology of prosperity and a theology of liberation, between a 'good life' and a 'good conscience' – may itself be a problem, but it at least highlights the limitations of prosperity theology in its current form.

Paul articulates an important principle when he says that all things are lawful, but not all things are beneficial. He had the right to be supported by the churches in which he had 'sown spiritual good', but he renounced that right rather than risk putting an 'obstacle in the way of the gospel of Christ' (1 Cor. 9:11-12). Perhaps we do have a right to be prosperous, but by claiming that right we may forfeit the right to speak with perceived integrity. It is similar to the problem of eating meat that has been sacrificed to idols. Meat is only meat – essentially a good gift of God to be enjoyed. But in certain cultural and religious contexts, for a Christian to eat meat may constitute a stumbling block to others and a hindrance to the gospel (cf. Rom. 14:20-21; 1 Cor. 8:8-13; 10:23-31). In the same way, in certain social and economic contexts, for a Christian to enjoy disproportionate prosperity may constitute a stumbling block to others and a hindrance to the gospel. This is an argument which today might apply globally as well as locally.

Prosperity teaching has begun to recognize that an adjusted set of values and a different sort of rhetoric are needed if the message is to be preached with any integrity in the context of extreme poverty. We may in the end conclude that Copeland's argument about the African convert is misguided, but it is not fundamentally immoral and arguably articulates a theologically realistic hope: 'Prosperity doesn't mean a Cadillac to this guy. It means God will show him how to get some water on his scorched village. It means God will do something about the alkaline poison that's ruined his land. It means God will show him how to grow crops, so his family can prosper instead of starving to death.'[26] But we will inevitably have reservations about the exportation of these doctrines to the Third World. There must be concern that these good intentions will be choked by the rampant weeds of materialism and greed. Gifford's account of the Victory '94 Conference in Lusaka illustrates the conflict between the Faith ethos and the socio-political analysis very well. Although the Ghanaian pastor Mensa Otabil has been a leading proponent of a success-oriented faith teaching in Africa, his address at the conference constituted a major change of direction with its emphasis on black pride and the need for political and economic restructuring: 'I prayed to God to prosper me [but] we have to change economic structures, we have to change social structures. If I don't have that opportunity, I can pray all I want and I'll still be poor.' In Gifford's view, he 'effectively destroyed the Faith Gospel', but his message simply fell on deaf ears.[27]

In a thoroughly materialistic and hedonistic culture the church will also find it very difficult to examine its own motives and ensure that the prosperity which it seeks is fundamentally *different* from the prosperity that the world seeks. There is a fine line between the hope of God-given prosperity and plain old covetousness. In an age of saturation advertizing, is it realistic to think that we may hope for prosperity and not become a slave to it? It *is*, as Jesus says, very difficult to serve both God and Mammon.

There is, finally, the very serious ethical question of whether the prosperity of the West, and of Western churches, is maintained at the expense of the poor (58). The Word of Faith movement foresees a transfer of wealth from the kingdom of Satan to the church, but others would argue that this is at best naïve and at worst a deeply immoral refusal to recognize the extent to which the rich nations of the world have exploited the poor. The church in the West is *already* prosperous – many would say indecently prosperous. A prosperity teaching that encourages giving and investment might be acceptable, but the acquisition of wealth at the expense of others cannot be justified. We are bound to ask whether prosperity teaching is not simply a means of excusing the lifestyle and assuaging the consciences of wealthy Christians.[28]

* * * *

We have dealt with the complex ethical and pastoral issues raised in this chapter only briefly. It is important that they are flagged, but we are conscious of the distortions that can easily arise in such a cursory and external analysis. The proper context for pursuing such an investigation ought to be one of long-term dialogue. Many evangelicals, however, will question whether such an objective is either achievable or desirable. In the final chapter we will explore the implications of our study for evangelical unity and ask what steps might be taken to promote détente.

Conclusions: Word of Faith and evangelical unity

The primary objective of this report has been to present and evaluate, as fairly as possible, the biblical and theological teachings that give shape to the Word of Faith movement. These teachings have appeared defective in three general areas: first, a narrative of salvation history that is at odds with mainstream evangelical thinking at a number of crucial points; secondly, an idealized and prescriptive conception of faith that diminishes the relational and personal dimensions of Christian spirituality; thirdly, an enthusiasm for material prosperity as a concrete expression of the goodness of God towards his people that is difficult to square with the high value placed, for various reasons, on 'poverty' in the Bible, and which is likely to compromise the church's prophetic voice.

We have also argued, however, that Word of Faith teaching should not be assessed solely according to its errors. Although in many respects the outward form of the movement may appear outlandish to evangelical sensibilities, we would suggest that at its heart lie certain instincts and convictions that are fundamentally biblical and which deserve respect. The first question to ask, therefore, in this final chapter is: What options are available to us for describing and responding to the peculiar mix of truth and error that we find in Word of Faith teaching? Secondly, we will review those aspects of Word of Faith teaching and praxis that may be broadly affirmed and which may offer mainstream evangelicalism an opportunity to recover some neglected emphases. Thirdly, we will outline some general recommendations with a view to encouraging better understanding between these two movements and, one would hope, some form of constructive dialogue.[1]

The question of orthodoxy

One approach would be to accept that the core of Word of Faith doctrine is sound while insisting, nevertheless, that a number of dubious teachings have been added to it or inferred from it. The movement itself not only regards its teachings as an authentic expression of the Word of God but also believes that it shares the fundamentals with evangelicalism. Hollinger quotes Kenneth Hagin Jr.'s apologetic for the movement: 'Our major tenets of faith are held in common by those in the evangelical world – beliefs such as the virgin birth and deity of our Lord Jesus Christ, the absolute necessity of the new birth through faith in the atoning work of Jesus on the cross, and other fundamental doctrines of the church.'[2] Douglas Moo appears to endorse this position: 'Most of the proponents of this movement do not seek to downplay the significance of spiritual salvation. What they believe about the basic doctrines of the faith is well within the parameters of orthodoxy. If, indeed, theirs is "another gospel," it is so not because any basic doctrines have been subtracted, but because certain questionable doctrines have been added.'[3]

A distinction is also readily drawn between a moderate faith-prosperity teaching and the more irresponsible and self-seeking forms that the argument has sometimes taken. Idealist movements invariably throw up extremists, some of them money-grabbing and unscrupulous, some of them merely self-deluding. Many evangelicals will want the option of affirming some of the fundamental assumptions about faith that have been elaborated into Word of Faith doctrine while distancing themselves both from the unbiblical augmentations and the excesses of some of the movement's proponents. Many

Pentecostals and charismatics would probably feel much more comfortable with a 'faith' emphasis that lacked the preoccupation with an individualistic material prosperity. Charles Farah endorses many Word of Faith distinctives, only really drawing the line at the presumption that the principles of faith must work the same way in every situation.[4]

Robert Bowman believes that 'at least some of the leading teachers of the movement do teach heresy' but argues that the movement as a whole should be classified as 'aberrant or sub-orthodox'.[5] He lists a number of reasons for this ambivalent conclusion.[6] First, Word of Faith teachers do not explicitly reject orthodox doctrine. Secondly, they sometimes *affirm* orthodox doctrine. Thirdly, the movement belongs to a radical wing of an orthodox Christian tradition, namely Pentecostalism. Fourthly, the movement teaches 'patently unbiblical ideas about the nature of God, the nature of human beings, and the person and redemptive work of Jesus Christ'. Fifthly, some Word of Faith teachers 'have espoused blatantly heretical and even blasphemous ideas'. Lastly, Word of Faith teaching is 'demonstrably detrimental to a sound Christian life'. None of these reasons is considered by Bowman to be conclusive one way or the other; to all of them he appends important caveats. But the classification is reckoned to be flexible enough to permit us to acknowledge the significant deviations from orthodoxy without ignoring either the substantial overlap with more conventional evangelical teaching or the undoubted presence of many genuine believers within the movement. Bowman thinks that few adherents actually take seriously the more extreme teachings. For this reason, if for no other, he believes that the movement should not be regarded as cultic.[7]

Bowman's assessment is important because it constitutes probably the most careful attempt to classify the doctrinal status of the Word of Faith movement available to us. The factors on which the assessment is based, however, are almost entirely theological; and while exegetical and theological concerns must be at the heart of any serious critique, there are a number of practical and historical factors that should also be taken into account. The reason for doing so is not to downplay or excuse the heterodoxy of the movement but to ensure that the theological judgment does not prove an impediment to further dialogue.

1. **The life of the movement**. The issues raised by the Word of Faith phenomenon have as much to do with personality and *praxis* as with the details of biblical exposition. At this level evaluation becomes much more problematic. On the one hand, these are difficult matters to judge from a distance. How are we properly to determine the authenticity of a testimony or the integrity of a ministry without actually being part of the event? On the other, while the movement may have attracted more than its fair share of charlatans and profiteers, there are undoubtedly many who genuinely love God, who seek to walk in faithful obedience to his Word, and who have experienced the power of the Holy Spirit. It would be no easy task to determine to what extent this is *because of* or *in spite of* the distinctive emphases of Word of Faith teaching. Nevertheless, it is important that due weight be given to the *life* of the movement. There are some exceptions to the generalization that Word of Faith ministries have a poor record of social and humanitarian engagement. For example, T.D. Jakes has been accused (by Eugene Rivers) of 'promoting black middle-class consumerism', but his Potter's House church in South Dallas is developing a 'City of Refuge' that will offer help for pregnant teenagers, vocational training and support for former prisoners and drug dealers, a home for the elderly, schools, a youth ministry, and a performing arts centre.[8]

2. **The fundamentalist imperative**. To a large extent the doctrinal errors apparent in Word of Faith teaching are historical in origin: they are the product of the confluence of different religious and philosophical traditions. But it could also be argued that the suborthodox doctrinal developments have been driven by the need to explicate and defend the fundamentalism of faith that lies at the heart of the

teaching. The Word of Faith movement has pushed the logic of faith to an idealized and absolute conclusion and in the process has severely distorted the fabric of biblical teaching. The fundamentalism is misguided, but it arises out of something authentically Christian – a deep appreciation for what God has done in Christ, a desire to take the Word of God with the utmost seriousness, and, most importantly, a determination to defend the life of faith against the forces of secularism. What invariably happens, though, is that entrenched fundamentalist movements are unable to respond when the hostile circumstances that provoked – and arguably justified – the initial obduracy disappear. The world changes, the war moves on, but the old guard remains in its bunker, doggedly holding out against an enemy that is no longer there.

3. **The need to read the rhetoric**. The idealization of faith has manifested itself not only in idiosyncratic biblical exposition but also in the flamboyant and histrionic rhetoric of the Word of Faith teachers and in the showmanship of their ministries. Although mainstream evangelicals will no doubt find the packaging all too flashy and superficial, it is important to understand the underlying purpose. We have to ask how the rhetoric of faith and prosperity teaching functions *within the context of Word of Faith ministry*. As we peer through the screen of an unfamiliar culture, it is easy to jump to the wrong conclusions about what is going on on the other side.

   The style and method of the Word of Faith ministries are geared towards actively enlisting believers to a life of radical faith in the promises of God. Such an existentially and psychologically precarious stance requires a high level of maintenance and motivational input, which goes a long way towards accounting for the obsessive and blinkered nature of the movement. The rhetoric of faith has to work very hard to shake people's grip on appearances and the dictates of common sense, to sustain conviction and resist doubt. There is a marked desire to shock, which goes with the showmanship of the Word of Faith movement[9] but which may also echo the background buzz of polemic and debate with mainstream Christianity. Word of Faith teachers have a habit of making theologically provocative statements that may appear much less scandalous when unpacked. The tabloid theologizing is designed to disrupt traditional assumptions and generate excitement about the life of faith on a routine basis. It may appear vulgar, it is open to abuse, and it produces more heat than light; but it is precisely heat rather than light that is needed to sustain this level of expectation.

4. **Adapatation and development**. This study has, for the most part, treated the body of Word of Faith teaching as a coherent and static whole. This has been a necessary procedure for the sake of clarity, but in reality the movement is neither coherent nor static. It presents a range of views, and there is some evidence both of an internal struggle to maintain integrity[10] and of a capacity for adaptation and development. It seems likely that there has been some adjustment in the light of criticism from within mainstream evangelicalism and fundamentalism. William DeArteaga suggests, for example, that Kenneth Hagin has made changes in response to the criticisms made by Farah, though Hagin makes a point of never responding publicly to his detractors.[11] He also quotes Hagin's admission that the Word of Faith movement has neglected to teach about the positive role of suffering in the Christian life:

> What's happened with the faith message is that we've told about the good things, but in telling only about the positive side, some people don't even realize that the suffering side exists. Certainly, we are to emphasize the positive aspects of walking in faith because there's victory in Jesus! But at one time or another, all of us suffer persecution, insults, and criticism that test and try us.[12]

Bruce Barron details the attempts of Hagin and Copeland to redress the balance with regard to prosperity teaching.[13]

Moreno Dal Bello quotes the 1981 edition of Hagin's *Zoe: The God-Kind of Life*: 'Even many in the great body of Full Gospel people do not know that the new birth is a real incarnation'. The 1997 printing, however, reads: 'Even many in the great body of Full Gospel people do not fully realize that in the new birth they become one spirit with God (1 Cor. 6:17).'[14] Hagin then develops the argument about the believer's 'union with God' in largely orthodox terms. R.M. Riss draws attention to Hagin's criticism of a self-generated faith: 'I do not understand how some people can go around spouting off things, endeavouring to believe, and calling it faith, when it is only presumption and folly.'[15] He also maintains that Hagin is candid about negative 'prophecies' which are not fulfilled.

Other Word of Faith leaders have also shown signs of a willingness to listen to their detractors. In 1995 John Avanzini published *Things that are Better than Money* (Tulsa, OK: Harrison House) in response to criticism. F.K.C. Price has apparently repudiated the belief that men are literally gods.[16] Kenneth Copeland's argument about God being a failure, which so upset Hank Hanegraaff, has been revised in his 1997 book *Managing God's Mutual Funds*.[17] Indeed, in a sermon in 1992 he went so far as to concede: 'I don't know all that much anyway. All I know is what I've learned and that's all I'm preaching.... I'm not 100 percent right. Dear Lord, I don't know what the percentage is, but I expect its [sic] probably pretty heavy on the wrong side.... there are certain things I am wrong about just simply because I don't know any better.'[18] Whether this admission should be read as a sign of humility or of irresponsibility is debatable, but it surely invites a more constructive response than mere condemnation and contempt.

5. **The problem of over-correction**. There is a case for saying, finally, that Word of Faith teaching has simply *over*-emphasized certain themes which have been neglected by mainstream evangelicalism. Price seems close to acknowledging the dangers inherent in attempting to redress the

balance: '*That's the way the old ship of Zion has been going* – it has listed so far to one side with erroneous doctrine or no doctrine, false teaching and faulty instruction, or mixed-up and messed-up instruction, that you almost have to appear to be completely fanatical to right the old ship and get her back on an even keel!'[19] The inevitable effect of shifting such themes as healing, prosperity, and positive confession to the centre stage is that those doctrines that evangelicals would normally regard as being of primary importance to the expression of Christian faith have – intentionally or otherwise – become marginalized, though Word of Faith teachers have sometimes tried to correct this impression. This may be regarded as a legitimate function provided that Word of Faith priorities are not allowed to set the whole agenda for the church and there can be some critical feedback into Word of Faith teaching. Kenneth Hagin Jr.'s complaint should be heard: 'The faith message is not the only message in the Word of God, but some people have latched onto the faith of God – what it can get them, and so forth – until they have perverted this greatest truth of God's Word.'[20]

Evangelicalism is bound to object to the centrality of even a reformed prosperity teaching, but the more tangential influence of a lobby within evangelicalism, having the aim of injecting a sound appreciation of the unique economy of God into the wider church, might prove acceptable.[21] Local Word of Faith churches in any case are often less strident and less fixated on a single issue than the propagandist parachurch ministries. Much of the extremism and many of the more esoteric teachings are quite naturally filtered out at the grassroots level. The Word of Faith movement is more than the sum of its teachers.

Could we then take the view that the Word of Faith churches are in effect testing the 'hypothesis' that God desires to bless his people materially as they seek to live faithfully in accordance with his will? Most churches tend to prioritize one aspect or other of collective devotional life and ministry: some emphasize charismatic experience, others place expository preaching at the centre of their ministry, others find their *raison d'être* in community service, and so on. We may not be entirely happy with the segregation and narrowness of focus which often results from these 'specializations'. But to the extent that we are willing to accept such a state of affairs as a function of evangelical diversity, it may be possible to regard prosperity teaching as an exploration of, or 'experiment' in, the economy of God. The extremism of the movement would then be recognized as being, in part at least, a consequence of its experimental character.[22] As an experiment it must also be open to rigorous evaluation in the light of Scripture and conscience, and subject to modification where necessary. But in the process it may become the means by which we bring into focus some important neglected aspects of biblical teaching.

What can evangelicalism learn from Word of Faith teaching?

Although evangelicalism has usually been highly suspicious of the arguments of the Word of Faith teachers, we take the view that there is enough common ground to justify a more constructive and ecumenical critique of the movement – that it is worth trying to disentangle the delicate wisteria of truth from the rampant Russian ivy of error. The assumption here is not just that the Word of Faith movement shares many of its core teachings with evangelicalism – enough to suggest consanguinity – but that there are some important lessons that evangelicalism might learn through dialogue and through exposure to the life of Word of Faith churches. Too little attention has been given to some important biblical emphases that can be found in this body of teaching. The challenge would then be to reconceptualize a theology of faith and prosperity, rescued from the current isolationism of the Word of Faith movement, stripped of the theological eccentricities and the cultural markers, and assimilated into the broader and more self-critical framework of evangelical theology.

1. **The priority given to the Word of God**. We have expressed serious concerns about the simplistic hermeneutic that governs the Word of Faith interpretation of Scripture and about the numerous exegetical errors that have been identified in this report. Nevertheless, we have recognized that Hagin, Copeland and other encourage a very thorough and practical commitment to be immersed in the Word of God and act in accordance with its precepts. In this respect the Word of Faith movement constitutes an extension of the Pentecostal/charismatic challenge to an evangelicalism which has become over-intellectualized, sanitized, reduced to something altogether too tame and ineffectual. The contractual hermeneutic has led to distortions, but it has also made the Bible a dynamic, authoritative and practical text at the centre of Word of Faith spirituality.

2. **Belief in a powerful God**. We may disagree with the methodology and the theological details in places and feel uncomfortable with the absolutism, but it is difficult to argue with the Word of Faith criticism of the widespread lack of commitment to the life of faith among Christians. Hagin makes the point: 'Our having to encourage believers to believe or have faith is a result of the Word of God's having lost its reality to us. We *are* believers.'[23] Many evangelicals, while committed to the intellectual truth of the gospel, would prefer to live out their faith within the normal parameters of everyday life. The Word of Faith movement is impatient with such constraints: it is a boisterous, self-confident faith that refuses to live within the confines of normality and must continually beat against the walls in order to extend its space. Moo's comment seems fair: 'the openness in this movement to the possibility of miraculous interventions of God may be more "biblical" than the skepticism that too many of us unwittingly share with our materialistic culture.'[24] We cannot properly evaluate the miracle claims in a study of this nature, but on the face of it many of the testimonies appear little different from accounts of divine intervention commonly heard within the

ambit of charismatic and Pentecostal evangelicalism.[25] That there are also stories of disappointment and failure is an embarrassment to the Word of Faith movement but does not in itself invalidate the claims for miraculous healing and divine provision. It does, however, point to the need for strong faith to be accompanied by an equally strong gift of discernment, informed both by the Spirit and by the Word of God, exercised both by the individual and by the believing community. Faith cannot be arbitrary, thoughtless, or presumptuous.

3. **A thoroughgoing optimism**. Word of Faith teaching promotes a fundamentally positive outlook on life. 'Learn to live on the good side of life,' T.L. Osborn urges.[26] The focus on prosperity can be construed in very humanistic and self-centred terms and at times hardly differs from secular self-help ideology. But the optimism is also quite consistent with the belief that our Father in heaven will 'give good things to those who ask him' (Mt. 7:11). Evangelical Christians, not least British evangelical Christians, could probably learn a lot from the exuberance and confidence that finds expression in the idealism of the Word of Faith movement. It may easily be confused with American feel-goodism and self-assertiveness, but we ought to be able to differentiate between such culturally determined attitudes and the profoundly hopeful trust in a loving and creative and generous God that we find in Scripture. If Word of Faith teaching overstates the dynamic of fulness and abundance and victory in the Christian life, this is largely as a corrective to the apathy and negativism that dominates the Christian mind-set in the West. The Word of Faith movement sees many Christians as cowed by the forces of secularism and anti-supernaturalism and has sought to reinforce the Christian self-perception as children of the King, heirs of divine promise. Colin Dye recognizes that prosperity teaching often inclines towards an over-realized eschatology, but he argues that 'a more widespread problem in British and European evangelicalism is the opposite

error of negativism'.[27] Despite his criticism of the faith movement Farah is careful to make the point that the church 'owes a tremendous debt to these teachers because of their great emphasis on positive faith and a God who answers prayer in the now. In a wholly negative world, this is a refreshing and needed message.'[28]

The phenomenal popularity of Bruce Wilkinson's small book *The Prayer of Jabez* (the website claims sales of more than 9 million)[29] suggests that there is a significant degree of overlap between evangelical spirituality and Word of Faith teaching that could be exploited in the interests of ecumenism. Wilkinson does not endorse 'the popular gospel that you should ask God for a Cadillac, a six-figure income, or some other material sign that you have found a way to cash in on your connection with Him',[30] but the spirituality which he evokes is not far from the more moderate, holistic forms of prosperity teaching. One can easily imagine Hagin and Copeland saying 'amen' to Wilkinson's statement that 'God really does have unclaimed blessings waiting for you' and his argument that we are not selfish enough in our prayers.[31]

4. **The subordination of Mammon to the kingdom of God**. There is always going to be a tension, even without a doctrine of prosperity, between the possession and the renunciation of material things – between enjoying the good things that God has given us and giving up what we have in order to alleviate the suffering of others or support Christian ministry. However, evangelicalism has not been especially successful at reconciling the spiritual and material sides of modern life. Some have responded to the dilemma by giving or by following a path of service and ministry that offers very little in the way of financial rewards. But there are many wealthy Christians who have failed to integrate their spiritual and material lives. The Sunday morning offering constitutes a very inadequate connection between the spiritual and material halves of the Christian life. Moo argues that advocates of the health and wealth gospel are 'justified in criticizing the

church in the west for too often unintentionally fostering an unbiblical anthropological dualism by confining God's concerns to the human soul'.[32] One has the impression at times that evangelicals feel that it is encumbent upon them to preserve the holiness of God by keeping him well away from the sordid business of earning, saving, and investing money. It is surely ironic, as Peter Gammons has complained,[33] that among the fiercest critics of prosperity teaching are the prosperous, middle-class churches.

This dichotomy at the heart of our spiritual allegiance is not helpful. We accept as a matter of central theological principle that Christ lays claim to a person's entire life and that our economic activity, as much as any other area, must be restructured in accordance with the Word of God. But we have lacked the commitment to work this through as a matter either of theological understanding or of spiritual practice. DeArteaga argues that it was the failure of mainline Protestant theology to provide a 'contemporary definition of godly motivation in the workplace' that allowed writers in the New Thought tradition to dominate the market for motivational literature.[34]

By stressing the intrinsic goodness of material things, the comprehensiveness of divine blessing, the requirement of righteousness, and the godly dynamic of giving and receiving, Word of Faith teaching has sought to shift prosperity from the kingdom of Mammon to the kingdom of God so that the believer may produce and enjoy wealth without being enslaved to it. In this way our economic life is redeemed. It is not merely that our wealth is consecrated to another purpose; it is redeemed in itself, and its intrinsic goodness restored, if only imperfectly prior to the creation of a new heaven and a new earth. There is some force to Copeland's argument that one of the main reasons why 'we've never won the world to Jesus is that we've never shown them how God could help them deal with the material monster that's eating them alive right now. Instead, we've acted like God was so far above material things that He wouldn't have anything to do with them.'[35]

Although the biblical arguments for debt-cancellation put forward by Word of Faith teachers are not fully convincing, it is undoubtedly the case that debt can be extremely detrimental to the well-being of believers and the effectiveness of Christian ministry. It is fair to say that prosperity theology is motivated to a large extent by the needs of people who have overreached themselves financially,[36] and in principle this aversion to debt should act as a brake on unbridled and irresponsible consumerism. There is a danger, of course, that people are attracted to the debt-reduction programmes purely for selfish financial reasons and not in order to achieve the spiritual freedom to pursue a more godly lifestyle. But the argument about the damaging effects of debt, both at the personal and the social level, certainly needs to be heard, and sound practical teaching about how to get out of debt is valuable.

5. **A theology of godly prosperity**. Historically the church has sought to address the complex challenges of poverty and wealth in one of three ways. The most radical approach – the classic religious response – has been to retreat from wealth and power into a lifestyle of simplicity and self-denial. Usually this has been accompanied by service to the poor and dispossessed. Secondly, the so-called Protestant work ethic has, in various guises, endorsed work as a God-given means of social and personal betterment and as providing the basis for supporting the work of the kingdom. John Wesley's austere rule exemplifies the position: 'Gain all you can, save all you can, give all you can.' Thirdly, there has been a strong emphasis, especially in recent years, on the pursuit of equality through economic restructuring and the redistribution of wealth. In some contexts this has taken the form of a liberation theology, but Western evangelicalism has been wary of the ideological commitments that this has entailed and has generally sought to take a more politically detached and 'prophetic' stance. The practical objective has been, on the one hand, to influence public opinion through the normal channels of persuasion, and on to the

other, to alleviate deprivation through humanitarian agencies. An analysis of these responses is beyond the scope of this report, but we would suggest that there are components of a proper biblical understanding of prosperity that are not adequately encompassed in these models.[37]

The first has to do with how we value our wealth and material possessions and with the integrity of our involvement in the material world. If our theology teaches us that wealth is merely something to be given away, for example, how are we to evaluate what we keep? Is there not a danger, in the end, that we acquire and keep wealth as a matter of theological *neglect*? Most Christians in the West, whether they like it or not, are an integral part of the economic system and have organized their lives and their finances largely in accordance with the opportunities and demands that this system presents. If we are bound to accept this situation, the challenge faced by the church in the West is: How do we make the modern, affluent, middle-class Christian lifestyle *godly*? Is it enough to insist on giving and self-denial? Is it enough to speak out against the excesses and injustices of the modern economy? Is our wealth an embarrassment, an impediment to spiritual growth, an offence in the eyes of God? If we must regard it as a blessing, if we are able to thank God for the abundant good things that we have received from his hands, why should we feel so uncomfortable with the view that a generous and gracious God might wish to add to that blessing as increasingly we learn to walk in righteousness and obedience? Prosperity teaching may be able to contribute a paradigm that will keep our economic activity usefully within the purview of the kingdom of God.[38]

Secondly, we cannot ignore the fact that wealth is a positive resource. It is a hazardous resource, certainly, but within a redeemed community there should be the wisdom and grace available to handle wealth responsibly.[39] Copeland quotes Proverbs 1:32 ('The prosperity of fools shall destroy them') but he asks: 'Does that mean you too should avoid being prosperous? ... No! It means you should avoid being a fool!'[40] If we are unconvinced by the argument that vast sums of money are needed to pay for mass-media evangelism on a global scale in the run up to the second coming, we can surely think of other ends to which the resources of a prosperous 'divine economy' might be put. It is perhaps a little odd that we constantly bemoan the lack of funds available to the church yet are so wary of a movement that believes that God is willing and able to bless his people financially as they learn to walk in faith and obedience.

The third gap in the traditional response to wealth and poverty has to do with the power of God. The problem is that all three traditional strategies simply presuppose the conditions of ordinary economic activity. They offer various answers to the question, What should we do with the wealth that we have acquired, or have the capacity to acquire, for ourselves? Do we give it away and opt out of the system? Do we work to produce more wealth to support Christian ministry? Do we campaign for a fairer distribution of wealth within society? Ron Sider's influential book *Rich Christians in an Age of Hunger* presents a well-developed theological critique of global economic injustice, but no mention is made of those New Testament texts (or for that matter the many Old Testament texts) which seem to promise some sort of *material* return on our giving.[41] The notion of 'abundance' is interpreted only in terms of the unselfish sharing of resources within the community.[42] It would be wrong to say that these approaches are merely humanistic or ungodly, but we miss an appreciation of the generosity of God and of his active involvement in our economic life. The Word of Faith movement has taken the course of seeking to demonstrate the viability of a positive, faith-based model of divine prosperity.

What prosperity teaching might help us grasp more effectively, therefore, is the possibility of being a wide conduit for God's material blessing – not a large container that has no outlet, but not a *narrow* conduit either. We have the prospect of enjoying prosperity as *it passes through our hands*.[43] This is Wilkinson's argument – that faithful and righteous people, whether in the ministry or in the secular world, should expect to receive greater opportunity and greater resources to influence the world for the glory of God: '*Everything you've put under my care, O Lord—take it, and enlarge it*.'[44] This could be a very powerful vision – a life of innocent and godly abundance, set free from the psychological and financial bondages of the secular economy, that counters the prevailing negativism, cynicism, and greed of contemporary culture; an economy of righteousness, that is not self-seeking but which generates and invests and redistributes wealth according to the purposes of God; a sanctified willingness to manage significant funds in order to support missionary work, relieve suffering, train workers, and bear witness to the goodness of God.

Does this simply ask too much of human nature? The Word of Faith teachers would argue that in the kingdom of God human nature has been radically transformed, brought back under divine sovereignty. Evangelicalism is likely to be less sanguine about the thoroughness of this transformation. Here again we encounter the fundamental divergence between the idealism of the Word of Faith movement and the more realistic and pragmatic stance of mainstream evangelicalism. It is the tension that emerges repeatedly in Paul between the indicative and the imperative of salvation, between those statements which affirm the spiritual transformation of the believer and the accompanying exhortations to put an end to sinful and worldly behaviour: 'once you were darkness, but now in the Lord you are light. Live as children of the light' (Eph. 5:8); we have been 'raised with Christ', and yet the reality is that we still struggle to keep our minds on 'things that are above' (Col. 3:1-2).

Both poverty and riches...?

There remains, however, a real tension between the wealth-affirming ethos of the Word of Faith movement and the more ascetic, anti-materialist, ethos of mainstream Christianity, including evangelicalism. To some extent this tension may be resolved simply by the two sides moving closer together. But an alternative, and more creative, approach suggests itself which may allow us to see in the conflict between these seemingly incompatible perspectives on prosperity an oscillation between two states of being that is intrinsic to the historical existence of the people of God. For it could be argued that underlying the tension between these two approaches to wealth is a real and important biblical distinction between two modes of discipleship: an unsettled discipleship of the road, on the one hand, and a settled discipleship of home and workplace, on the other.

The first is a characteristically, though not exclusively, New Testament model, shaped by the course of Jesus' ministry, the crisis of the kingdom of God, and the missionary activity of the early church. It requires the abandonment of previous securities, a radical trust in God to provide for material needs – Abraham setting out from Haran or the Israelites fleeing Egypt in response to a divine calling would count as valid precedents for this mode of discipleship. The provision of manna in the wilderness (Ex. 16:11-35) – no more than was needed for each day – may be taken as a paradigm for the Christian's reliance on God to provide sufficient for his material needs,[45] but we should not overlook the fact that this was a supernatural provision in a time of transition and crisis. It is not how God provided for the settled community. Jesus taught the disciples to pray for their 'daily bread' (Mt. 6:11; Lk. 11:3), but the context is again one of extreme insecurity. It is a form of discipleship that often has to deal with the prospect of persecution or martyrdom; it is where a 'theology of the cross' finds its most natural setting. Much of the teaching about self-denial and suffering in the New Testament, as Word of Faith teachers have been quick to observe, presupposes this context and pattern of discipleship. In terms of classical spirituality, we are on the *via negativa*. In such circumstances a theology of material prosperity appears irrelevant; wealth is likely to be a hindrance or distraction; a lifestyle of poverty may seem more consistent with the spiritual and emotional demands of following Christ. The rich young ruler was confronted with the challenge of this sort of discipleship. Jesus instructed him to give away his wealth not primarily for the sake of the poor, as a matter of economic justice, but *for the sake of discipleship*. To those who have left everything is promised substantial relational and material compensation in the present age – and, of course, much more in the age to come.

The second mode of discipleship is better represented by Old Testament patterns of spirituality. It is the discipleship of a settled community with more or less reliable means of income and potentially a high standard of living. It is the discipleship of the New Testament churches when they are relatively free from the threat of persecution (cf. 1 Tim. 2:1-2).[46] This sort of discipleship requires a contextually appropriate theology of prosperity that emphasizes the need not only for economic justice but also for the active recycling of wealth through the virtuous circle of God's economy. There may not be the same sense of having abandoned everything for the sake of the gospel, and the scope for radical faith may be restricted, but the demand for a fully God-centred lifestyle is no less urgent. Prosperity is seen less as the product of a worldly economic system or a measure of personal success and more as a gift of grace, given for enjoyment and well-being of the people, just as other gifts are given to individuals for the benefit of the body. Concern for the poor and oppressed as an expression of the righteousness that is ours in Christ becomes a goal in its own right – a quite natural extension of the Old Testament ideal. It is within this context, too, that a theology of work finds its place: the dynamic of giving and receiving does not replace the more mundane process of acquiring wealth through labour.[47] A divine economy is not an alternative to the secular economy but rather an extension and heightening of it. There is also much greater scope here for the development of a creation theology that is able to affirm the intrinsic value of material things, work, culture, creativity, and so on (cf. 1 Tim. 4:4-5; 6:17; Tit. 1:15). Here we are on the *via positiva*. There is no reason why our definition of 'prosperity' should not be expanded beyond the narrow economic definition that has traditionally characterized prosperity theology to include social, environmental and aesthetic values. Indeed, this brings us back to the Old Testament idea of *shalom*: a holistic notion of prosperity that encompasses not only peace with God but also relational and material well-being. We are not bound to accept the restrictive definition foisted upon us by the historical anomaly of contemporary American prosperity teaching.

The distinction between these two forms of discipleship is not a hard and fast one. If it can be explained in terms of a contrast between an Old Covenant spirituality and a New Covenant spirituality, this is merely an historical, not an absolute, distinction: it is simply that one model is better illustrated from the New Testament, the other from the Old. They should be regarded as complementary rather than as contradictory modes – though any discipleship of prosperity will always be dependent for its life and authenticity both on Christ's eschatological self-giving and on our own willingness, in the final analysis, to lose everything for the sake of the gospel. Churches and even individuals will shift from one to the other according to circumstances. We might venture, then, to amend Craig Blomberg's negative slogan ('neither poverty nor riches'), which was intended in its original context less as the expression of an ideal attitude to wealth than as a prudential safeguard against sin: 'give me neither poverty nor riches; ...or I shall be full, and deny you, and say, "Who is the Lord?" or I shall be poor, and steal, and profane the name of my God' (Prov. 30:8-9). If, in Christ, prosperity need not lead to denying God nor poverty to stealing, can we not affirm instead *both* poverty *and* riches? Even under the difficult circumstances of an itinerant apostolic ministry Paul could say: 'I know what it is to have little, and I know what it is to have plenty. In any and all circumstances I have learned the secret of being well-fed and of going hungry, of having plenty and of being in need' (Phil. 4:12).[48]

Too often, however, the model of eschatologically oriented discipleship that is found in the New Testament is imposed quite unrealistically on Christian communities for whom the prospect of eschatological crisis is little more than a vague theological hypothesis. The church does not always face upheaval, dislocation, or persecution. The fundamental mistake of the Word of Faith movement could also be diagnosed as a mismatch of these two modes of discipleship. The movement has taken a *radical* notion of faith that properly belongs in the context of an insecure and unsettled discipleship and linked it to a definition of prosperity that is only really workable under settled conditions. The result is that both faith and prosperity are misapplied. Radical faith is made to serve mammon rather than the kingdom of God; and a divine economy that blesses through industry and giving is subjected to the uncertainties and liabilities of a misplaced faith. Ironically, the sort of faith advocated by the Word of Faith movement becomes relevant at precisely the moment at which we are called to abandon the life of the prosperous settled community and walk the fateful road from Galilee to Jerusalem.

Finally, we might consider how the dynamic of giving and receiving, underwritten by the goodness of God, might bind these two modes of discipleship together. There is much to be said for the Word of Faith vision of a busy and productive economy of giving and receiving, on the one hand, as a means of introducing grace into our daily lives and of generating resources for ministry and mission, and on the other, as an antidote to the prevailing individualism and selfishness of modern life. Jacques Ellul writes that giving is 'the penetration of grace into the world of competition and selling'.[49] But when properly understood, this is no less true of receiving – because God is no less a giver than we are.

If the basic argument about giving and receiving is correct, then we may begin to grasp how our economic life, or at least a large part of it, may take on a fundamentally godly dynamic: by giving generously we draw into the whole process the much greater generosity and resources of God; we activate grace in our lives. The receiving from God makes this more than just an individualistic and unilateral act: it is productive, interactive, it engages others, it promotes interdependence and community. It overcomes the alienation of wealth: we do not give to an indifferent God, we do not simply pour our money into a void, we do not stand outside the system injecting money in. We have become part of it and we are blessed by it. We must be careful not to reduce the interaction to an automated and formulaic process, the predictable operation of spiritual laws to the exclusion of a sovereign and intentional deity. Ellul warns against making 'God's kingdom an object of shrewd calculation, for God does not like schemers, and he never gives them what they have banked on'.[50] We must also be clear in our own minds that the economy of God is never an escape from servanthood and compassion. But we must also not lose the challenge of faith, which motivates the church to centre itself around a good and generous God.

Towards a final position

If there is to be a worthwhile rapprochement between the Word of Faith movement and mainstream evangelicalism, then a number of steps need to be taken on both sides towards overcoming the current stand-off. What we are recommending, therefore, is a constructive or progressive dialogue. Too often when we attempt to deal with divisions of this nature within the church, we are presented with a stark choice: either a superficial unity or doctrinal soundness.[51] We do not at all wish to downplay the significance of the doctrinal differences between Word of Faith and traditional evangelical teaching. But we would argue, nevertheless, that there is a large enough overlap between the two to justify a serious commitment to work together to understand and resolve the causes of division. There is no need for self-deception in such an undertaking; but there is no need either for a defensive, judgmental ideological separatism.

The challenge to those outside the Word of Faith movement

1. In the first place, we would suggest that those outside the Word of Faith movement need to recognize and resist the

pressure to prejudge matters. The problem is perhaps less acute in Britain than in the US, but there is still a widespread tendency to condemn the movement on the basis of an ingrained and largely unexamined moral revulsion. Much of what passes for doctrinal integrity, however, is often little more than spiritual snobbery and disdain for what appears to be the uneducated, status-seeking vulgarity of Word of Faith religion.

2. The Word of Faith movement should be recognized as being *at its best* a serious attempt to explore and be blessed by the generosity and faithfulness of God. If there is to be any progress in dialogue, evangelicals must be ready to affirm those aspects of Word of Faith teaching and practice that coincide with their own biblical convictions. Evangelicalism has become so sensitized to the doctrinal shortcomings of the movement that we find it difficult to acknowledge the large body of general teaching that is biblically centred, that exalts Christ, that inspires faith in God, and that encourages a lifestyle of integrity and righteousness.

3. Evangelicalism generally should take up the challenge of developing a more positive understanding of the role of wealth within the divine economy. The argument about giving and receiving has often been overstated and twisted by the Word of Faith movement, but the core of the doctrine is sound and may offer a powerful way to reintegrate our economic and spiritual lives. The Word of Faith critique of the prevailing 'poverty gospel' has some force to it and should be a stimulus to a renewed examination of Scripture.

4. To some extent it lies in our hands to dismantle the caricatures and stereotypes into which the church and the secular media have tended to box Word of Faith and prosperity teachers. Caricatures help to highlight excess and hypocrisy, but they are an indiscriminate instrument of polemic. They make it much more difficult to identify and approach those more moderate leaders who seek to be

effective, responsible and faithful ministers, and much more difficult to maintain good standards of integrity.

5. Evangelicals need to be sensitive to the impact that an aggressive critique may have on ordinary believers within the Word of Faith movement. The danger is that such an approach will either reinforce the position or will undermine faith altogether. The point has been made more than once that there is more to the teaching of Hagin and Copeland than is found in the one-sided analyses of their opponents; and there is more to the Word of Faith movement than is found in the ministries of its most prominent evangelists.

The challenge to those inside the Word of Faith movement

1. The leaders of the Word of Faith movement clearly need to reverse the tendency towards isolationism. They are not entirely to blame for this state of affairs: whenever evangelicals have sought to engage with the Word of Faith movement, it has generally been with a view to censuring some aspect or other of its teaching and ministry. John Ankerberg and John Weldon accuse Copeland and others of spiritual pride because they have refused to 'enter into dialogue with other Christian brothers who have, out of love, attempted to correct the Faith teachers'.[52] One wonders whether, instead of attempting to correct, an offer to pray together or worship together or minister together might not have borne more fruit. Dialogue on the basis of criticism only, where there is no trust, is only likely to exacerbate the situation.

   Nevertheless, the suspicion remains that these high profile organizations find it advantageous to maintain their outsider status, not least because it allows them to preserve a distinctive (and marketable) identity within the highly competitive world of global Christianity.[53] But if Word of Faith teachers genuinely believe that their message about faith and prosperity needs to be heard by the whole church, they must begin to dismantle some of the ideological and organizational distinctives that underpin their separatism, even if in the process they risk losing something of their own identity.

2. The Word of Faith movement must take steps to engage in serious biblical scholarship in dialogue with other evangelical scholars. There is no question that Word of Faith theology is fundamentally flawed at a number of critical points, to the extent that we can hardly avoid applying to it some such label as 'suborthodox' or 'heterodox'. We believe, however, that a serious and open-minded conversation between the two communities and a greater interaction between students and scholars across the boundaries will lead to the resolution of many of these disagreements. But the Word of Faith movement must demonstrate a willingness to be heard as one voice among many others within evangelicalism, in dialogue with others, open to reproof and correction. Tightly-controlled, exclusivist, and strongly doctrinaire training institutions are an anomaly today and an unnecessary means of safeguarding the deposit of biblical truth that has been entrusted to us. The development of critical Pentecostal scholarship in recent decades offers a valuable precedent and model for the sort of change that is needed (see above page 82).

3. The Word of Faith movement must address the ethical and pastoral dangers that are inherent in the practice of radical 'faith' ministries. When expectations regarding the efficacy of faith and the availability of material blessings and physical healing are raised to such a great height, pastors and evangelists will find themselves under pressure to make faith work, to create the *appearance* of success, and to conceal failure. This will not always be the case, but the risk of slipping from faith to presumption, from grace to legalism, from transparency to deception, is inevitably much greater when the credibility of the ministry appears to be so dependent on getting results from God. Great faith must be

matched by great integrity. This requirement of integrity, of course, applies to all aspects of Word of Faith ministry, which is too often discredited by financial and pastoral controversy.

4. Although some allowance can be made for a rhetoric that may not always mean quite what it appears to mean, which frequently aims to provoke rather than to inform, and which is often cited out of context by opponents, the question must still be asked whether such rhetoric is helpful. Is the provocation really necessary? We can hardly avoid the conclusion that the power to motivate faith has been gained at the expense both of the general theological project and of Christian unity.

5. Serious questions must be asked about the dominant role models found in the Word of Faith movement. If prosperity teachers appear wealthy and successful, we should not forget that their wealth and success has been acquired through Christian ministry – they are the beneficiaries of the generosity of their supporters. That is a unique position to be in: it cannot be emulated by ordinary Christians and is clearly open to abuse. More importantly, whatever the motives and intentions of the particular minister may be, it is all too easy for the image of the prosperous, high-profile, charismatic leader to replace Christ as the object of adulation and imitation. Hank Hanegraaff quotes the words of the former wife of a televangelist:

   > I know a lot of people were blessed and sincerely ministered to by what we sang on TV, and by what we said—but the overall picture, I'm afraid, seemed to say, "If you follow our formula, you'll be like us," rather than, "If you do what Jesus says, you'll be like Him." It was certainly more exciting to follow us, because to follow us was to identify with success, with glamour, with a theology that made everything good and clean and well-knit together. To identify with Jesus, however, meant to identify with the Cross.[54]

6. If the Word of Faith movement is to remain committed to the ideal of godly prosperity, then something must be done to dissociate this in the public mind – and not least in the evangelical mind – from the materialism and hedonism of contemporary Western culture. On the one hand, there must be an unequivocal critique of economic injustice and excess; on the other, any godly prosperity must be manifestly associated with righteousness, compassion, and a willingness to give to the poor and invest wealth in the kingdom of God. The church cannot afford to have its prophetic voice compromised by an appearance of greed and indifference to economic injustice. We would hope to see develop a more balanced and holistic understanding of 'blessing' that sets material prosperity firmly within the context of relational, developmental, and spiritual prosperity.

* * * *

We do not wish to underestimate the extent of the gulf between the Word of Faith movement and mainstream evangelicalism. But it would be foolish to assume that this situation cannot change. Neither the Word of Faith movement nor Western evangelicalism is a fixed ideological entity: both are in a state of flux and this should encourage an openness on both sides of this controversy to work towards some sort of resolution of the points of disagreement. This will not happen without a commitment on both sides to drop the prejudgments, suspend the antipathies, and re-evaluate the relation between prosperity teaching and mainstream evangelicalism. Such a re-evaluation does not have to be naïve or uncritical. But it does need to be generous, less hasty to condemn than in the past, capable of discerning and affirming what is right and good, and committed to creating mechanisms for mutual understanding and respect.

Statement of the World Evangelical Fellowship on Prosperity Theology and the Theology of Suffering (1995)

Definition

A distinction should be made between 'prosperity theology' and the biblical teaching on prosperity. The former expression refers to a contemporary theological teaching stressing that God always blesses his people materially, with wealth and health, as well as spiritually when they have a positive faith and are obedient to him. It is a teaching that is found frequently, though not exclusively, in some charismatic and Pentecostal circles, where it is also frequently criticized. The accent is not placed on the stewardship of the wealth that God has given to a person, but rather on understanding the biblical concepts of faith, prayer, and blessing, and the consequences of this teaching for one's daily life. A biblical theology of prosperity, on the other hand, would emphasize the responsibilities of the successful or prosperous to use their wealth for the glory of God and for the alleviation of the suffering of the poor and the weak.

Biblical teaching on Wealth and Prosperity

The Old Testament is full of promises of blessing to the person who walks obediently before the Lord and keeps his commands. The book of Deuteronomy, for example, promises the people abundant material blessing in their lives in the land of Canaan if they remain true to the Lord. At the same time, there are checks and balances written into the biblical laws to prevent those who become wealthy from failing to share from their abundance with the poor – for example the laws of the gleanings, the sabbatical year, and the Year of Jubilee. The ideal in ancient Israel was that there should not be a very big gap between the rich and the poor, though in time, this ideal seems to have been lost sight of by many of the rich families in Israel and Judah. This neglect of the poor and needy called forth the scathing denunciations of the prophets of the Lord.

While the Old Testament promises abundance, including both spiritual and material blessings, to the faithful, this emphasis must be balanced by other Old Testament texts that warn the people concerning the accumulation of great wealth and the neglect of the needs of the poor, namely, the widow, the orphan, the alien, and the physically disabled. God is the champion of the poor, and God's people are called upon to manifest his love and graciousness in reaching out to the needy (Ex. 22:22; Deut. 10:18; 14:29; Is. 1:17; 10:2; Jer. 22:3). Both the Old Testament and the New Testament teach that a faith that does not care for the weakest members of the human community is no faith at all (Is. 1:11-17; Jas. 1:27; 1 Jn. 3:17).

While the Bible teaches that all wealth comes from the Lord and is his possession, it does not teach that those who have wealth are more godly than others who do not. God in his providence causes his sun to rise on the evil and the good, and sends his rain on the just and the unjust (Mt. 5:45). The wicked frequently prosper (Ps. 72:3-12) and the righteous are frequently poor even though they are rich in faith (Rom. 15:26; 1 Cor. 1:26; 2 Cor. 6:10; Gal. 2:10; Jas. 2:3-6). The consequences of the fall have permeated the created order so that all are affected, yet God is still the benevolent creator who showers his blessings upon all (Ps. 127:2).

The good news of the kingdom proclaimed by Jesus and ultimately made real by his death, burial and resurrection is good news for the whole created order (1 Cor. 15:1-5). He did not preach a message of the salvation of the soul after death but of the fullness of life; he announced good news to the poor, the imprisoned, the blind, the hungry, the weeping and the persecuted (Lk. 4:18; 6:20-22; Mt. 5:3-11). And he demonstrated the power of the kingdom by restoring people to wholeness, (Heb. *shalom*) in their relationships with God and with their neighbours (Mk. 2:1-12; Lk. 19:9; 7:36-50), by driving out demons (Mk. 1:23-28; Mk. 5:1-20), and by healing the sick (Mk. 1:40-45; 10:46-52; Lk. 7:18-23). What Jesus promised by his Kingdom proclamation, he wrought through his death on the cross and his resurrection from the dead.

The values of the kingdom of God proclaimed by Jesus were set by a radical commitment to the double command to love God with all one's being and to love one's neighbour as oneself (Mk. 12:29-31). To trust God completely frees the disciple of Jesus from being overly concerned about material things. The desire to accumulate wealth, to have security and personal happiness represents the values of the old order, which is passing away (1 Jn. 2:15-17). To share what one has with others is a core value of the new community of the kingdom of God (Lk. 3:11; 12:33; 18:22; Acts 2:35; 2 Cor. 9:2, 7, 11; Eph. 4:28). The disciple of Jesus is called to a life of self-denial and servanthood, following the example set by the Lord himself (Mk. 8:34-35; 10:45; 1 Pet. 2:21).

Both Testaments teach that everything that exists belongs to the Lord and that anything anyone of us possesses is held in trust from the Lord. Thus, no followers of the Lord should regard anything they possess as their own. What we have is blessing from God, but it is not ours to use in any way we desire. We are responsible for using whatever wealth we have for the Lord, particularly in the service of those who are in need. Our motivation for giving is gratitude, rather than to gain more. God has lavished his love upon us by his many gifts to us, the greatest of which is the life of his Son (Rom. 5:8; Eph. 1:7-8; 1 Jn. 3:1). Therefore, we find it natural to respond by sharing what he has given to us with others who have less of this world's goods than we have.

If our wealth comes from God, why is it that so many people, including many Christians, are poor? The bible suggests a variety of reasons. Some are poor because they are lazy (Prov. 10:4 *et passim*). But many others are poor because of circumstances totally outside of their control – because of injustice being done against them by people more powerful than themselves, because of war or famine, because of the death of the husband and father who is able to provide for his family. As it was in the Old Testament period and in the first century church, so it is today.

The Scriptures teach that it is the responsibility of those who have to share with those who have not, and thus to fulfil God's command to love our neighbour as ourselves. The kingdom of God proclaimed by Jesus and inaugurated by his healing mission, death, burial and resurrection has brought salvation to all who come to God through him; however, our experience of salvation is only begun in this life. Christians live between the ages – the age dominated by sin and rebellion and the age of the coming new world order that will be established at Christ's return. At the present time, we experience a foretaste of the age to come through the liberating power of the Holy Spirit, by signs and wonders, by the fruit of the Spirit, the experience of joy and the assurance of the hope that we have in Christ. Jesus' saving work has touched our lives and transformed them, and he, through us, reaches out to bring health, wholeness, and well-being to others; yet we must still resist the temptation to live selfishly and to invest our energies in matters of less importance, giving greater priority to spiritual matters. Hence the New Testament writers constantly urge believers to live in the light of the eschaton, the day when each and every one will experience full health, wealth and eternal prosperity (Mk. 10:25-31; Col. 3:1-4; Heb. 12:1-2; 2 Pet. 3:11-13; Rev. 21:1-4).

A Search for Balance

The Bible does not, unlike some other religious and philosophical traditions, denigrate the physical and material. Wealth is not per se a negative. Viewed and handled properly, it can be an instrument for great blessing. On the other hand, it should not be given too high a value. Wealth can become a substitute for God; it can become an idol. Therefore, the Lord Jesus frequently warned his disciples concerning the dangers of riches (Mk. 10:25; Lk. 6:24; Mt. 6:4; 16:19-23, etc).

It is imperative that the church be taught a balanced perspective on wealth and prosperity. While there may have been times in the past history of the church where there was a danger of denigrating material things, that does not seem to be the present problem of the world Christian community. Rather, with the development of modern industrial and consumer capitalism, all too many Christians are obsessed with material things. Moderation is the true biblical perspective; 'Better is little with the fear of the Lord than great treasure and trouble with it' (Prov. 15:16). 'Give me neither poverty nor riches..., or I shall be full and deny you..., or I shall be poor, and steal, and profane the name of my God' (Prov. 30:7-9). 'Godliness with contentment is great gain. For we brought nothing into the world, and we can take nothing out of it. But if we have food and clothing, we will be content with that' (1 Tim. 6:6-8). Scripture teaches 'those who are rich in this present world not to be arrogant nor to put their hope in wealth, which is so uncertain, but to put their hope in God' and 'to do good, be rich in good deeds, and to be generous and willing to share' (1 Tim. 6:17-18). Through the writings of Proverbs, scripture teaches the poor to learn the disciplines of careful planning, hard work, frugality, and honesty, so that they will 'have something to share with the needy' (Eph. 4:28).

Conclusion

Wealth and prosperity can be a blessing from God, but they can also be Satan's temptation (Lk. 4:5-7). Wealth can be used in a manner that brings great glory to the Lord and great blessing to his people, or it can subtly supplant the place of the Lord in one's life. Jesus warns us that we cannot serve both God and Mammon (Wealth) (Mt. 6:24). This message is as urgent in our day as it was in the first century and must be heeded. In the model prayer (Mt. 7:11; Lk. 11:3), Jesus taught us to trust God for our daily bread, ie. the necessities of life rather than the luxuries. Moderation and sufficiency mark the lifestyle of the biblically sensitive Christian. Paul had learned the secret of being content with whatever he had, whatever circumstances came his way, even in prison (Phil. 4:11-14). In another passage, Paul reminds us of 'the grace of our Lord Jesus Christ, that though he was rich, yet for your sake he became poor, so that you through his poverty might become rich' (2 Cor. 8:9).

Jesus thus provides the Christian with a model of sacrificial and truly altruistic love (*agape*). Whatever wealth an individual Christian or a Christian community has provides an opportunity for *koinonia,* for sharing. All the world's wealth belongs to the Lord. And if God's people could learn to be content with what is sufficient for a full and healthy life rather than the excesses that mark the overly developed world, there would be more than enough to go around. The earth is rich enough to support all those who are alive today and who will be born in the near future at a level of sufficiency but not at the level of prosperity and affluence presently attained by only a few. Both the creation ethic of the Old Testament and the kingdom ethic announced by Jesus call those who would be true worshippers of the living God to take steps to see that the basic needs of all are met. As God blessed Abraham so that he could make him a blessing to the nations (Gen. 12:2), so God has blessed rich Christians to make them a blessing to others.

* * * *

Excerpts from the Declaration of the Consultation organised by the Theological Commission of the World Evangelical Fellowship at Torch Centre, Seoul, Autumn 1994. 50 theologians from 6 continents participated.

Endnotes

INTRODUCTION

[1] E.g., T.L. Osborn, *The Message That Works*, 27, 40-41, 52-58.

[2] J. Avanzini, 'Dr. Drydust, Sister Wonderful, and You', 25.

[3] K. Copeland, *Our Covenant with God*, introduction; cf. K.E. Hagin, *The Believer's Authority*, 6, and T. Newport, *Your Provision and Prosperity*, 53, for similar stories.

[4] G. Copeland, 'Do You Know What Time It Is?', 30.

[5] F.K.C. Price, *Prosperity on God's Terms*, 7; cf. K.E. Hagin, *Mountain Moving Faith*, 131.

[6] D.W. Bebbington, *Evangelicalism in Modern Britain* (London: Unwin Hyman, 1989), 2-17; cf. A.E. McGrath, *Evangelicalism and the Future of Christianity* (London: Hodder & Stoughton, 1988), 49-82.

[7] See, e.g., C. Colson and R.J. Neuhaus (eds.), *Evangelicals and Catholics Together: Toward a Common Mission* (Dallas: Word Publishing, 1995); R.E. Webber, *Ancient Future Faith* (Grand Rapids: Baker Books, 1999).

PART ONE – CHAPTER ONE

[1] K.E. Hagin, *I Believe in Visions*, 58-59.

[2] See Hagin, *Visions*, 1-12; K.E. Hagin, *Zoe: The God-Kind of Life*, 13-14; K.E. Hagin, Understanding the Anointing, 23-27; K.E. Hagin, 'Jesus Christ – The Same Yesterday, Today, and Forever', 19-21; cf. D.R. McConnell, *A Different Gospel*, 56-59.

[3] Hagin, *Visions*, 24-25.

[4] K.E. Hagin, *Must Christians Suffer?*, 32; cf. Hagin, *Anointing*, 51.

[5] D.E. Harrell describes Hagin as 'an able preacher with a homey and humorous Texas style,' who has 'always been more a student and teacher than platform performer' (D.E. Harrell, *All Things Are Possible: The Healing and Charismatic Revivals in Modern America*, 185–186).

[6] Hagin, *Anointing*, 52-53; see also Hagin, *Visions*, 99-102.

[7] Hagin discusses the prophet's ministry in *Visions*, 103-109.

[8] Cf. S. Sizer, 'A Sub-Christian Movement', 46-47.

[9] See *Believer's Voice of Victory* 25.7 (July/Aug. 1997), 19. This edition celebrates 30 years of the Copelands' ministry.

[10] See Hagin, *Anointing*, 65.

[11] See M. Hemry, 'Grand Slam', 10-13 on Jerry Savelle.

[12] See M. Hemry, 'His Father's Business', 8-11.

[13] McConnell, *Gospel*, 82-85.

[14] Frederick K.C. Price grew up as a Jehovah's Witness, entered Christian ministry in 1955, and wandered through Baptist, African Methodist Episcopal, Presbyterian, and Christian and Missionary Alliance denominations before founding the Crenshaw Christian Center in 1973. The multiracial congregation of more than 15,000 occupies the 32 acre site of the former Pepperdine University.

[15] Charles Capps, a former farmer, heard Hagin preach in 1969 and in 1973 began an itinerant ministry emphasizing the power of the spoken word for victorious Christian living. He was ordained by Copeland in 1980 and became a minister in the ICFCM.

[16] Robert Tilton, a former occultist and briefly a devotee of the spiritualist Edgar Cayce, built a multi-million dollar 'ministry' out of a religious infomercial called *Success-N-Life*. His ministry, however, has been hit by repeated financial scandals. Tilton's first wife filed a fraud lawsuit in 1996, and his Word of Faith Outreach Center in Dallas was sold off in 1999. Tilton currently broadcasts on Black Entertainment Television. See J. Ankerberg and J. Weldon, *The Facts on the Faith Movement*, 21.

[17] Avanzini, founder and president of His Image Ministries, has developed a reputation as an expert on divine economics and on the practicalities of getting out of debt. His web site (www.avanzini.org, accessed June 2002) invites people to enlist in his 'debt-free

army' by purchasing a 'Debt Terminator' kit for $59.95, described as 'The Most Powerful Financial Information That our Lord Jesus Christ has ever Released to His Church'.

[18] The eccentricities and excesses of many of these figures are well documented by prominent critics such as Hanegraaff (H. Hanegraaff, *Christianity In Crisis*, 32-39; H. Hanegraaff, 'What's Wrong with the Faith Movement? Part One'); cf. Ankerberg and Weldon, *Facts*, 20-22.

[19] See N. Justice, 'Bakker Apologizes for Prosperity Gospel', 49; also J. Bakker, 'Does God Want Me to be Rich?', and his book: J. Bakker, *Prosperity and the Coming Apocalypse* (Nashville: Thomas Nelson, 1998). Cf. Hanegraaff, *Crisis*, 214-215.

[20] See Hanegraaff, *Crisis*, 343-344; and comments in T. Smail, A. Walker, and N. Wright, '"Revelation Knowledge" and Knowledge of Revelation: The Faith Movement and the Question of Heresy', 59; Ankerberg and Weldon, *Facts*, 23.

[21] G.R. Fisher and M.K. Goedelman, *The Confusing World of Benny Hinn*. In an article in *Now* magazine in 1998 Andre Kole expressed considerable frustration over the difficulty of getting documented evidence of healings from Hinn (A. Kole, 'Illusion and Reality', *Now* (Jan. 1998), 12). A documentary broadcast on British Television by ITV on 22nd April 2001 ('Miracles') also did little to allay the doubts about the ethical integrity of Hinn's ministry and the authenticity of the claims for divine healing.

[22] See D.E. Harrell, *All Things Are Possible: The Healing & Charismatic Revivals in Modern America*, 171.

[23] S. Brouwer, P. Gifford, and S.D. Rose, *Exporting the American Gospel*, 191.

[24] Hemry, 'Grand Slam', 13; D. Hollinger, 'Enjoying God: An Historical/Sociological Profile of the Health and Wealth Gospel', 138-139.

[25] P. Gifford, 'The Gospel of Prosperity', 1390; P. Gifford, 'Prosperity: A New and Foreign Element in African Christianity', 374-375.

[26] See C. Cutrer, 'Come and receive your miracle', 41-49.

[27] P. Gifford, *African Christianity: Its Public Role*, 337-338; M.A. Ojo, 'Charismatic Movements in Africa', 106.

[28] Gifford, 'Foreign Element', 383.

[29] Gifford, 'Gospel of Prosperity', 1390; see also Kim, Sang-Bok D., 'A Bed of Roses or a Bed of Thorns', 15.

[30] See B. Beresford, 'Building up the body of Christ: What Is ... Rhema Church?'; A. Anderson, 'Pentecostals and Apartheid in South Africa during Ninety Years 1908-1998'; and Gifford, 'Gospel of Prosperity', 1390.

[31] Accessed May 2002 at www.rhema.co.za.

[32] Gifford, 'Gospel of Prosperity', 1390; cf. Gifford, 'Foreign Element', 383; Ojo, 'Charismatic Movements', 106.

[33] Gifford, *African Christianity*, 335.

[34] See S. Buckley, "'Prosperity Theology' Pulls on Purse Strings"; A.C. Barro, 'Wrestling with Success'.

[35] Brouwer, et al., *American Gospel*, 68-73.

[36] Hanegraaff, 'What's Wrong with the Faith Movement? Part One'.

[37] See S. Coleman, 'Charismatic Christianity and the Dilemmas of Globalization', 247-248, 249-253; Gifford, *African Christianity*, 40-41. For the history of the church see www.ulfekman.org/the_church/history.htm (accessed June 2002).

[38] See G. Lie, 'The Charismatic/Pentecostal Movement in Norway: The Last 30 Years'.

[39] 'Turning 30... in a Year That Was Like Heaven', *Believer's Voice of Victory* 26.1 (Jan. 1998), 22; also 'A Tidal Wave of Glory', *Believer's Voice of Victory* 26.3 (March 1998), 26.

[40] See also W.K. Kay, *Pentecostals in Britain*, 88. Kay thinks that 'The Hagin/Copeland faith teaching is more likely to be held by older ministers and ministers who have not received full-time training' (102).

[41] Smail, et al., 'Revelation Knowledge', 59.

[42] See www.pgmi.org (accessed June 2002).

[43] Newport, *Provision*, 41.

[44] Cf. R. Jackson, 'Prosperity theology and the faith movement', 22.

[45] Morris Cerullo World Evangelism eventually resigned from the Evangelical Alliance in September 1996.

[46] Coleman, 'Charismatic Christianity', 246.

[47] Gifford, 'Gospel for champions', 1256.

[48] Hanegraaff, *Crisis*, 14. For a comprehensive index of the more alarmist online criticism of the Word of Faith movement see www.deception-inthechurch.com/word-faith.html (accessed June 2002).

[49] R.M. Bowman, '"Ye Are Gods?" Orthodox and Heretical Views on the Deification of Man', 5; cf. Smail, et al., 'Revelation Knowledge', 58-60.

[50] Hanegraaff, *Crisis*, 13.

[51] A. Brandon, *Health and Wealth*, 142.

[52] See, e.g., Harrell, *All Things*, 99-116; cf. W. DeArteaga's account of the opposition of Buckley and Warfield to the Faith-Cure movement and Pentecostalism (W. DeArteaga, *Quenching The Spirit*, 128-139).

[53] See DeArteaga, *Quenching The Spirit*, 247-263.

[54] See, e.g., H.T. Newman, 'Cultic Origins of Word-Faith Theology Within the Charismatic Movement', *Pneuma: The Journal of the Society for Pentecostal Studies*, Spring 1990, 32-55; cf. W.J. Hollenweger, *Pentecostalism: Origins and Developments Worldwide*, 229-233.

[55] See, e.g., C. Farah, *From the Pinnacle of the Temple*, 1-4, 20-21; cf. DeArteaga, *Quenching the Spirit*, 225-231.

[56] R.M. Bowman, *The Word-Faith Controversy: Understanding the Health and Wealth Gospel*, 12.

[57] McConnell's book was published in the UK under the title *The Promise of Health and Wealth* (London: Hodder & Stoughton, 1990). An updated American version appeared in 1995.

[58] E.g., McConnell, *Gospel*, 101-111; Jackson, 'Prosperity Theology', 20; Smail, et al., 'Revelation Knowledge', 61-62.

[59] See, e.g., Hanegraaff, 'What's Wrong with the Faith Movement? Part One'.

[60] Bruce Barron's 'Appendix on Methodology' in *The Health and Wealth Gospel*, 171-174, provides some helpful guidelines for this sort of research.

[61] Barron makes this criticism in his review of *Christianity in Crisis* (B. Barron, 'Sick of Health and Wealth', 28). Cf. J. McIntyre, *E.W. Kenyon and His Message of Faith*, 258: 'Some who call themselves researchers have mastered the ability to quote out of context and to paint a warped view of what others in the body of Christ teach.'

[62] E.g., J. MacArthur, *Whose Money Is It Anyway?*, 26-27, 137.

[63] See, e.g., DeArteaga, *Quenching The Spirit*, and McConnell's response (McConnell, *Gospel*, 199-211).

CHAPTER TWO

[1] See, e.g., B. Hinn, *The Biblical Road to Blessing*; T. Bakare, *Operating in High Finances*.

[2] See R. Tucker, *Strange Gospels*, 81.

[3] Kenneth Copeland ministry letter, 21 July 1977, cited in Hanegraaff, 'What's Wrong with the Faith Movement? Part Two'; see further quotes in Bowman, *Controversy*, 116-117.

[4] Bowman, *Controversy*, 116-117. Hanegraaff discusses the possibility that this was a description of Jesus (Hanegraaff, *Crisis*, 393 n.1).

[5] K.E. Hagin, *Foundations for Faith*, 29-30.

[6] Hagin, *Zoe*, 37.

[7] Copeland, 'Following the Faith of Abraham I', side 1, cited in Hanegraaff, 'What's Wrong with the Faith Movement? Part Two'. Elsewhere, with reference to Ps. 8:5, Copeland speaks of Adam and Eve sharing the visible 'glory' of God (K. Copeland, 'Expect the Glory', 5).

[8] Hagin, *Authority*, 19.

[9] Cf. K. Copeland, 'Living at the End of Time', 6; K. Copeland, *Living at the End of Time*, 19; Hagin, *Mountain*, 132. Kenyon taught that man was given a 'lease' to rule the universe at creation, but when Adam sinned this lease was legally transferred to Satan: see the discussion in Bowman, *Controversy*, 138-139.

[10] K. Copeland, 'To Know the Glory', 6. Cf. G. Copeland, *God's Will is Prosperity*, 1: 'Spiritual death – the nature of Satan – overtook his once righteous spirit, and he became one with Satan. Sin and death consumed him spiritually. He was born again from life into death.' The connection between eating the fruit and death made in Gen. 2:17 is the basis for the argument about 'spiritual death' since Adam did not die physically until many years later (Copeland, *Our Covenant*, 6).

[11] Gloria Copeland, *God's Will For You* (Fort Worth: Kenneth Copeland, 1972), 3, cited in B. Onken, 'The Atonement of Christ and the "Faith" Message'; cf. K. Copeland, *The Force of Faith*, 13-14. Copeland attributes the transfer of sovereignty to a 'law of genesis' according to which 'man takes on the nature of his spiritual father or lord' (Copeland, *Covenant*, 3).

[12] Hanegraaff quotes Price: 'When God gave Adam dominion, that meant God no longer had dominion. So, God cannot do anything in this earth unless *we let* Him. And the way we let Him or give Him permission is through prayer' (Hanegraaff, *Crisis*, 85).

[13] Copeland, *Covenant*, 8-10.

[14] Copeland, *Covenant*, 17.

[15] C. Capps, *The Tongue, A Creative Force*, 19 (original emphasis). Cf. Capps: 'This is the key to understanding the virgin birth. God's Word is full of faith and spirit power. God spoke it. God transmitted that image to Mary. She received the image inside of her.... The embryo that was in Mary's womb was nothing more than the Word of God.... She conceived the Word of God' (C. Capps, *Dynamics of Faith and Confession* (Tulsa, OK: Harrison House, 1987), 86-87, cited in Hanegraaff, 'What's Wrong with the Faith Movement? Part One').

[16] See Bowman, *Controversy*, 155-156.

[17] Copeland, *Believer's Voice of Victory* (Aug. 1988), 8, cited in M. Dal Bello, 'Atonement Where?'; cf. Hagin, *Anointing*, 4-5.

[18] Copeland, *Believer's Voice of Victory* (Aug. 1988), 8, cited in Dal Bello, 'Atonement Where?' DeArteaga (*Quenching The Spirit*, 272) quotes a taped sermon by Copeland: 'There had to be a man, but it also had to be man as pure as that first one [Adam], and there wasn't anybody left like that but God. Now somehow or another there's got to be an incarnation, there's got to be a man filled with God – there's got to be a God-man come into the earth.' See also Hagin, *Anointing*, 135.

[19] K. Copeland, 'Take Time to Pray', *Believer's Voice of Victory* (Feb. 1987), 9, cited in Hanegraaff, *Crisis*, 137-138. Copeland's statement elicited immediate condemnation from CRI: see Bowman, *Controversy*, 150-151.

[20] Cf. K. Copeland, 'Signs and Wonders... Without the Wonder', 6; Copeland, *Covenant*, 40-42.

[21] Hagin, *Anointing*, 6 (cf. 134-136), his italics.

[22] Copeland, *Covenant*, 40.

[23] K. Copeland, 'Turning up the Power', 3.

[24] The Word of Faith understanding is that when Jesus cried 'It is finished', he was referring not to the work of redemption but to the old covenant (cf. Hagin, *Zoe*, 44).

[25] Hagin, *Anointing*, 135.

[26] F.K.C. Price, *Ever Increasing Faith Messenger* (June 1980), 7, cited in McConnell, *Gospel*, 117-118.

[27] Copeland, 'To Know the Glory', 6.

[28] The mythology of a double atonement appears to have originated with Kenyon, who 'knew this for many years, but... had no

scriptural evidence of it' until he noticed the marginal reading of Is. 53:9 (E.W. Kenyon, *Identification*, 16). DeArteaga also points to a possible background in ransom theories of the atonement (DeArteaga, *Quenching The Spirit*, 240-243). Kenyon argues that Jesus, who had an immortal body like Adam's, had to die spiritually and become mortal before he could die physically (E.W. Kenyon, *Identification*, 16).

[29] K. Copeland, 'What Happened From the Cross to the Throne?' (Fort Worth, Texas: Kenneth Copeland Ministries, n.d.), audiotape, side 2, cited in Onken, 'Atonement'.

[30] McConnell, *Gospel*, 118. Price argues that this transformation took place in Gethsemane, which appears to echo Mormon teaching (Hanegraaff, *Crisis*, 157). Kenyon identified Jesus' cry of abandonment on the cross (Mt. 27:46; Mk. 15:34) as the moment of spiritual death, three hours before his physical death (E.W. Kenyon, *What Happened from the Cross to the Throne*, 43-44).

[31] K. Copeland, 'What Happened From the Cross to the Throne?' (Fort Worth, Texas: Kenneth Copeland Ministries, n.d.) audiotape, side 2, cited in Onken, 'Atonement'.

[32] K. Copeland, in McConnell, *Gospel*, 119. See also Hanegraaff, *Crisis*, 169-171.

[33] Copeland, 'To Know the Glory', 6. Cf. K. Copeland, 'Absolute Life', *Believer's Voice of Victory* (Sept. 1980), 6, cited in Onken, 'Atonement', 3: God's 'purpose was to put Jesus through all the torments of hell. He bore our sins, our sickness, our disease, our griefs, our sorrow, and our pain. Then, at the command of God the Father the Spirit of God came blasting down through the eons of time and injected the very "zoe" life, light, and glory of God into Jesus' spirit and He came out of that place victoriously!'

[34] Hagin, *Zoe*, 50-53; Hagin, *Authority*, 32.

[35] K. Copeland, 'Worthy to Be Anointed', 5.

[36] Cf. Hagin, *Foundations*, 46; Hagin, *Authority*, 4, 11, 31-33; Kenyon, *Identification*, 38.

[37] Copeland, 'End of Time', 6.

[38] Copeland, 'End of Time', 6; cf. Copeland, *End of Time*, 8-9, 21-24; Copeland, 'Signs and Wonders', 5; Copeland, 'Expect the Glory', 4-7; and Hagin, *Visions*, 47-48.

[39] Cf. Copeland, *End of Time*, 26. The influence of figures such as Hagin, the Copelands, and Benny Hinn on the genesis of the 'Toronto' blessing is recorded in Hilborn, D. (ed.), *'Toronto' in Perspective*, 46-47, 131-147.

[40] K. Copeland, *The Miraculous Realm of God's Love*, 62.

[41] K. Copeland, *Managing God's Mutual Funds*, 112-113; cf. J. Avanzini, *The Wealth of the World*, 85. See also Coleman, 'Charismatic Christianity', 246.

[42] Hagin, *Foundations*, 34. Copeland argues that the 'law of sin and death' from which we have been set free by the 'law of the Spirit of life in Christ Jesus', includes mankind's bondage to sickness and poverty and failure (Copeland, 'When the Devil', 5-6); also Price, *Prosperity*, 37; Gloria Copeland, *God's Will is Prosperity*, 33-34.

[43] Copeland, *The Troublemaker*, 6, cited in Hanegraaff, 'What's Wrong with the Faith Movement? Part Two'.

[44] Copeland, 'Worthy to be Anointed', 6; cf. Copeland, *Miraculous Realm*, 17-18. Sarles comments: 'At the very least this is an unguarded way of referring to the believer's new nature and the indwelling of the Spirit' (Sarles, 'Evaluation', 342).

[45] K. Copeland, 'Anointed All the Time', 5.

[46] Copeland, 'Worthy to be Anointed', 6.

[47] Hagin, *Foundations*, 44; cf. Hagin, *Zoe*, 58-60.

[48] Hagin, 'The Incarnation', *The Word of Faith* (Dec. 1980), 14, cited in Bowman, '"Ye Are Gods"'. Hanegraaff notes ('What's Wrong with the Faith Movement? Part One') that the same statement is found in E. W. Kenyon, *The Father and His Family*, 17th ed. (Lynnwood, WA: Kenyon's Gospel Publishing Society, 1964), 100.

[59] Dal Bello, 'Atonement Where?', quoting: Hagin, *Zoe*, 40 (the statement has been modified in the 1997 printing (41) with the omission of the idea that the believer becomes a 'human-divine being'); K. Copeland, 'The Force of Love', audiotape BCC-56; Copeland, *Believer's Voice of Victory* (March 1982), 2; Copeland, 'The Force of Love', audiotape BCC-56; B. Hinn, 'Praise-a-thon' program on TBN, 6th Nov. 1990.

[50] M. Cerullo, 'The Endtime Manifestation of the Sons of God', audiotape 1, cited in Hanegraaff, *Crisis*, 109.

[51] Copeland, *Miraculous Realm*, 24.

CHAPTER THREE

[1] Cf. Hagin, *Authority*, 3: 'We must have this spirit of wisdom and revelation of Christ and His Word if we are to grow. It is not going to be imparted to us through our intellect, either. The Holy Spirit must unveil it to us.'

[2] E.g. Hagin, *Authority*, 29-33; Copeland, *Miraculous Realm*, 75-76.

[3] Hagin, 'Jesus Christ', 22; cf. Hagin, *Understanding the Anointing*, 70. The incident is also related (with some slight variation: Hagin finds himself in the back of the car) by Hanegraaff, 'What's Wrong with the Faith Movement? Part One', citing Kenneth E. Hagin, *The Glory of God* (Tulsa, OK: Kenneth Hagin Ministries, 1987), 13-15. Cf. Copeland: 'My friend, Jesse Duplantis, has been to heaven and seen that glory. He said it's so thick around the throne of God that you can't see through it. You can just see an outline of God the Father through that brilliant cloud.... There's so much power in that glory, Jesse lost all strength in the presence of it. He fell on his face and could hardly *move*. Yet, he watched as Jesus walked right into it and spent time in there with the Father' (Copeland, 'To Know the Glory', 6).

[4] See Hagin, *Anointing*, 65-85.

[5] In its early days, students at Rhema Bible Training Center were not allowed to ask questions during class (DeArteaga, *Quenching The Spirit*, 228).

[6] Copeland, *Force*, 10 (his italics).

[7] Copeland, *Force*, 8; cf. Hagin, *Zoe*, 2-8. See the discussion in Bowman, *Controversy*, 98-104.

[8] Copeland, *Force*, 12.

[9] Cf. Jackson, 'Prosperity theology', 20-21.

[10] Hagin, *Visions*, 122.

[11] K. Copeland, 'How to Receive Revealed Knowledge' (tape, n.d.), cited in McConnell, *Gospel*, 115.

[12] The transcript can be found at www.rapidnet.com/%7ejbeard/bdm/exposes/hinn/general.htm (accessed June 2002). Bowman records another intemperate harangue by Hinn: "Somebody's attacking me because of something I'm teaching. Let me tell you something, brother: You watch it!... You know, I've looked for one verse in the Bible – I just can't seem to find it – one verse that said, "If you don't like them, kill them." I really wish I could find it!...

You stink, frankly – that's the way I think about it.... Sometimes I wish God will give me a Holy Ghost machine gun – I'll blow your head off!'" ('Praise-a-thon,' TBN, 2 April 1990, in Bowman, *Controversy*, 16).

[13] Dal Bello, 'Atonement Where?'

[14] Copeland, *Mutual Funds*, 26.

[15] K. Copeland, *The Laws of Prosperity*, 15-16.

[16] K. Copeland, 'Authority of the Believer II', audiotape #01-0302, cited in Hanegraaff, *Crisis*, 69. The argument is also found in C. Fillmore, *Prosperity*, 161.

[17] Hagin, *Foundations*, 60.

[18] Copeland, 'When the Devil', 5; cf. Hagin, *Mountain*, 3-4.

[19] K.E. Hagin, *New Thresholds of Faith* (Tulsa: Kenneth Hagin Ministries, 1980), 74, cited in McConnell, *Gospel*, 139.

[20] *Believer's Voice of Victory* 25.7 (July/Aug. 1997), 19.

[21] K.E. Hagin, *Having Faith in Your Faith* (Tulsa: Kenneth Hagin Ministries, 1980), cited in McConnell, *Gospel*, 134.

[22] Copeland, *Force*, 14; cf. Copeland, *Miraculous Realm*, 53-54; C.A. Dollar, *Total Life Prosperity*, 57; Osborn, *Message*, 46-47.

[23] Newport, *Provision*, 62 (italics removed).

[24] Cf. Hagin's summary: '*First*, have God's Word for what ever you may be seeking; *second*, believe God's Word; *third*, refuse to consider the contradictory circumstances, or what your physical senses may tell you about it; and, *fourth*, give praise to God for the answer.... Follow these four steps, and you always will get results' (Hagin, *Foundations*, 22). Copeland draws from Mark 11:22-25 a more detailed set of conditions (K. Copeland, 'Words at Work', 10): '1. You must have faith in God. 2. You must be willing to "say" something to your mountains (problems, needs, etc.). 3. You must not doubt. 4. You must have confidence in your own words. You must believe in your heart that what you say will come to pass. 5. You must believe you receive what you desire *when you pray* – not when you see it happen. 6. You must "say" what you believe. 7. You must forgive everyone.'

[25] Copeland, *Laws of Prosperity*, 47; and 88: 'The very first rule – the predominant rule – about believing God is *faith cometh by hearing, and hearing by the word of God.* Acting on God's Word brings results.'

[26] Dollar, *Prosperity*, 59.

[27] Dollar, *Prosperity*, 56.
[28] Copeland, *Laws of Prosperity*, 19 (italics removed).
[29] Hagin, *Foundations*, 59.
[30] K.E. Hagin, *The Name of Jesus* (Tulsa: Kenneth Hagin Ministries, 1981), 16, cited in McConnell, *Gospel*, 140.
[31] Copeland, *Force*, 19.
[32] Copeland, *Force*, 9.
[33] P. Gifford, 'Gospel for Champions', 1256.
[34] Copeland, 'Inner Image of the Covenant', audiotape #01-4406, cited in Hanegraaff, *Crisis*, 81.
[35] Copeland, *Mutual Funds*, 58-59.
[36] D. Roberts, 'Discerning the Truth', 17.
[37] P.Y. Cho, *The Fourth Dimension* (1979), 42, 44, cited in D.J. Wilson, 'Cho, Paul Yonggi', 162.
[38] Copeland, *Force*, 18.
[39] Copeland, 'Turning Up the Power', 4; cf. Copeland, *Laws of Prosperity*, 81.
[40] Hagin, *Foundations*, 18; cf. Hagin, *Mountain*, 107-115.
[41] See *Believer's Voice of Victory* 25.7 (July/Aug. 1997), 19. Cf. Kenyon's phrase, 'What I confess, I possess', cited in McConnell, *Gospel*, 135.
[42] Copeland, 'Turning Up the Power', 4.
[43] Capps, *The Tongue*, 136.
[44] Cf. Copeland, *Covenant*, 51.
[45] Copeland, *Laws of Prosperity*, 80 (emphasis removed).
[46] Hagin, *Foundations*, 63.
[47] Cf. Copeland, 'Words at Work', 10; Jackson, 'Prosperity theology', 21 cols. 1-2).
[48] Hagin, *Foundations*, 63.
[49] J. Avanzini, *God's Debt-Free Guarantee*, 42-43 (his italics).
[50] Copeland, 'Turning Up the Power', 4.
[51] Copeland, *Miraculous Realm*, 37.
[52] Cf. DeArteaga, *Quenching The Spirit*, 221-222.
[53] Cf. DeArteaga, *Quenching The Spirit*, 230-231.
[54] Dollar, *Prosperity*, 90-91.
[55] Avanzini, 'Dr. Drydust', 25. By 'notes' Avanzini means 'debts'; 'bank notes' refers to his indebtedness to banks.
[56] Copeland, *Force*, 31.

[57] Dollar, *Prosperity*, 71.
[58] Dollar, *Prosperity*, 41.
[59] Hagin, *Authority*, 51; cf. Copeland, *Mutual Funds*, 109: 'If something is wrong, it's not with God or faith or His Word. So it must be with me.'
[60] See Hagin, *Foundations*, 6-9; Hagin, *Mountain*, 156; cf. Copeland, Force, 24.
[61] F.K.C. Price, *Is Healing For All?* (Tulsa: Harrison House, 1976), 122, cited in Jackson, 'Prosperity theology', 20 (original emphasis).
[62] Hagin, *Foundations*, 7.
[63] Hagin, *Foundations*, 16.
[64] Hagin, *Authority*, 63-64.
[65] Copeland, *Force*, 28; cf. Copeland, *Miraculous Realm*, 75. It is not certain that 'all things' is meant to include bad experiences, or for that matter that it is the subject of the verb. It is possible that the subject is either God or the Spirit, who 'works together in all things for good' or who 'causes all things to work for good' (cf. D. Moo, *The Epistle to the Romans*, 527-528).
[66] Avanzini, 'Was Jesus Poor?', 8.

CHAPTER FOUR

[1] Hagin, *Zoe*, 1.
[2] Hagin, *Zoe*, 2 (*zōē* is the word used in the New Testament for the new 'life' that the believer receives from God).
[3] Hagin, *Must Christians Suffer?*, 23; cf. Kenyon, *Identification*, 19: 'It is an abnormal thing in the mind of the Father for a child of God to be sick.'
[4] Cf. Osborn, *Message*, 132; F.F. Bosworth, *Christ the Healer*, 23-30; Kenyon, *Identification*, 14-15. The argument goes back at least to Otto Stockmayer in the nineteenth century (see P.G. Chappell, 'Healing Movements', 356).
[5] Cf. Hagin, *Mountain*, 79.
[6] Hagin, *Foundations*, 15-16.
[7] Hagin, *Visions*, 69.
[8] Copeland, *Covenant*, 34.
[9] Hagin, *Mountain*, 77.
[10] Hagin, *Mountain*, 77 (original italics); cf. Hagin, *Anointing*, 123-124.

[11] The statement in Acts 10:38 that 'God anointed Jesus of Nazareth with the Holy Spirit and with power' is cited as further support for this.

[12] Hagin, 'Jesus Christ', 22-23; see also Hagin, *Anointing*, 136-145; Hagin, *Visions*, 53-54.

[13] Cf. J.R. Goff, 'The Faith that Claims', 21; Barron, *Health and Wealth*, 83-86; McConnell, *Gospel*, 153-154. Bowman believes that 'all of the major Word-Faith teachers are careful to say that Christians should not discontinue medical treatment unless they are sure of their healing' (Bowman, *Controversy*, 91). He attributes this moderate position to the influence of Oral Roberts.

[14] Hagin, *Anointing*, 25; cf. Hagin, *Mountain*, 44-48.

[15] Hagin, *Visions*, 91-92.

[16] Hagin, *Visions*, 97-102.

[17] Newport, *Provision*, 13.

[18] Hagin, *Foundations*, 37; cf. Hagin, *Mountain*, 131-135; G. Copeland, *God's Will is Prosperity*, 1-2.

[19] Hagin, *New Thresholds of Faith*, 54-55, cited in McConnell, *Gospel*, 174.

[20] F.K.C. Price, *High Finance – God's Financial Plan* (Tulsa: Harrison House, 1984), 41, cited in Jackson, 'Prosperity theology', 18.

[21] G. Copeland, *God's Will is Prosperity*, 2-4.

[22] Avanzini, *Wealth*, 25.

[23] G. Copeland, *God's Will is Prosperity*, 8; cf. Copeland, *Laws of Prosperity*, 31-38; Price, *Prosperity*, 29-37.

[24] G. Copeland, *God's Will is Prosperity*, 9 (emphasis removed).

[25] Copeland, *Laws of Prosperity*, 17.

[26] K.E. Hagin, 'The Law of Faith', *Word of Faith* (Nov. 1974), 2-3, cited in McConnell, *Gospel*, 171. Also W. George, 'The Hand of the Diligent', 18-19. Copeland adds a slightly disturbing aside to his statement that what God taught Abraham and his descendants about 'operating financially' is just as valid today: 'If you don't believe it, you've never met a Jew!' (Copeland, *Laws of Prosperity*, 17).

[27] E.g. Copeland, *Mutual Funds*, 71-80; G. Copeland, *God's Will is Prosperity*, 41-56; Price, *Prosperity*, 56-57; Newport, *Provision*, 33-36. Cf. McConnell, *Gospel*, 170-171.

[28] Gloria Copeland, *God's Will is Prosperity*, 44-45.

[29] E.g. Copeland, *Laws of Prosperity*, 11-13; Price, *Prosperity*, 9; Osborn, *Message*, 131; P. Gammons, '30 Reasons Why God Wants You to

Prosper'. Hanegraaff records the importance of this verse for Oral Roberts' conversion to the prosperity ideal (*Crisis*, 223-224).

[30] Gammons cites a range of verses in Proverbs, most of which attribute poverty to indolence, greed, dissipation, and waywardness (Gammons, '30 Reasons'). For example, Proverbs 11:24: 'One man gives freely, yet gains even more; another withholds unduly, but comes to poverty'.

[31] Cf. Price, *Prosperity*, 71-72.

[32] Dollar, *Prosperity*, 47; cf. Newport, *Provision*, 11, 48-51.

[33] Copeland, *Laws of Prosperity*, 19 (his italics); cf. Copeland, *End of Time*, 33-34. Benny Hinn in his book *The Biblical Road to Blessing* places a strong emphasis on relationship with God and focus on ministry, giving out of love rather than obligation, blessing as more than finances, and the connection between prosperity and the character of God (Hinn, *Biblical Road*, 48-52, et passim).

[34] K. Hagin Jr., *Itching Ears*, 17.

[35] Avanzini, *Wealth*, 78. MacArthur is not well-disposed towards prosperity teaching but he questions the traditional view that 'Christian poverty leads to righteousness' (MacArthur, *Whose Money?*, 33).

[36] Price, *Prosperity*, 14; cf. Copeland, *End of Time*, 34-35; Copeland, *Mutual Funds*, 85. Similar arguments can be found outside the Word of Faith movement (see e.g. S. Murray, *Beyond Tithing*, 30-31). In a passage that could have been lifted from the pages of prosperity teaching MacArthur affirms: 'If you sow material goods, you'll get material goods from God in return. If you give your money and possessions to God, He will lavish material goods back to you. The principle is simple: The generous giver will always have plenty' (MacArthur, *Whose Money?*, 142).

[37] Somewhat less to the point Copeland also quotes Gen. 8:22; Mk. 4:30-32 (K. Copeland, 'Sowing and Reaping an End-Time Harvest', 5).

[38] Copeland, 'Sowing and Reaping', 7; cf. Copeland, *End of Time*, 52-58.

[39] E.g. Newport, *Provision*, 40-45.

[40] Cf. Dollar, *Prosperity*, x.

[41] Copeland, *Mutual Funds*, 115.

[42] Cf. Avanzini, *Wealth*, 130-131.

[43] Avanzini, *Wealth*, 132-137; cf. Newport, Provision, 19-20.

[44] Copeland, *Laws of Prosperity*, 57-63; cf. Copeland, *Mutual Funds*, 99.

[45] Copeland, *Laws of Prosperity*, 75-86.

[46] Avanzini gives a particularly disingenuous example of the sort of 'God idea' that the Spirit might put in the mind of the believer: 'He'll speak to you one moment and say, *Write a check for $1,000, send it to Kenneth and Gloria*, and your soulish man may try to stop you. And you'll say, "Shut up, soul." Then out of a place where you might not even expect it, He can start bringing your hundred-fold return,' (J. Avanzini, 'How to be a Money Magnet', 27). Copeland argues that tithes should be given to churches and ministries that are actively feeding God's people (Copeland, *Laws of Prosperity*, 68-69).

[47] Michael Bassett, *Expect the Best*, 52, cited in Jackson, 'Prosperity theology', 18 col.1.

[48] Cf. Avanzini, *Wealth*, 38-41; Newport, *Provision*, 9-10. Colin Dye defines biblical prosperity as: 'Having an abundant provision for your needs so that you can meet the needs of others' ('Prosperity Teaching in Pastoral Practice', unpublished paper for the ACUTE working group on the Prosperity Gospel).

[49] J. Avanzini, *How Much Money is Enough.*

[50] Quoted in G. Copeland, *God's Will is Prosperity*, 17.

[51] Copeland, *Mutual Funds*, 30.

[52] MacArthur, *Whose Money?*, 26-27, 55; cf. WEF 'Statement on Prosperity Theology and Theology of Suffering', above page 237: the Bible 'does not teach that those who have wealth are more godly than others who do not'.

[53] Copeland, *Mutual Funds*, 97.

[54] MacArthur, *Whose Money?*, 138.

[55] Cf. W. George, 'Hand', 18-19. Note also MacArthur, *Whose Money?*, 40-49, on 'God-honoring ways of acquiring money'.

[56] Cf. Copeland, *Laws of Prosperity*, 19, 45-46; Copeland, *Mutual Funds*, 81-84; Newport, *Provision*, 23-27.

[57] Avanzini, *God's Debt-Free Guarantee*, 42 (Avanzini's italics).

[58] Cf. Copeland, *Laws of Prosperity*, 26; Dollar, *Prosperity*, 10; R. Joyner, *Overcoming the Spirit of Poverty*, 7, 19-22.

[59] Cf. Gammons, '30 Reasons'; Newport, *Provision*, 13.

[60] G. Copeland, *God's Will is Prosperity*, 54-56. Avanzini suggests that something similar took place, though on a lesser scale, when Constantine legalized Christianity and the wealth of the Roman world was transferred to the church (Avanzini, *Wealth*, 97-98).

[61] E.g. Avanzini, *Wealth*, 52-53, 145.

[62] G. Copeland, 'Build Your Financial Foundation', 29.

[63] G. Copeland, 'Build Your Financial Foundation', 30; G. Copeland, 'Do You Know?', 30; cf. G. Copeland, *God's Will is Prosperity*, 18; and Copeland's emphasis on a holistic prosperity in *Laws of Prosperity*, 12-14. Also Price, *Prosperity*, 10; Dollar, *Prosperity*, 59: 'When a man is doing God's Word, He will empower him to prosper. He will give him godly ideas or set him up for favor from men. He will open doors that the man could never have opened by himself. By blessing him at every turn. God has put this man in a position to prosper because he delighted in His commandments.'

[64] Price, *Prosperity*, 59.

CHAPTER FIVE

[1] D.W. Dayton, *Theological Roots of Pentecostalism*, 122. Noll points to the underlying enlightenment premise, that the spiritual world functions no less rationally and predictably than the physical world, to the extent that it is quite appropriate to speak of the effects of spiritual laws (Noll, M., *The Scandal of the Evangelical Mind*, (Grand Rapids: Eerdmans), 1995, 96).

[2] See DeArteaga, *Quenching The Spirit*, 109-112; McIntyre, *Kenyon*, 46-49, 71-72. The same thought appears in the writings of Samuel Logan Brengle, Daniel Steele, George D. Watson, and Hannah Whithall Smith (see McIntyre, *Kenyon*, 50-56).

[3] Dayton argues that 'the rise of the healing doctrines was largely a radicalization of the perfectionist push of the Holiness teachings' (Dayton, *Roots*, 136). Cf. Chappell: 'By propagating the doctrine of Christian perfection or the baptism of the Holy Spirit as purification from sin, the enduemcnt with power, and the living of a consecrated life of holiness, the nineteenth-ccntury Holiness movement provided the basic theological milieu in which the supernatural gifts of God, and in particular divine healing, would flourish' (Chappell, 'Healing Movements', 357).

[4] Chappell, 'Healing Movements', 357.
[5] Chappell, 'Healing Movements', 358.
[6] From C.J. Montgomery, *The Prayer of Faith* (Alameda County: Office of 'Triumphs of Faith', 1894), 14-15, cited in McIntyre, *Kenyon*, 74 (original italics).
[7] The same argument was put forward by A.J. Gordon (Chappell, 'Healing Movements', 362). Cf. Dayton, *Roots*, 124-125.
[8] Dayton, *Roots*, 122-127.
[9] Judd, 'Faith Reckonings', *Triumphs of Faith* 1 (Jan. 1881), 2-3.
[10] See DeArteaga, *Quenching The Spirit*, 118-120.
[11] A.B. Simpson, *In Heavenly Places* (1892, reprinted Harrisburg, PA: Christian Publications, 1968), 98, cited in McIntyre, *Kenyon*, 65-66.
[12] The quotations are from Dayton, *Roots*, 127-132. The failure of devout missionaries to resist African fevers by faith, leading to the death of many, also contributed to a crisis within the healing movement (Dayton, *Roots*, 131-132; DeArteaga, *Quenching The Spirit*, 126).
[13] Chappell, 'Healing Movements', 358, 362-363.
[14] Chappell, 'Healing Movements', 366-367; DeArteaga, *Quenching The Spirit*, 124-125.
[15] Quoted in Chappell, 'Healing Movements', 367.
[16] Chappell, 'Healing Movements', 367.
[17] Hagin approves of Dowie's faith but admits that 'In his latter years, Dowie had missed God' (Hagin, *Anointing*, 101).
[18] Chappell, 'Healing Movements', 367.
[19] Chappell, 'Healing Movements', 368.
[20] Hagin acknowledges the importance of this 'classic' book (Hagin, *Anointing*, 41). George Müller and Smith Wigglesworth are also regarded as forerunners of the modern Faith movement (Hagin, *Mountain*, 40).
[21] Bosworth, *Healer*, 8. Bosworth applies to this process Heb. 6:11-12; 10:35-36, which in context refer to the endurance of faith under persecution, not to waiting for healing.
[22] See Bowman, *Controversy*, 88-89.
[23] Quoted in Chappell, 'Healing Movements', 372.
[24] Hollinger, 'Enjoying God', 141-142; also Harrell, *All Things*, 158.
[25] Hollinger, 'Enjoying God', 146.
[26] Harrell, *All Things*, 103. Possibly these unaccounted elements developed as a result of the need to expand and make more

efficient the fund-raising machinery that supported the growing Word of Faith ministries. The scale of the undertakings, and the ballooning culture of prosperity in the States, required a much more sophisticated theological underpinning. It may also be that these developments were a substitute for real scholarship.

[27] A.A. Allen, *The Secret to Scriptural Financial Success* (Miracle Valley, AZ: A.A. Allen Publications, 1953), cited in Harrell, *All Things*, 75.

[28] Quoted by Harrell (*All Things*, 105).

[29] See Hollinger, 'Enjoying God', 141.

[30] Harrell, *All Things*, 105.

[31] Hollinger, 'Enjoying God', 141.

[32] Cf. the parallels outlined by Bowman between Kenyon's teaching and the doctrines of the Faith-Cure and Pentecostal movements: 'Kenyon's controversial teachings have significant antecedents in the teachings of the faith-healing teachers (e.g., Simpson) and parallels in the early Pentecostal evangelists (e.g., Lake)' (Bowman, *Controversy*, 69; cf. 69-78). Also Gifford ('Prosperity', 378-379): 'Copeland stands squarely and recognizably within pentecostal Christianity'; he argues that it is only in his emphasis on prosperity that Copeland differs significantly from Pentecostal/fundamentalist Christianity.

[33] Cf. McIntyre, *Kenyon*, 60-61.

[34] Note Hollinger, 'Enjoying God', 141.

[35] D.T. Williams puts the emphasis on the influence of contemporary prosperity teachers such as Norman Vincent Peale (D.T. Williams, 'Prosperity Teaching and Positive Thinking'). Hunt and McMahon note that Glenn Clark's Camps Far Out organization, Robert Schuller, and Peale have preserved the influence of New Thought and Positive Thinking on the fringes of the church. He also quotes Kenneth Hagin Jr.'s description of God as 'the greatest Positive Thinker who ever was' and his observation that the 'two most prominent teachers of positive thinking are ministers' (D. Hunt and T.A. McMahon, *The Seduction Of Christianity: Spiritual Discernment in the Last Days*, 151-153, citing K. Hagin Jr., *The Word of Faith* (Nov. 1984), 3).

[36] H.W. Dresser, *The Quimby Manuscripts*, chapter 14.

[37] Quoted in Dresser, *The Quimby Manuscripts*, chapter 12.

[38] H.W. Dresser, *Handbook of New Thought*, cited in Tucker, *Strange Gospels*, 177.

[39] From the International New Thought Alliance statement of purpose, accessed online June 2002 at www.newthought.net/defined 1916.htm.

[40] H. Emilie Cady, *Lessons in Truth*, 56.

[41] Cady, *Lessons*, 52.

[42] DeArteaga, *Quenching The Spirit*, 189.

[43] C. Fillmore, *Jesus Christ Heals*, 3.

[44] DeArteaga argues that the New Thought emphasis on material prosperity was filling a vacuum left by the failure of the church in the nineteenth century to sustain a theology of work and motivation (DeArteaga, *Quenching The Spirit*, 177-184). New Thought was in this respect a more or less secularized form of Puritanism.

[45] See DeArteaga, *Quenching The Spirit*, 185.

[46] This argument has been advocated most strongly by McConnell in *A Different Gospel*. See also Hollenweger, *Pentecostalism*, 231.

[47] See McConnell, *Gospel*, 29-33; McIntyre, *Kenyon*, 25-27. McIntyre stresses the strong links between the Free Will Baptists and the Wesleyan Holiness revival (McIntyre, *Kenyon*, 28-29).

[48] Article 9, 'Constitution of Bethel Bible Institute', *Reality* (April 1907), 209, cited in McConnell, *Gospel*, 31. See also DeArteaga, *Quenching The Spirit*, 216; McIntyre, *Kenyon*, 99.

[49] McIntyre, *Kenyon*, 126.

[50] See McIntyre, *Kenyon*, 15-22.

[51] McConnell, *Gospel*, 48; cf. Bowman, *Controversy*, 45: 'Kenyon believed that the rise of the metaphysical cults was due to the unpaid debts of the church, a church torn by the fundamentalist-modernist controversy and rapidly giving way to liberalism in its theology and anti-supernaturalism in its ministry'; and McIntyre, *Kenyon*, 280: Kenyon felt that 'a spirit of unrest had seized the heart of Christendom due to the Higher Criticism'.

[52] McConnell, *Gospel*, 6-11. Hagin is not the only one to have plagiarized Kenyon. Lie reports that the Norwegian born Pentecostal evangelist 'Tommy' Hicks published a Swedish translation of Kenyon's *The Wonderful Name of Jesus* under his own name and with a different title (*Atomkraften I Jesu Namn*) (Lie, 'E.W. Kenyon', 5.3).

[53] Hagin, *Zoe*, 18; cf. Hagin, *Anointing*, 52. Lie considers Hagin's claim that owing to his 'prodigious memory, he could have

quoted others verbatim and that transcriptions may have been produced without the usual credit being given to those who were quoted' (Lie, 'E.W. Kenyon', 4.3).

[54] Cf. McConnell, *Gospel*, 12.

[55] Cf. R.M. Riss, 'Kenyon, Essek William', 517: 'Kenyon's writings also became seminal for the ministries of Kenneth Hagin, Kenneth Copeland, Don Gossett, Charles Capps, and others in the Word of Faith and Positive Confession movements.'

[56] McConnell, *Gospel*, 119-120, quoting Kenyon, 'Incarnation', *Reality* (Dec. 1911), 49.

[57] McConnell, *Gospel*, 149.

[58] Trine, *In Tune with the Infinite*, 135, cited in McConnell, *Gospel*, 172.

[59] Cf. McConnell, *Gospel*, 135.

[60] DeArteaga, *Quenching The Spirit*, 243-245.

[61] DeArteaga, *Quenching The Spirit*, 214-215; cf. McIntyre, *Kenyon*, 11-13.

[62] DeArteaga, *Quenching The Spirit*, 165-167, 173, 175, 217-219; cf. McIntyre, *Kenyon*, 223-224.

[63] McIntyre, *Kenyon*, 125.

[64] McIntyre, *Kenyon*, 13. Lie quotes an excerpt from a letter from Dr. Dale H. Simmons (Simmons, letter to author, Aug. 10, 1991, in Lie, 'E.W. Kenyon', footnote 765): 'Kenyon was living in an age when the liberal wing of the Christian church was presenting Jesus' death as merely a "moral influence" intended as an object lesson on suffering love – it had no objective merit in securing anyone's salvation. In trying to answer this, Kenyon goes too far in the opposite direction – arguing in favor of a substitutionary atonement which goes far beyond what most Christians have held over the centuries.'

[65] McIntyre, *Kenyon*, 151.

[66] There is some evidence from Kenyon's contemporaries that his thinking was influenced by Mary Baker Eddy (McConnell, *Gospel*, 25-26).

[67] McConnell, *Gospel*, 44.

[68] DeArteaga, *Quenching The Spirit*, 235; cf. Lie, 'E.W. Kenyon', 3.4.3; McIntyre, *Kenyon*, 223-224; Bowman, *Controversy*, 59. McIntyre is at pains to stress the direct influence of the Holiness tradition on Kenyon (McIntyre, *Kenyon*, e.g. 28-29, 36-40, 42-59, 228) and the

fact that this movement predated the emergence of the metaphysical cults (229, 296).

[69] Bowman, *Controversy*, 64.

[70] McIntyre, *Kenyon*, 16-18; cf. Bowman, *Controversy*, 65. Lie similarly plays down the influence of Minot J. Savage and Unitarianism on Kenyon's intellectual development (Lie, 'E.W. Kenyon', 3.1).

[71] DeArteaga, *Quenching The Spirit*, 246.

[72] Cf. Bowman, *Controversy*, 40: 'Perhaps the origins of the Word-Faith movement are more complex than drawing a straight line to either Pentecostalism or the metaphysical movement. Perhaps both traditions contributed significantly to the Word-Faith teaching.'

[73] Against, e.g., W. Ward Gasque, 'Prosperity Theology and the New Testament', 40.

[74] Hagin, *Foundations*, 9. Barron makes the point that 'several critics had likened positive confession to Christian Science, but no one had bothered to examine Kenneth Hagin's own explanations of how the two differ' (Barron, *Health and Wealth*, 65).

[75] Bowman, *Controversy*, 94.

PART TWO – CHAPTER SIX

[1] Note Copeland's reliance on the study notes in the nineteenth century *Companion Bible* of E.W. Bullinger (Copeland, *End of Time*, 17).

[2] On this point generally, see Mark Noll's critique of evangelical anti-intellectualism: Noll, M.A., *The Scandal of the Evangelical Mind* (Grand Rapids: Eerdmans, 1994).

[3] Cf. Hanegraaff, 'What's Wrong with the Faith Movement? Part Two'.

[4] See e.g. F.D. Macchia, 'The Struggle for Global Witness', 10-13. In the same volume Wonsuk Ma comments, 'It is a pleasant surprise that the rise of Pentecostal critical scholarship and the employment of critical methods have not raised significant suspicion among ecclesial leadership' ('Biblical Studies in the Pentecostal Tradition: Yesterday, Today, and Tomorrow', 61).

[5] K. Copeland, 'Jesus: Our Lord of Glory,' *Believer's Voice of Victory* (April 1982), 3, cited in Onken, 'Atonement', 3.

[6] E.g. P.T. O'Brien, *Colossians, Philemon*, 50-51.

[7] Copeland, *Laws of Prosperity*, 51.

[8] Farah accepts the 'faith *of* God' translation, but the thought is less of the faith that God exercises than of a unique gift of

extraordinary faith that transcends our capacity to engender belief (Farah, *Pinnacle*, 100-105, 123-125).

[9] Price, *Prosperity*, 52.

[10] Price, *Prosperity*, 53.

[11] If the giving of alms is normally understood to mean the giving of a *portion* of one's wealth, Jesus' statement in Lk. 12:33 ('Sell your possessions, and give alms') may not entail the dispersal of the entire proceeds of the sale. However, the continuation of the verse suggests that he did not expect the disciples to carry literal purses with them (cf. Lk. 10:4; 22:35).

[12] Gammons, '30 Reasons'.

[13] See G.J. Wenham, *Genesis 1-15*, 64-65.

[14] Newport, *Provision*, 34-35.

[15] Dollar, *Prosperity*, 46-47.

[16] Against Avanzini, *Guarantee*, 22-23.

[17] Copeland, *Laws of Prosperity*, 49-50.

[18] Hagin, *Understanding the Atonement*, 135.

[19] Hinn, *Biblical Road*, 8.

[20] H. Osgood explains: 'the words of Scripture cease to be just informative and become exact, legally-framed language to be used as arguments for obtaining rights. In turn, faith becomes the confidence we need in order to press our claims in heaven's court' (Osgood, "Prosperity Teaching and 'Contractual' Exegesis", 3).

[21] K. Copeland, 'Surviving the Counterattack', 6; cf. Copeland, *Covenant*, 64.

[22] Copeland, 'Counterattack', 7.

[23] Copeland, *Laws of Prosperity*, 17; cf. Price, *Prosperity*, 38.

[24] See e.g. Copeland, *Miraculous Realm*, 40-42.

[25] Cf. Jackson, 'Prosperity Theology', 18.

[26] See Brandon, *Health & Wealth*, 82-84. It is difficult to make sense of Newport's comment that the New Covenant is 'a more powerful covenant and deals with the whole man, not just the spiritual part of things' (Newport, *Provision*, 35). Young Hoon Lee, *The Case for Prosperity Theology*, 29: '...the material side of the blessing is never denied in the New Testament. Since the Old and the New Testament have complete unity and harmony, we must accept the fact that their ideas of blessings do not differ in essence but are the same.'

[27] D. Moo, 'Divine Healing In The Health And Wealth Gospel', 195.

[28] Is. 1:19 and 61:4-5 are also used indiscriminately to support a prosperity message. In fact, they promise restoration to a nation that has suffered divine judgment. See Avanzini, *Wealth*, 74.

[29] Against Gammons, '30 Reasons'. The same argument applies for Zech. 1:17 which Gammons also quotes. The phrase 'abundant prosperity' in the NIV translates a simpler Hebrew expression meaning 'all the good things'.

[30] E.g., Farah, *Pinnacle*, 20-21.

[31] Against, e.g., Gammons, '30 Reasons'; Price, *Prosperity*, 33-37.

[32] Against J. Avanzini, 'How to be a Money Magnet', 26.

[33] Avanzini, *God's Debt-Free Guarantee*, 19-22.

[34] Price, *Prosperity*, 24.

[35] See Hanegraaff, *Crisis*, 223-224. Cf. Sarles, 'Evaluation', 339: 'A standard salutation is forced by prosperity interpreters to carry far more weight than it can possibly bear.' But note C. Kee Hwang's argument that the greetings in the New Testament letters are not without contemporary significance ('Response' to Gasque, 'Prosperity Theology', 48).

[36] Benny Hinn admitted as much in an interview in *Charisma*, August 1993, 25: 'People can take a few verses of Scripture and say, "see, it says here." But they need to read the entire chapter or the entire book. When I taught the little gods doctrine, I was using scriptures that didn't fit.'

[37] Farah, *Pinnacle*, 131.

[38] Osgood regards this as a consequence of the Word of Faith movement's insistence on the covenantal or contractual nature of Scripture: 'We need to remember that a contractual understanding of Scripture sets a lot of weight on the exact words. Distinctions between figures of speech become largely irrelevant and all figurative language (even anthropomorphism) is believed to be more readily understood literally' (Osgood, 'Prosperity Teaching', 7).

[39] Hanegraaff, 'What's Wrong with the Faith Movement? Part Two'.

[40] Copeland, 'Worthy to Be Anointed', 6. Cf. Kenyon, *Identification*, 13-14. See also Osgood, 'Prosperity Teaching'.

[41] Against, e.g., Bakare, *High Finances*, 63-64.

[42] See the arguments in W.D. Mounce, *Pastoral Epistles*, 253.

[43] Against, e.g., Gammons, '30 Reasons'. Ps. 122:6-7 is also cited, where the thought is of peace rather than specifically of material prosperity.

[44] Against Gammons, '30 Reasons'.

[45] R.L. Harris, G.L. Archer, B.K. Waltke, *Theological Wordbook of the Old Testament* (Chicago: Moody Press, 1980).

[46] Against Gammons, '30 Reasons'.

[47] Cf. 2 Chron. 20:20; Ps. 1:3.

[48] Bakker comments rather astutely on this common misinterpretation in 'Does God Want Me to be Rich?', 40-41.

[49] John prays that he may prosper '*in* all things' (*peri pantōn*), not 'above all' as in KJV.

[50] Cf. Sarles, 'Evaluation', 337. According to Osgood ('Prosperity Teaching'): "Copeland appears to dislike the subjectivity of any approach that requires special confirmation by God, be it by personal divine visitation or any other 'sense-knowledge' confirmation. He opts for 'just reading the Word and believing'."

[51] The priority of the spirit is attributed sometimes to a dichotomist (cf. Jackson, 'Prosperity theology', 20-21) and sometimes to a trichotomist (cf. Bowman, *Controversy*, 98-104) anthropology.

[52] Copeland, *Miraculous Realm*, 75-76.

[53] Hagin, 'Jesus Christ', 22-23.

[54] Hagin, 'Jesus Christ', 21.

[55] While *arrōstos* may suggest a less serious form of illness, the word is used only a few verses later in much more positive circumstances (Mk. 6:13; cf. 16:18; Mt. 14:14). It would be hazardous, then, to place too much theoretical weight upon its use in Mark 6:5.

[56] Note Sarles, 'Evaluation', 337. Ankerberg and Weldon (*Facts*, 30-31) make a similar case against Oral Roberts' seed-faith principles.

[57] See Allen, L.C., *Psalms 101-150*, 38, who says that the expression 'my anointed ones' is used in a 'secondary sense': 'The psalmist is transferring to the patriarchal period a term especially associated with the Davidic monarchy.'

[58] The statement may also have been linked with the story of the Amalekite who claimed to have killed Saul and was killed by David because he had not been afraid to lift his hand 'to destroy

the Lord's anointed' (2 Sam. 1:14). This provides the justification for the claims that people had died because they did not accept the teaching of the 'anointed' Word of Faith leaders.

[59] The word 'fundamentalist' is used here not with reference to any particular historical movement but in more general terms to designate a doctrinaire and exclusivist adherence to a rather narrow set of religious principles.

[60] Cf. McIntyre's assertion that Kenyon did not belittle the intellect but 'saw a harmony and fellowship between the mind and spirit to be the desired goal' (McIntyre, *Kenyon*, 218-219).

[61] Macchia, 'Struggle', 11. Note, for example, Dollar, *Prosperity*, 17: 'I never attended a school of theology. I've always gone to the place of "kneeology." That's where I got my degree. That's where I go to get my credentials to lead so great a number of people, even to this day.'

[62] Copeland, 'Following the Faith of Abraham I', side 2, cited in Hanegraaff, 'What's Wrong with the Faith Movement? Part Two'.

[63] Cf. Hanegraaff, *Crisis*, 133-135.

[64] Hanegraaff, 'What's Wrong with the Faith Movement? Part One' (Copeland's italics).

[65] Hanegraaff, 'What's Wrong with the Faith Movement? Part One', footnote 24; K. Copeland, *The Troublemaker* (Fort Worth, TX: Kenneth Copeland Publications, n.d.), 23. Critics are quick to point to the contradictions in Word of Faith teaching (cf. McConnell, *Gospel*, 120), but this may well only confirm the fact that the more extreme statements have a rhetorical rather than a precisely theological function.

[66] T. Tillin, 'Wells Without Water: The Errors of the Word-of-Faith Movement', 4b, extract 6.

[67] R. Sider, *Rich Christians in an Age of Hunger*, 41-66. For a similar critique of evangelical anti-materialist exegesis see R.H. Nash, *Poverty and Wealth: The Christian Debate over Capitalism*, 159.

CHAPTER SEVEN

[1] Note the argument in Copeland, *Covenant*, 4-5.

[2] See also Bowman, *Controversy*, 141-145.

[3] Sarles proposes two criteria for determining whether an illness is of demonic origin (Sarles, 'Evaluation', 345). First, there must be sufficient evidence; secondly, 'no more causes for an effect should

be assumed than sufficiently explain the effect'. However, Sarles offers no test of the evidence other than the testimony of Christ and the apostles; and the fact that 'a physical malady has a known physical cause' does not rule out demonic influence any more than an unknown physical cause would entail demonic influence – or any more than a known physical cause of a healing would rule out divine intervention.

[4] See B.E. Foster, 'Kenoticism', 364.

[5] A.E. McGrath, *Christian Theology: An Introduction*, 306-308; G. Newlands, 'Christology', 103. Hanegraaff's defence of an orthodox christology is not especially helpful. The self-abasement described in Phil. 2:6-7 must be more than a mere veiling of Christ's divine glory (Hanegraaff, *Crisis*, 140).

[6] Cf. G.D. Fee, *Paul's Letter to the Philippians*, 210-211. If the description of the 'suffering servant' in Isaiah is in the background, Christ's 'self-emptying' may also be an allusion to Is. 53:12: 'he poured out himself to death' (cf. Fee, *Philippians*, 212; R.P. Martin, *Carmen Christi*, 184-185).

[7] R.A. Whitacre, *John*, 270.

[8] G.R. Beasley-Murray, *John*, 174.

[9] Beasley-Murray, *John*, 139.

[10] Copeland, *Covenant*, 41.

[11] Copeland, *Covenant*, 40; cf. 31-32.

[12] Cf. Farah, *Pinnacle*, 140: 'I am convinced that the healing ministry of Jesus related much more to His humanity than to His divinity. Otherwise, our emulation of Him would be futile.'

[13] Hanegraaff, *Crisis*, 138-139.

[14] Bowman, *Controversy*, 150-153.

[15] Hanegraaff, *Crisis*, 140.

[16] See Fee, G.D., *The First Epistle to the Corinthians*, 788-789.

[17] Cf. Smail, et al., 'Revelation Knowledge', 68-69.

[18] E.g. McConnell, *Gospel*, 126. The expression may also mean 'in his grave' (cf. J.D.W. Watts, *Isaiah* 34-66, 226 n.9b).

[19] Author's translation. Bowman's observation that 'death' is singular in 53:12 is not particularly helpful because the idiom is different. In Ezek. 31:14, for example, the same phrase ('to death') is used with a plural subject.

[20] Cf. D.A. Hagner, *Matthew 14-28*, 845: 'one of the most impenetrable mysteries of the entire Gospel narrative'.

[21] Cf. P. Barnett, *The Second Epistle to the Corinthians*, 314 n.65; R.P. Martin, *2 Corinthians*, 140, who suggests also the related view that 'Christ identified himself with sin in his incarnation'. Bowman's argument that Christ became 'sin-for-us' is difficult to understand (Bowman, *Controversy*, 169-171). He argues that God 'inflicted suffering and death on Jesus, his own Son, as if Jesus were our sin' (170). But it is not sin, either as an abstract quality or as particular actions, that comes under judgment but the one who sins.

[22] Kenyon argued on the basis of the sacrificial typology presented in Heb. 9:11-12 that the atonement was not fully accomplished until the blood of Christ entered heaven and was accepted by the Father (see the discussion in McIntyre, *Kenyon*, 180-181).

[23] See R.J. Bauckham, 'Descent into Hell', 194; cf. Smail, et al., 'Revelation Knowledge', 72-73.

[24] See the discussion in A.T. Lincoln, *Ephesians*, 244-247.

[25] 1 Pet. 4:6 is more likely to have in view those who died after believing in Christ, who will not be alive at the end (cf. 4:7). They have not escaped the judgment of death, but they they will 'live in the spirit as God does'. There is some discussion of these texts in the ACUTE report, *The Nature of Hell* (Carlisle: ACUTE, Paternoster, 2000), 89-92.

[26] Cf. J.D.G. Dunn, *The Epistles to the Colossians and to Philemon*, 97-98.

[27] Kenyon, *Identification*, 16-26.

[28] Kenyon, *Identification*, 16; McIntyre, *Kenyon*, 179, has a different form of the statement.

[29] DeArteaga, *Quenching The Spirit*, 242-243; cf. McIntyre, *Kenyon*, 183-197. Calvin insisted that Christ's bodily death alone would have been ineffectual (*Institutes*, b.2.16.10). He also had to 'grapple hand to hand with the armies of hell and the dread of everlasting death'. But this describes a mental struggle *before* death. McIntyre argues that Kenyon's teaching about identification and the regeneration of Christ in the resurrection has its origins in the Holiness and Faith-Cure traditions (McIntyre, *Kenyon*, 201-203). Smail et al. ('Revelation Knowledge', 70-75) think that Kenyon's soteriology is a misreading of certain strands of teaching found in the early church, notably the ransom theory of the atonement, the descent into hell, and the doctrine of *theosis*.

[30] DeArteaga regards the influence of dispensationalism as one of the reasons why the Word of Faith movement has met such a hostile reaction from conservative evangelicalism (DeArteaga, *Quenching The Spirit*, 100-106, 141).

[31] Copeland, 'Signs and Wonders', 4-5; cf. Copeland, *End of Time*, 67-69.

[32] Gifford, 'Gospel for champions', 1257.

[33] Avanzini, *Wealth*, 85.

[34] Hagin, *Authority*, 11-13, 17; cf. Copeland, *End of Time*, 28. The argument that to be seated at the right hand of a person signifies authority is doubtful: in the biblical context at least, the figure has to do with the imputation of honour, with the recognition of worth, rather than with the bestowal of authority (see A.C. Perriman, *Speaking of Women*, 43-44).

[35] See Hanegraaff, *Crisis*, 117; Bowman, '"Ye Are Gods?"'.

[36] Gen. 5:1-3 may add a filial dimension to the motif. Gen. 9:6 perhaps suggests that it also conveys something of the intrinsic value of human life, but since in v.7 the command to 'be fruitful and multiply' is reiterated (cf. 1:28), it seems likely that the main idea is that the taking of life reduces mankind's productive and creative function.

[37] Cf. Bowman, *Controversy*, 128-130.

[38] Hagin, *Authority*, 19.

[39] Paulk, E., *Held in the Heavens Until*, (Atlanta: Kingdom, 1985), 171, cited in Bowman, *Controversy*, 127.

[40] Copeland, *Our Covenant*, 2-3. Cf. Bowman's response (*Controversy*, 133-135).

[41] Against, e.g., Osborn, *Message*, 24: 'The Garden of Eden exhibited the lifestyle and circumstances for which God designed you.' Also Gammons, '30 Reasons': 'Prosperity does not stand alone, it is part of what Adam lost and what Christ came to restore.'

[42] Hanegraaff, *Crisis*, 113.

[43] Hunt and McMahon, *Seduction*, 84-88. Note also Bowman, '"Ye Are Gods?"'.

[44] See Beasley-Murray, *John*, 176. It has also been suggested that the psalm has Israel's judges in view (cf. Bowman, *Controversy*, 132; L. Morris, *The Gospel According to John*, 525) or angelic powers.

[45] There is perhaps also the idea that the righteous will be among the 'gods' who sit in the divine council (Ps. 82:1).

[46] For the arguments see R.J. Bauckham, *Jude, 2 Peter*, 179-183. Note 4 Macc. 18:3: 'those who gave over their bodies in suffering for the sake of religion were not only admired by mortals, but also were deemed worthy to share in a divine inheritance (*theias meridos katēxiōthēsan*).'

[47] See Hanegraaff, *Crisis*, 109.

[48] Bowman, *Controversy*, 14-16.

[49] The Word of Faith position is also not far removed from the Orthodox doctrine of *theosis* or 'deification'. Orthodox theology, however, makes a distinction between a participation in the divine essence, which would amount to pantheism, and a participation in the 'energies' of God, which appears little different to the familiar notion that the believer receives the Spirit of God in power. See *Evangelicalism and the Orthodox Church* (Carlisle: ACUTE, Paternoster), 2001, 126. Smail et al. ('Revelation Knowledge', 73-75) argue that the Faith doctrine of deification is closer to the teaching of the metaphysical cults than to that of Eastern Orthodoxy.

[50] McIntyre, *Kenyon*, 205; cf. Bowman, *Controversy*, 71, with reference to Kenyon's teaching that we were created 'in God's class of being'.

[51] Hanegraaff, *Crisis*, 112.

[52] Hagin, *Foundations*, 35-36; cf. Hagin, *Zoe*, 36, 48; Hagin, *Authority*, 39-40; and also 16: 'The trouble with us is that we've preached a "cross" religion, and we need a "throne" religion.... The cross is actually a place of defeat, whereas the Resurrection is a place of triumph. When you preach the cross, you're preaching death, and you leave people in death. We died all right, but we're raised with Christ. We're seated with Him. Positionally, that's where we are right now: We're seated with Christ in the place of authority in heavenly places.'

[53] See J.D.G. Dunn, *Romans*, 282: 'their rule will be a consequence of their... final vindication'. But note Moo's qualification (Moo, *Romans*, 340).

[54] Hagin, *Zoe*, 46.

[55] E.g., Hagin, *Foundations*, 36-37; Copeland, *Covenant*, 25-29, 33-34; Copeland, *Mutual Funds*, 5; Gammons, '30 Reasons'; cf. Osgood, 'Prosperity Teaching', 10-12.

[56] Cf. Sarles, 'Evaluation', 347; A. Brandon, 'Prosperity and Hermeneutics'.

[57] E.g., Gammons, '30 Reasons'.

[58] Cf. F.F. Bruce, *The Epistle to the Galatians*, 168. Price interprets 'the promise of the Spirit' to mean the promise of prosperity made *by the Spirit* to Abraham (Price, *Prosperity*, 29; cf. Copeland, *Covenant*, 49-50), but the context makes it clear that the issue is the inheritance of the Spirit (Gal. 3:1-5; 4:6).

[59] Also Brandon, 'Hermeneutics', 4.

[60] See also Sarles, 'Evaluation', 339-340.

[61] Note Sarles, 'Evaluation', 339: 'sickness is either physical or psychological but not moral. It may indeed result from sin, but it does not bear the penal character of sin. Since illness is not sinful in itself, it does not need atonement.'

[62] Jackson, 'Prosperity theology', 20. Note also Hinn: 'So I believe with all my heart that healing is part of our inheritance as believers. It's a provision of God's covenant with us. But now I have come to realise that God is sovereign, and there are things I just don't understand' (cited in S. Strang, 'Benny Hinn Speaks Out').

[63] Hanegraaff's argument that Is. 53:4 refers to physical healing but verse 5 to spiritual healing is unconvincing (Hanegraaff, *Crisis*, 249-251).

[64] This perhaps weighs against Carson's argument: 'the Cross is the basis for all benefits that accrue to believers but this does not mean that all such benefits can be secured at the present time on demand, any more than we have the right and power to demand our resurrection bodies' (cited in Jackson, 'Prosperity theology and the faith movement', 19). At least, we should be wary of making such a case on the basis of Is. 53:4-5. Sarles, following Unger, considers the healing to be 'spiritual in nature, descriptive of the remission of sins' (Sarles, 'Evaluation', 339). Cf. Bowman, *Controversy*, 210: 'I understand Isaiah 53:5 to be speaking primarily of spiritual "healing," with physical sickness as a type representing or picturing sin as a kind of sickness.'

[65] Against J.C. Thomas (*The Devil, Disease and Deliverance*, 173), Matthew may have discerned a 'deep connection' between the healing of the sick and the vicarious suffering of the Servant without meaning that 'such activity is part of Jesus' atoning work'. The fact that Matthew preferred the Hebrew text of Is. 53:4 over the more spiritualized LXX is irrelevant: Jesus' healed *real* diseases.

[66] Hanegraaff points out that Jesus fulfilled this prophecy 'before His atonement on the cross', with the result that this verse 'does not guarantee our healing today' (*Crisis*, 251; cf. Sarles, 'Evaluation', 339). But people were also *forgiven* before Jesus bore our sins on the cross.

[67] See Allen, *Psalms 101-150*, 19-20.

[68] Cf. Bosworth, *Healer*, 9-10.

[69] Note in particular Prov. 14:30; 15:4.

[70] Cf. Moo, 'Divine Healing', 204: 'We would prefer... to say that physical healing is one *effect* of the atoning death of Christ.'

[71] Cf. Moo, 'Divine Healing', 196-197.

[72] Cf. Moo, 'Divine Healing', 198: the health and wealth gospel is 'right to proclaim that God has promised to remove all our physical infirmities; but they are wrong to claim that we can expect this to take place in this life.' Also Bowman, *Controversy*, 210: 'I think it is actually correct to teach that healing is guaranteed to us by Christ's atonement. I would simply qualify this guarantee as prospective.'

[73] F.K.C. Price, 'Knowing Our Territory', excerpted from *Living in Hostile Territory* (1999), accessed online June 2002 at www.eifm.org /cfide/smartsurf/user/Monthly_Messages/Jan.html.

[74] Cf. Hagin, *Must Christians Suffer?*, 10, 14, 41; Hinn, *Biblical Road*, 76.

[75] E.g., Hagin, *Must Christians Suffer?*, 2-3; Young Hoon Lee, 'Prosperity Theology', 33.

[76] Moo, 'Divine Healing', 199-200. The suffering of the faithful recounted in Heb. 11:36-39 is not an argument against prosperity teaching (against Sarles, 'Evaluation', 340-341; Sang-Bok, 'Bed of Roses', 22-23; Gasque, 'Prosperity Theology', 43). See also 'Statement on Prosperity Theology and Theology of Suffering' (Ev. Rev. Th. 20-1, 1996), 10-12.

[77] Hagin, *Visions*, 100.

[78] Cf. Thomas, *Devil*, 61.

[79] Cf. the use of the image of the 'thorn' in Num. 33:55; Ezek. 28:24. See Moo, 'Divine Healing', 200; Barnett, *Second Corinthians*, 569-570.

[80] Cf. Martin, 2 *Corinthians*, 414-415; Moo, 'Divine Healing', 201; Thomas, *Devil, 66-69*. It is interesting to note that Num. 33:55 says the Canaanites who are not driven from the land will be as 'barbs (*skolopes*) in your eyes and thorns (*bolides*) in your sides'. Does

this add support to the view that Paul suffered from an eye problem (cf. Gal. 4:13-15)?

[81] So, e.g., Hawthorne, *Philippians*, 118. Others, however, doubt that Paul's language is meant to exclude the possibility of divine healing: see Fee, *Philippians*, 279; Thomas, *Devil*, 80-81.

[82] Thomas, *Devil*, 87.

[83] Hagin, *Foundations*, 42.

[84] Cf. McIntyre's defence of Kenyon's belief that the believer is 'absolute master of satanic forces in the name of Jesus' (McIntyre, *Kenyon*, 265-275).

[85] Copeland, 'Expect the Glory!', 6.

CHAPTER EIGHT

[1] E.g., Sang-Bok, 'Bed of Roses', 17.

[2] Against, e.g., S. Hunt, 'Magical Moments: An Intellectualist Approach to the Neo-Pentecostal Faith Ministries', 274-276.

[3] See, e.g., N. Turner, *A Grammar of New Testament Greek*, 210-211.

[4] 1 Sam. 21:3 LXX has the phrase *en tōi topōi tōi legomenōi theou pistis*, which means 'in the place that is called "the faithfulness of God"'.

[5] Similar forms are found in Josephus, *Ant*. 17.179 (*pistin tou theiou*), a variant reading of Acts 19:20 (*hē pistis tou theou*), 1 Clement 3.4 (*pistei autou*); cf. 27:3; Hermas, *Mand*. 11:9 (*pistis theiou pneumatos*).

[6] Cf. Dunn, *Galatians*, 138-139, 195-196; R.N. Longenecker, *Galatians*, 87-88. The suggestion that the phrase might be translated 'you have the faithfulness of God' (cf. W.L. Lane, *The Gospel of Mark*, 409) makes little sense of the connection with the preceding verse.

[7] M.D. Hooker, *The Gospel According to Mark*, 269.

[8] Heb. 11:3 is sometimes cited, but 'by faith' attaches to 'we understand', not to the preparation of the ages by the word (*rhēmati*) of God. It is by faith that we see the hidden divine purpose behind the visible reality.

[9] Cf. Hanegraaff, *Crisis*, 92-93; G. Lie, 'The Theology of E.W. Kenyon: Plain Heresy or Within the Boundaries of Pentecostal-Charismatic "Orthodoxy"?', 106-107.

[10] Cf. Bowman, *Controversy*, 109-112.

[11] Cf. DeArteaga, *Quenching The Spirit*, 256-257; McIntyre, *Kenyon*, 304.

[12] DeArteaga, *Quenching The Spirit*, 257. Note DeArteaga's discussion of the background to the idea of spiritual laws, especially the

influence of the Sandfords (DeArteaga, *Quenching The Spirit*, 188-200). Lie argues that Kenyon's theory of spiritual laws is essentially functional; it presupposes not a 'deistic *Weltanschauung*' but the experience of the believer (Lie, 'Theology of E.W. Kenyon', 104-105). He then suggests that 'the belief that God has declared once and for all his unalterable will to always respond affirmatively to the believer's prayer' is not incompatible with an affirmation of divine sovereignty.

[13] Copeland, *Miraculous Realm*, 46 (italics removed).

[14] Cf. the 'kingdom law' of sowing and reaping in Gal. 6:7-8 (Copeland, *End of Time*, 40).

[15] McIntyre, *Kenyon*, 266.

[16] Copeland, *Miraculous Realm*, 32-33.

[17] E.g. Hanegraaff, Crisis, 80-84; Hunt, *Seduction*, 140-141.

[18] Cf. Copeland, *Mutual Funds*, 59-60: 'Quite often when I talk about building an inner image with the Word of God, I find believers are wary of such things. They say it sounds like positive thinking or New Age techniques.... Well, where do you think the devil got those things? You don't think he ever came up with anything on his own, do you? Of course not! He's a thief!'

[19] Copeland, *Mutual Funds*, 58, 60.

[20] DeArteaga, *Quenching The Spirit*, 206; quoting J. Edwards, *The Distinguishing Marks of a Work of the Spirit of God*.

[21] DeArteaga, *Quenching The Spirit*, 210-211.

[22] This is a common argument against visualization: see, e.g., Ankerberg and Weldon, *Facts*, 33.

[23] Copeland, *Mutual Funds*, 60.

[24] Cf. Brandon, *Health & Wealth*, 37: 'Faith is not rooted in a warm, loving relationship with God, but is something extra, a magical power imprisoned in words that will inevitably bring them to pass. This seems more like primitive animism than the elevated monotheism of the Bible. In the most affluent civilization on earth, Christianity has been reduced to a stone-age religion, a superstitious hotchpotch of pagan high priest, spells and magic power.'

[25] Hunt, 'Magical Moments', 276.

[26] Copeland, *Force*, 18.

[27] Coleman sees a 'parallel' between positive confession and 'those aspects of Austinian speech-act theory which describe

how discursive practice can produce that which it names' (Coleman, 'Charismatic Christianity', 248). However, it is only a parallel: the performative function of ordinary language is dependent on certain socially derived conventions: there is no suggestion either that the words are inherently powerful or that they invoke some actor or force not already involved in the speech act.

[28] Dollar, *Prosperity*, 50.

[29] Cf. Hanegraaff, *Crisis*, 76. Dollar cites Prov. 18:20-21 (Dollar, *Prosperity*, 45), but there is no reason to attribute the 'power of the tongue' to some esoteric spiritual or metaphysical law: the tongue is powerful because it *communicates* and communication is powerful.

[30] Copeland, 'Counterattack', 7.

[31] Dollar, *Prosperity*, 46.

[32] Copeland, 'Counterattack', 7.

[33] Copeland, *Covenant*, 54, cf. 59-61.

[34] Hagin, *Mountain*, 121; cf. Hagin, *Authority*, 21-22.

[35] Lane, *Mark*, 410; cf. Sarles, *Evaluation*, 348-349.

[36] Hooker thinks that the saying was originally proverbial but that Mark has made it a word of judgment against the temple (Hooker, *Mark*, 270).

[37] Note also Jesus' response to the disciples in Lk. 17:6 (cf. Mt. 17:20): 'If you had faith the size of a mustard seed, you could say to this mulberry tree, 'Be uprooted and planted in the sea,' and it would obey you.' Given the context, which has to do with the disciple's willingness to forgive, it seems likely that the uprooting of the 'mulberry tree' is meant symbolically. Possibly Jer. 1:10 is in the background, which would suggest a prophetic role.

[38] E.g., Farah, *Pinnacle*, 25-30, 49-51, 133-134; DeArteaga, *Quenching The Spirit*, 228. This is a little different to the use of *rhema* to signify the word which is spoken by faith and which is therefore powerful. Rom. 10:8 is generally cited: '"The word is near you, on your lips and in your heart" (that is, the word of faith (*to rhēma tēs pisteōs*) that we proclaim).'

[39] Cf. Hooker, *Mark*, 270.

[40] Cf. Bowman, *Controversy*, 197:

CHAPTER NINE

[1] Cf. Gowan, 'Wealth and Poverty in the Old Testament', 16; against Brandon, 'Hermeneutics', 2.

[2] Cf. Hinn, *Biblical Road*, 81.

[3] Note Prov. 22:2: 'The rich and the poor have this in common: the LORD is the maker of them all.'

[4] C.L. Blomberg, *Neither Poverty nor Riches*, 40.

[5] See Blomberg, *Poverty*, 49; and the discussion in J. Stott, *New Issues Facing Christians Today*, 271.

[6] Cf. Blomberg, *Poverty*, 48.

[7] Cf. Blomberg, *Poverty*, 45-46.

[8] The possibility that this provision might be abused was recognized (Deut. 15:9).

[9] See Blomberg, *Poverty*, 46-47; Murray, *Tithing*. Hinn distinguishes three types of giving: tithes, offerings, alms (*Biblical Road*, 113-155).

[10] This third year provision came to be interpreted later as a third tithe, added to the other two (cf. Blomberg, *Poverty*, 46).

[11] Cf. Gowan, 'Wealth and Poverty', 16.

[12] See Blomberg, *Poverty*, 47-49.

[13] Cf. Sider, *Rich Christians*, 76.

[14] There is no systematic commitment to correct structural economic injustice: 'Care of the poor was the king's responsibility, as the representative of Yahweh (Ps. 72:2-4), but the law establishes no programs that might endure from one administration to another' (Gowan, 'Wealth and Poverty', 18).

[15] Against Blomberg, *Poverty*, 49; D.A. Hughes and M. Bennett, *God of the Poor*, 49. In Isaiah it is the servant of the Lord who is described as a 'light to the nations' (Is. 42:6; 49:6).

[16] See, e.g., D.A. Hay, *Economics Today: A Christian Critique*, 40.

[17] Cf. Pss. Sol. 5:16 (Brenton): 'Happy is the one whom God remembers with a moderate sufficiency; for if a man is excessively rich, he sins.'

[18] See Blomberg, *Poverty*, 70.

[19] Cf. Sider, *Rich Christians*, 44; Hay, *Economics*, 39-40.

[20] Blomberg, *Poverty*, 71-77.

[21] Though note Ps. 37:25: 'I have been young, and now am old, yet I have not seen the righteous forsaken or their children begging bread.'

[22] Cf. Blomberg, *Poverty*, 70.

[23] 'The dominant thrust of the Prophets... is that God will judge the exploitative rich as part of his eschatological plan to create a perfectly just society and redeemed material world' (Blomberg, *Poverty*, 82).

[24] Note Blomberg, *Poverty*, 61; though David's claims to be 'poor and needy' (Ps. 40:17; 86:1; 109:22) are perhaps not the best evidence of this.

[25] Note Blomberg's comments on this text (Blomberg, *Poverty*, 67-68); and Gowan, 'Wealth and Poverty', 16.

CHAPTER TEN

[1] Cf. P.H. Davids, 'Rich and Poor', 703.

[2] The 'lure of wealth' is one of the things which choke the word of God so that it produces no yield (Mt. 13:22; Mk. 4:19).

[3] Copeland, *Laws of Prosperity*, 52; cf. Copeland, *Mutual Funds*, 130-133.

[4] Price, *Prosperity*, 50-51.

[5] See above page 84.

[6] T.E. Schmidt, 'Burden, Barrier, Blasphemy: Wealth In Matt 6:33, Luke 14:33, And Luke 16:15', 185.

[7] Cf. J. Nolland, *Luke*, 827.

[8] Copeland, *Laws of Prosperity*, 58-60. He finds the same argument in 1 Tim. 6:18-19: by their generosity and good works the rich will store up for themselves 'the treasure of a good foundation for the future, so that they may take hold of the life that really is life.' Paul, however, is concerned in this letter about the spiritual dangers that believers will face 'in later times' (4:1). By urging those who are rich 'in the present age' not to put their trust in uncertain riches but to do good works he believes that they will develop a foundation of spiritual maturity that will enable them to persevere and take hold of that which really is life.

[9] On the proclamation of the Jubilee year see Davids, 'Rich and Poor', 707.

[10] See, e.g., Sider, *Rich Christians*, 47-48. It is misleading to say that 'The Bible clearly and repeatedly teaches that God is at work in history exalting the poor and casting down the rich who got that way by oppressing or neglecting the poor' (*ibid.* 63) because we

only really see God at work *within Israel*. We would certainly not deny that God is concerned about the condition of the world's poor, but this sort of interpretation both obscures the deeper purpose underlying God's concern for the poor within Israel and misrepresents the mission of the people of God within the world. Poverty becomes a problem because it is inextricably bound up with a failure at the level of covenant, but the purpose of the covenant was not primarily to ensure economic equality.

[11] Against Copeland, *Mutual Funds*, 20-21.

[12] T.E. Schmidt, *Hostility to Wealth in the Synoptic Gospels*, 164.

[13] Avanzini, 'Was Jesus Poor?', 8-9; cf. Avanzini, *Wealth*, 81-84. Newport thinks that the disciples' perplexed question in Mk. 10:26 ('Then who can be saved?') implies that they were all wealthy (Newport, *Provision*, 12). But as Peter points out in verse 28, whatever wealth they may have had, they have now 'left everything' in order to follow Jesus. Note also MacArthur, *Whose Money?*, 34-35.

[14] Beasley-Murray, *John*, 347; cf. Whitacre, *John*, 459.

[15] As evidence for his claim that many of the early Christians were legitimately poor Gasque quotes Jesus' statement that God 'makes his sun rise on the evil and on the good, and sends rain on the righteous and on the unrighteous' (Mt. 5:45; Gasque, 'Prosperity Theology', 42). However, this is not quite Jesus' point. The saying supports the assertion that the disciples should love their enemies (5:44). Just as God does not withhold the blessings of sun and rain from the unrighteous, so the disciples should love not only their friends but also their persecutors. See also Schmidt, *Hostility*, 119-120, who finds attractive Buchanan's argument that Jesus was originally a prosperous skilled craftsman who deliberately renounced his wealth and background.

[16] Cf. Blomberg, *Poverty*, 108.

[17] See, e.g., Hagner, *Matthew 1-13*, 149-150.

[18] Copeland, *Laws of Prosperity*, 53.

[19] Hagin, *Must Christians Suffer?* 14-15.

[20] Note Blomberg, *Poverty*, 145-146: "...the main focus of his ministry, the road to the cross, and his call to disciples to imitate him in similar self-denying sacrifice rather than basking in glory,

suggests the overarching paradigm of generous giving, rather than 'godly materialism', for the one who would faithfully follow Christ."

CHAPTER ELEVEN

[1] Cf. Blomberg, *Poverty*, 147-148; R.P. Martin, *James*, lxxiii.

[2] Cf. I.H. Marshall, *Acts*, 108: 'This way of putting the matter brings out the fact that the things which each person possessed evidently continued to be his own property until it was found necessary to sell them for the common good.' See also Blomberg, *Poverty*, 164-165; Sider, *Rich Christians*, 81.

[3] Marshall, *Acts*, 341-342; F.F. Bruce, *The Acts of the Apostles*, 389.

[4] Cf. Blomberg, *Poverty*, 161-162; MacArthur, *Whose Money?*, 69-71.

[5] Whether this situation lasted through to the Roman invasion is unclear. James may provide evidence for more complex socio-economic patterns in the latter part of this period. There is also the question of whether the selling of possessions exacerbated the later suffering of the church in Judea during the famine (cf. Blomberg, *Poverty*, 162-163; MacArthur, *Whose Money?*, 72-74).

[6] Cf. Blomberg, *Poverty*, 147.

[7] See Blomberg, *Poverty*, 149-150.

[8] The letter begins with reference to the 'trials' that its recipients will face and through which they will become mature (1:2-4). Given this and the fact that in the parable of the sower the heat from the sun that causes the seed sown on the rocky ground to 'wither away' is interpreted as persecution (Mt. 13:20-21 and pars.), the thought may be that the rich are likely to succumb in the face of opposition. Jas. 4:13-17, however, perhaps again suggests that it is the transience and fragility of human life that should give the money-makers pause for thought.

[9] Note the argument that this is not the gathering for worship but a quasi-legal meeting for the purpose of settling disputes among Christians (Blomberg, *Poverty*, 153).

[10] Against Newport, *Provision*, 88.

[11] See Mounce, *Pastoral Epistles*, 342, for the religious and philosophical background to the argument.

[12] Price, *Prosperity*, 47; cf. Copeland, *Mutual Funds*, 106.

[13] See Perriman, *Speaking of Women*, 168-169.

[14] Hinn, *Biblical Road*, 71-72.
[15] Copeland, *Laws of Prosperity*, 63-65.
[16] Copeland, *Mutual Funds*, 116.
[17] Cf. MacArthur, *Whose Money*, 103.
[18] Copeland, *Mutual Funds*, 117.
[19] The comprehensiveness of the promise cannot be missed: *en panti pantote pasan autarkeian.*
[20] Cf. Fee, *Philippians*, 431-432 n.37. In the Septuagint version of Proverbs 30:8, to have *ta autarkē* means to avoid both poverty and wealth. *Autarkeia* is used in Pss. Sol. 5:16-17 to describe financial circumstances that are compatible with righteousness: if a man is excessively rich, he sins, but moderation (*to metrion*) permits a 'satisfaction with righteousness' (*plēsmonēn en dikaiosynē*) and with that the blessing of God.
[21] Against Price, *Prosperity*, 92-93.
[22] Blomberg thinks that *autarkeia* denotes spiritual sufficiency, arguing that Paul has spiritualized the Old Testament prosperity theme. But this seems motivated by a desire to refute 'prosperity theology' (Blomberg, *Poverty*, 196). Cf. MacArthur, *Whose Money?*, 58-59. John Stott repudiates the 'health and wealth' gospel by pointing out that although Israel as a nation was promised material blessings as a reward for obedience, in Christ God has blessed us 'with every spiritual blessing' (Stott, *New Issues*, 276). But it may infer too much from Paul's argument to say that the affirmation of 'spiritual blessings' in Eph. 1:3 *excludes* material blessings.
[23] There is no strong reason to think that God is the subject of the quotation (against Barnett, *Second Corinthians*, 440) if we assume that Paul has the whole of Ps. 112 in view: the prosperity of the righteous is the basis for the assurance that the Corinthians will always have sufficiency and be able to 'share abundantly in every good work' (2 Cor. 9:8).
[24] In Hos. 10:12 Israel is intructed: 'Sow for yourselves righteousness, reap steadfast love'. The spiritualization of the formula in this case, however, may depend on the argument about judgment and repentance. In the case of a faithful people the material interpretation may still apply. But does this carry over into the New Testament?
[25] See Mounce, *Pastoral Epistles*, 309.

[26] Cf. G.W. Knight, *The Pastoral Epistles: A commentary on the Greek text*, 232.
[27] Avanzini, *How Much?*, 8 (his italics).

CHAPTER TWELVE

[1] Cf. Kenyon's struggle with the demands of entire sanctification and his eventual realization that sanctification could only come about through the indwelling of the Spirit (McIntyre, *Kenyon*, 45-46).
[2] Sarles, 'Evaluation', 343.
[3] H. Osgood, 'Prosperity Teaching and Evangelical Unity'.
[4] See e.g., Copeland, 'Signs and Wonders', 5.
[5] Hagin, *Anointing*, 114-116.
[6] Copeland, 'Signs and Wonders', 5; cf. Copeland, *End of Time*, 72-73.
[7] Hollenweger, *Pentecostalism*, 233.
[8] 'Miracles', ITV 22nd April 2001.
[9] Farah, *Pinnacle*, 33.
[10] Cf. Farah, *Pinnacle, passim*; DeArteaga, *Quenching The Spirit*, 227; Hanegraaff, *Crisis*, 61-63, 237-239; L. Parker, *We Let Our Son Die* (Eugene: Harvest House, 1980); Barron, *Health and Wealth*, 46-47, 127-131; Brandon, *Health & Wealth*, 48-49; Ankerberg and Weldon, *Facts*, 40-41; 'Death by Faith', Let Us Reason Ministries (www.letusreason.org/Wf25.htm, accessed June 2002); 'The effectiveness of faith healing', ReligiousTolerance.org (www.religioustolerance.org/medical3.htm, accessed June 2002).
[11] J.R. Goff, 'The Faith that Claims', *Christianity Today*, Feb. 19, 1990, 21; Barron, *Health and Wealth*, 14-34; Moo, 'Divine Healing', 133.
[12] Farah, *Pinnacle*, 151-152; cf. Hanegraaff, *Crisis*, 259-260, 261-269.
[13] Cf. Bakker, 'Does God Want Me to be Rich?', 41; R. Warner, 'Postscript: Reflections following the EA Consultation'.
[14] Copeland, *End of Time*, 31-32.
[15] Hagin, *Authority*, 16.
[16] Copeland says that the seed sown by the missionaries 'who preached, shed tears and gave their lives, and it looked like the devil had the upper hand' will produce a harvest in the end-time (Copeland, *End of Time*, 60-61).
[17] Hagin, *Must Christians Suffer?*, 12.
[18] See, e.g., Hagin's story about the 'unnecessary' sufferings of a bereaved woman (Hagin, *Must Christians Suffer?* 19-22).

[19] See, e.g., Copeland, *Miraculous Realm, passim.*

[20] Cited in Strang, 'Benny Hinn'.

[21] Note, e.g., Osborn, *Message*, 38, 64-66. Osborn lists seven basic human needs which are met through redemption (76-81 for overview). The programme is not especially God-centred, either for this age or for the age to come.

[22] Cf. Gasque, 'Prosperity Theology', 44: 'Except for the fact that they are ostensibly quoting from the Bible, their message is more akin to the doctrines of self-actualization and self-esteem of the contemporary pop-psychologists than it is to the motifs of classical Christian theology.' See also Young Hoon Lee, 'Prosperity Theology', 34.

[23] Cf. Macchia, 'Struggle', 21: 'The problem with much of the popular teaching of Pentecostal evangelists on healing is its implicit isolation of sickness from the broader plight of human injustice and suffering.'

[24] Gifford, 'Foreign Element', 381; for an analysis of the relation of liberation to prosperity theology see G. Grogan, 'Liberation and Prosperity Theologies'.

[25] Stott, *New Issues*, 277.

[26] Copeland, *Mutual Funds*, 29; cf. Barron, *Health and Wealth*, 96-97; Hollinger, 'Enjoying God', 135.

[27] Gifford, *African Christianity*, 236, 240.

[28] Cf. Gifford, 'Gospel of Prosperity', 1388–90.

CONCLUSIONS

[1] Cf. the appeal for a more constructive approach made by Jack Hayford in 'To Avoid a Modern Inquisition', *Ministries Today* (Sept.-Oct. 1993), 8ff (see Smail, et al., 'Revelation Knowledge', 75).

[2] Hollinger, 'Enjoying God', 132. The Kenneth Hagin Ministries statement of faith can be found at www.rhema.org/about/tenets_faith.asp (accessed June 2002); the Copelands' statement of faith is given at www.kcm.org/about/faith_statement/index.html (accessed June 2002). Bowman quotes a statement by Michael Bruno, a Word of Faith writer, with reference to the Athanasian Creed: 'There is not a teacher of faith or a Christian I know who holds the doctrine of faith who would not agree with the above' (in Bowman, *Controversy*, 148). Evangelical individuals and organizations are sometimes mentioned with tacit

approval – Billy Graham, for example (Hemry, 'His Father's Business', 10).

[3] D. Moo, 'Divine Healing', 191.

[4] Farah, *Pinnacle*, 115-164.

[5] According to Bowman, the Word of Faith movement is 'suborthodox' in that 'its teachings in certain crucial respects fall below the standards of orthodoxy'; by 'aberrant' he means that in other respects they 'deviate from orthodoxy in ways difficult to classify easily' (Bowman, *Controversy*, 227; see also R.M. Bowman, *Orthodoxy and Heresy: A Biblical Guide to Doctrinal Discernment*).

[6] Bowman, *Controversy*, 226-227.

[7] Bowman, *Controversy*, 228.

[8] See L.F. Winner, 'T.D. Jakes Feels Your Pain'.

[9] Note Benny Hinn's admission that 'There is pressure to produce when you're up there on that platform – especially in a healing ministry. People don't come just to hear you preach; they want to see something' (Strang, 'Benny Hinn', 29).

[10] See, e.g., Harrell, *All Things*, 234: 'Every evangelist knew that some of their number had succumbed to the evil triumvirate—"women, money, and popularity." Admitted evangelist Kenneth Hagin, "It is no more than a con game with many."'

[11] DeArteaga, *Quenching The Spirit*, 272. Cf. Hagin, *Must Christians Suffer?*, 3: 'I just keep putting out the truth; I don't take time to answer critics.'

[12] K.E. Hagin, 'Suffering Unto Perfection: Part 3', *Word of Faith* (Nov. 1995), 16, cited in DeArteaga, *Quenching The Spirit*, 232.

[13] Barron, *Health and Wealth*, 95-98.

[14] Hagin, *Zoe*, 42; Dal Bello, 'Atonement Where?'

[15] K.E. Hagin, *What to Do When Faith Seems Weak and Victory Lost* (1979), 25, cited in R.M. Riss, 'Hagin, Kenneth E.', 345. Cf. Hagin's comments on people who 'try to "make" the gifts happen': 'Instead of letting the Spirit use us, so often folks are trying to use the Spirit' (Hagin, 'Jesus Christ', 22).

[16] See Bowman, '"Ye Are Gods?"'.

[17] Copeland, *Mutual Funds*, 92-93.

[18] Dal Bello, 'Atonement Where?'

[19] Price, *Prosperity*, 25. Cf. Hagin (*Authority*, 18): 'It seems like it's the most difficult thing in the world for the Church to stay balanced.

You can take any subject – including the authority of the believer – push it to the extreme, and it becomes harmful and ceases to bless.'

[20] Cf. K. Hagin, Jr., *Itching Ears*, 7.

[21] Atkinson has defended the imbalance in Avanzini's teaching on the grounds that it is the result of 'God's individual calling on his life' (Atkinson, 'Prosperity Teaching').

[22] Cf. Donald Gee's remarks on the relation between the healing revivalists and the local Pentecostal churches: 'We need the extremist to start things moving, but we need the balanced teacher to keep them moving in the right direction. We need extremism for a miracle of healing, but we need balanced sanity for health. We need extreme fervor to launch a movement, but we need repudiation of extremes to save it from self-destruction. Only a wisdom from above can reveal the perfect synthesis' (cited in Harrell, *All Things*, 111). It is generally instructive to consider the current tension between the Word of Faith movement and mainstream evangelicalism in the light of the earlier conflict between the healing revivalists and the AOG (Harrell, *All Things*, 107-116).

[23] Hagin, *Foundations*, 63 (his italics).

[24] D. Moo, 'Divine Healing', 196. Similarly Barron notes that 'Even New Testament scholar Gordon Fee, no admirer of faith teachers, commends them for recovering this text [Mk. 11:23-24] from oblivion and rebelling against the typical style of prayer, in which people go through the motions but really don't expect anything to happen' (Barron, *Health and Wealth*, 103).

[25] See, for example, the testimonies in *Believer's Voice of Victory* 25.11 (Dec. 1997), 24-25.

[26] Osborn, *Message*, 63.

[27] Dye, 'Prosperity Teaching'.

[28] Farah, *Pinnacle*, 136.

[29] See www.prayerofjabez.com (accessed June 2002).

[30] B. Wilkinson, *The Prayer of Jabez*, 24.

[31] Wilkinson, *Jabez*, 17, 19.

[32] Moo, 'Divine Healing', 202.

[33] Gammons, '30 Reasons': 'One Anglican Vicar announced that he could not support one of my conventions because one of the guest speakers "believed in prosperity". I satirically replied, "Not as

much as your Bishop practices it!" I went on to explain that his Bishop lived in a medieval palace, with priceless oil paintings on the wall and was driven around by a chauffeur. My guest speaker had none of these and what is more, he preached prosperity for all! The Bishop preached against prosperity, yet he lived it!'

[34] DeArteaga, *Quenching The Spirit*, 183-187.

[35] Copeland, *Mutual Funds*, 27.

[36] Cf. Hinn, *Biblical Road*, 9-12.

[37] On this issue see also Nash, *Poverty*, 156-171.

[38] There is a parallel here with the debate over creation-centred spirituality: evangelicalism has generally found it rather difficult to affirm and enjoy the products of divine and, more importantly, human creativity.

[39] Roger Forster argues that the church is slowly learning to react more positively to the perennial hazards of sex, power and money (audio tape 'Debt and Money', Ichthus Media Services, 2001). Traditionally the solution has been avoidance and abstinence, often to the point of asceticism and withdrawal from the world. The church has loosened up somewhat and is now willing to promote a much more positive understanding of the role of sex within marriage. We have remained much more wary of power and wealth, but the option is there for the church to redeem these things, to exercise godly power and maintain a godly economy.

[40] Copeland, *Mutual Funds*, 11.

[41] See especially Lk. 6:38; 2 Cor. 9:10-11, and the discussion in chapters 9 to 11 above. Similarly, Meilaender, 'Problem', 79-80, whose reasonably balanced argument about possessions nevertheless can envisage only simplicity, renunciation, and generosity as the outcome of a theology of possessions. We can enjoy and we can give up material things, but the reciprocal dynamic is missing: the active, responsive generosity of God is factored out of the equation.

[42] Sider, *Rich Christians*, 78-80.

[43] Cf. Copeland, *Laws of Prosperity*, 27.

[44] Wilkinson, *Jabez*, 31.

[45] Cf. J.V. Taylor, *Enough is Enough*, 49-50.

[46] Cf. Price, *Prosperity*, 73-74. We do not have to agree, however, with Price's contention that 'Things should get progressively better as

the influence of the Gospel dulls the edge of the sword of the wicked one.'

[47] P. Mills ('Christians and Financial Security', 191-192) asks whether the birds of the air who are fed by God (Mt. 6:19, 26) are more spiritual than the ant which works hard to gather food for itself (Prov. 6:6-8).

[48] Mills ('Financial Security', 199) puts forward a similar argument for a contextualized theology of wealth: "when witness is to be given of the imminence and power of the kingdom of God, a 'reckless' attitude towards wealth and possessions is entirely appropriate in order to display more powerfully Christian love and faith. However, greater prudence is required when physical conditions are more hostile and endurance is the order of the day." The historical perspective, however, is missing, and a certain ethical caution is evident in the affirmation of 'prudence' rather than of prosperity.

[49] Ellul, *Money*, 110.

[50] Ellul, *Money*, 41.

[51] See, e.g., Ankerberg and Weldon, *Facts*, 13-14.

[52] Ankerberg and Weldon, *Facts*, 15.

[53] See Barron's sensitive discussion of this issue in *Health and Wealth*, 137-139.

[54] Hanegraaff, *Crisis*, 192.

Bibliography

Allen, L.C., *Psalms 101-150* (Waco: Word Publishing, 1983)

Anderson, A., 'Pentecostals and Apartheid in South Africa during Ninety Years 1908-1998', *Cyberjournal for Pentecostal Charismatic Research*, vol. 9, Feb. 2001 (http://www.pctii.org/cyberj/cyber9.html)

Ankerberg, J. and J. Weldon, *The Facts on the Faith Movement* (Eugene, Oregon: Harvest House Publishers, 1993)

Atkinson, W., 'Prosperity Teaching: As Bad as it Seems?' (unpublished paper for the ACUTE working group on the Prosperity Gospel, 1998)

Avanzini, J., 'Dr. Drydust, Sister Wonderful, and You', *Believer's Voice of Victory* 23.10 (Oct. 1995), 24-25

—, *God's Debt-Free Guarantee* (Tulsa OK: Harrison House, 1994)

—, *How Much Money Is Enough* (HIS Publishing Company, n.d.)

—, 'How to be a Money Magnet', *Believer's Voice of Victory* 25.9 (Oct. 1997), 26-27

—, *The Wealth Of The World* (Tulsa: Harrison House, 1989)

—, 'Was Jesus Poor?', *Believer's Voice of Victory* 24.1 (Jan. 1996), 8-9

Bakare, T., *Operating in High Finances* (London: Mattyson Media Company, 1993)

Bakker, J., 'Does God Want Me to be Rich', *Renewal* (winter 1998), 38-41

Barnett, P., *The Second Epistle to the Corinthians* (Grand Rapids and Cambridge: Eerdmans, 1997)

Barro, A.C., 'Wrestling with Succcess', *Christianity Today* 42.13 (Nov. 1998), 70

Barron, B., 'Sick of Health and Wealth', *Christianity Today* (Nov. 1993), 27-28

—, *The Health and Wealth Gospel* (Downers Grove: InterVarsity Press, 1987)

Bauckham, R.J., 'Descent into Hell', in Ferguson, S.B. and D.F. Wright, *New Dictionary of Theology* (Leicester and Downers Grove: Inter-Varsity Press, 1988), 194-195

—, *Jude, 2 Peter* (Waco: Word Inc., 1983)

Beasley-Murray, G.R., *John* (Dallas: Word Publishing, 1987)

Bebbington, D.W., *Evangelicalism in Modern Britain* (London: Unwin Hyman, 1989)

Beresford, B., 'Building up the body of Christ: What Is ... Rhema Church?', The Mail & Guardian, Johannesburg (January 26, 2000), accessed online at http://www.mg.co.za/mg/news/2000jan2/26jan-rhema.html

Blomberg, C.L., *Neither Poverty nor Riches* (Leicester: IVP, Apollos, 1999)

Bosworth, F.F., *Christ the Healer* (Grand Rapids: Fleming H. Revell, 1973; first published 1924)

Bowman, R.M., *Orthodoxy and Heresy: A Biblical Guide to Doctrinal Discernment* (Grand Rapids: Baker, 1992)

—, *The Word-Faith Controversy: Understanding the Health and Wealth Gospel* (Grand Rapids: Baker Books, 2001)

—, '"Ye Are Gods?" Orthodox and Heretical Views on the Deification of Man', *Christian Research Journal* (Winter/Spring 1987), 18ff., accessed online June 2002 at http://www.iclnet.org/pub/resources/text/cri/cri-jrnl/web/crj0018a.html

Brandon, A., *Health & Wealth* (Eastbourne: Kingsway, 1987)

—, *Health And Wealth: Hooked On Heresy – Daily Notes, January to March 1993* (Scripture Union, UK)

—, 'Prosperity and Hermeneutics' (unpublished paper for the ACUTE working group on the Prosperity Gospel, 1998)

Brouwer, S., P. Gifford, and S.D. Rose, *Exporting The American Gospel* (New York and London: Routledge, 1996)

Bruce, F.F. *The Acts of the Apostles* (Grand Rapids: Eerdmans, 1951)

—, *The Epistle to the Galatians* (Exeter: Paternoster Press, 1982)

Buckley, S., "'Prosperity Theology' Pulls on Purse Strings", Washington Post (Feb. 13, 2001), A16, accessed online at http://www.washingtonpost.com/wp-dyn/articles/A61379-2001Feb12.html

Burgess, S.M. and G.B. McGee (eds.), *Dictionary of Pentecostal and Charismatic Movements* (Grand Rapids: Zondervan, 1988)

Cady, H.E., *Lessons in Truth* (Unity Village, MO: Unity Books, n.d.)

Calvin, John, *Institutes of the Christian Religion*, ed. J.T. McNeill (Philadelphia: The Westminster Press, 2 vols., 1960)

Capps, C., *The Tongue, A Creative Force* (Tulsa: Harrison House, 1995, 1976)

Cerullo, M., *Giving and Receiving* (Robertsbridge: Battle Books for MCWE, 1995)

Chappell, P.G., 'Healing Movements', in S.M. Burgess and G.B. McGee (eds.), *Dictionary of Pentecostal and Charismatic Movements* (Grand Rapids: Zondervan, 1988), 353-374

Coleman, S., 'Charismatic Christianity and the Dilemmas of Globalization' (*Religion* 28, 1998), 245-256

Copeland, G., 'Build Your Financial Foundation', *Believer's Voice of Victory* 25.9 (Oct. 1997), 28-31

—, 'Do You Know What Time It Is?', *Believer's Voice of Victory* 25.11 (Dec. 1997), 28-31

—, *God's Will for Your Healing* (Tulsa: Harrison House, 1972)

—, *God's Will Is Prosperity* (Fort Worth: Kenneth Copeland Publications, 1978)

Copeland, K., 'Anointed All the Time', *Believer's Voice of Victory* 24.8 (Sept. 1996), 4-7

—, 'Expect the Glory!', *Believer's Voice of Victory* 26.2 (Feb. 1998), 4-7

—, *Honor: Walking in Honesty, Truth, & Integrity* (Tulsa: Harrison House, 1992, 1994)

—, 'Living at the End of Time', *Believer's Voice of Victory* 25.10 (Nov. 1997), 4-7

—, *Living at the End of Time* (Fort Worth: Kenneth Copeland Publications, 1997, 1998)

—, *Managing God's Mutual Funds* (Fort Worth: Kenneth Copeland Publications, 1997)

—, *Our Covenant With God* (Fort Worth: Kenneth Copeland Publications, 1976)

—, *Prosperity: The Choice is Yours* (Fort Worth: Kenneth Copeland Publications, 1985)

—, 'Signs and Wonders... Without the Wonder', *Believer's Voice of Victory* 26.1 (Jan. 1998), 4-7

—, 'Sowing and Reaping an End-Time Harvest', *Believer's Voice of Victory* 25.11 (Dec. 1997), 4-7

—, 'Surviving the Counterattack', *Believer's Voice of Victory* 25.9 (Oct. 1997), 4-7

—, *The Force of Faith* (Fort Worth: Kenneth Copeland Publications, 1983)

—, *The Laws of Prosperity* (Fort Worth: Kenneth Copeland Publications, 1974)

—, *The Miraculous Realm of God's Love* (Fort Worth: Kenneth Copeland Publications, 1980)

—, 'To Know the Glory', *Believer's Voice of Victory* 24.11 (Dec. 1996), 4-7

—, 'Turning Up the Power', *Believer's Voice of Victory* 23.10 (Oct. 1995), 2-5

—, 'When the Devil Runs for Cover', *Believer's Voice of Victory* 24.1 (Jan. 1996), 4-7

—, 'Words at Work', *Believer's Voice of Victory* 24.1 (Jan. 1996), 10

—, 'Worthy to Be Anointed', *Believer's Voice of Victory* 24.9 (Oct. 1996), 4-7

Cutrer, C., 'Come and Receive Your Miracle', *Christianity Today* 45 (Feb. 2001), 41-49

Dal Bello, M., 'Atonement Where?', Cross and Word Christian Resource: Banner Ministries, accessed online June 2002 at www.banner.org.uk/wof/moreno1.html

Davids, P.H., 'Rich and Poor', in Green, J.B., S. McKnight and I.H. Marshall (eds.), *Dictionary of Jesus and the Gospels* (Downers Grove, Leicester: InterVarsity Press, 1992), 701-710

Dayton, D.W., *Theological Roots of Pentecostalism* (Metuchen and London: The Scarecrow Press, 1987)

DeArteaga, William, *Quenching The Spirit* (2nd Edn., Orlando: Creation House, 1996)

Dempster, M.W., B.D. Klaus and D. Petersen (eds.), *The Globalization of Pentecostalism* (Carlisle: Regnum, Paternoster, 1999)

Dollar, C.A., *Total Life Prosperity* (Nashville: Thomas Nelson Publishers, 1999)

Dresser, H.W., (ed.), *The Quimby Manuscripts* (New York: Thomas Y.C, 1921), accessed online June 2002 at http://www.ppquimby.com/hdresser/manscpts/manscpt.htm

Dunn, J.D.G., *Romans* (2 vols.) (Dallas: Word Books, 1988)

—, *The Epistles to the Colossians and to Philemon* (Grand Rapids: Eerdmans, Carlisle: Paternoster, 1996)

—, *The Epistle to the Galatians* (London: A & C Black, 1993)

Ellul, J., *Money and Power* (Basingstoke: Marshall Pickering, 1986)

Farah, C., *From the Pinnacle of the Temple* (Plainfield: Logos International, n.d.)

Fee, G.D., *Paul's Letter to the Philippians* (Grand Rapids: Eerdmans, 1995)

—, *The First Epistle to the Corinthians* (Grand Rapids: Eerdmans, 1987)

Fillmore, C., *Jesus Christ Heals* (Kansas City: Unity School of Christianity, nd.)

—, *Prosperity* (Kansas City: Unity School of Christianity, 1936)

Fisher, G.R. and M.K. Goedelman, *The Confusing World of Benny Hinn* (Personal Freedom Outreach, 1995)

Foster, B.E., 'Kenoticism', in Ferguson, S.B. and D.F. Wright, *New Dictionary of Theology* (Leicester and Downers Grove: Inter-Varsity Press, 1988), 364

Frame, R., 'Critics Claim "Word-Faith" Is Cultic', *Christianity Today* (Oct. 24, 1994), 85

Gammons, P., '30 Reasons Why God Wants You to Prosper' (unpublished paper for the ACUTE working group on the Prosperity Gospel, 1998)

—, *Vital Truths* (Walton On Thames: Reach Out Ministries International, n.d.)

Gasque, W. Ward, 'Prosperity Theology and the New Testament' (*EvRevTh* 20, 1996, 40-46)

George, W., 'The Hand of the Diligent', *Believer's Voice of Victory* 25.3 (March 1997), 18-19

Gifford, P., *African Christianity: Its Public Role* (London: Hurst & Company, 1998)

—, 'Gospel for Champions', *The Tablet* (Sept. 18, 1999), 1256-57

—, 'Prosperity: A New and Foreign Element in African Christianity', *Religion* 20 (1990), 373-388

—, 'The Gospel of Prosperity', *The Tablet* (Dec. 3, 1988), 1388-90

Goff, J.R., 'The Faith that Claims', *Christianity Today* (Feb. 19, 1990), 18-21

Gowan, D.E., 'Wealth and Poverty in the Old Testament: The Case of the Widow, the Orphan and the Sojourner', in Packer, J.I. and H. Smith (eds.), *The Best in Theology*, vol. 3 (Illinois: Christianity Today Inc., 1989), 9-20

Green, J.B., S. McKnight and I.H. Marshall (eds.), *Dictionary of Jesus and the Gospels* (Downers Grove, Leicester: InterVarsity Press, 1992)

Grogan, G., 'Liberation and Prosperity Theologies', *Scottish Bulletin of Evangelical Theology* 9.2 (1991), 118-132

Hackett, R.I.J., 'New Directions and Connections for African and Asian Charismatics', *Pneuma* 18.1 (1996), 69-77

Hagin, K., Jr., *Itching Ears* (Tulsa: Kenneth Hagin Ministries, 1982)

Hagin, K.E., *Foundations for Faith* (Tulsa: Kenneth Hagin Ministries, 1998)

—, *I Believe In Visions* (Tulsa: Kenneth Hagin Ministries, 1984)

—, 'Jesus Christ — The Same Yesterday, Today, and Forever', *The Word of Faith* 31.4 (April 1998), 18-23

—, *Mountain Moving Faith* (Tulsa: Kenneth Hagin Ministries, 1993)

—, *Must Christians Suffer?* (Tulsa: Kenneth Hagin Ministries, 1982)

—, *The Believer's Authority* (2nd Edn., Tulsa: Kenneth Hagin Ministries, 1984)

—, *Understanding the Anointing* (Tulsa: Kenneth Hagin Ministries, 1983)

—, *Zoe: The God-Kind of Life* (Tulsa: Kenneth Hagin Ministries, 1981)

Hagner, D.A., *Matthew* (2 vols.) (Dallas: Word Books, Publisher, 1993, 1995)

Hanegraaff, H., *Christianity In Crisis* (Eugene: Harvest House Publishers, 1993)

—, 'What's Wrong with the Faith Movement? Part One: E.W. Kenyon and the Twelve Apostles of Another Gospel', accessed online June 2002 at http://www.iclnet.org/pub/resources/text/cri/cri-jrnl/web/crj0118a.html

Hanegraaff, H., and E.M. de Castro, 'What's Wrong with the Faith Movement? Part Two: The Teachings of Kenneth Copeland', accessed online June 2002 at http://www.iclnet.org/pub/resources/text/cri/cri-jrnl/web/crj0119a.html

Harrell, D.E., *All Things Are Possible: The Healing & Charismatic Revivals in Modern America* (Bloomington: Indiana University Press, 1975)

Harrison, B., *Just Do It* (Tulsa: Harrison House, 1985, 1991)

Hawthorne, G.F., R.P. Martin and D.G. Reid (eds.), *Dictionary of Paul and his Letters* (Downers Grove and Leicester: InterVarsity Press, 1993)

Hay, D.A., *Economics Today: A Christian Critique* (Leicester: IVP, Apollos, 1989)

Hemry, M., 'Grand Slam', *Believer's Voice of Victory* 25.10 (Nov. 1997), 10-13

—, 'His Father's Business', *Believer's Voice of Victory* 26.1 (Jan. 1998), 8-11

Hilborn, D. (ed.), *'Toronto' in Perspective* (Carlisle: ACUTE/Paternoster), 2001

Hinn, B., *The Anointing* (Nashville: Thomas Nelson Publishers, 1992, 1997)

—, *The Biblical Road to Blessing* (Nashville: Thomas Nelson Publishers, 1997)

Hollenweger, W.J., *Pentecostalism: Origins and Developments Worldwide* (Peabody, Mass.: Hendrickson Publishers, 1997)

Hollinger, D., 'Enjoying God Forever: An Historical/ Sociological Profile of the Health and Wealth Gospel', *TrinJ* 9.2 NS (1988), 131-149

Hooker, M.D., *The Gospel According to Mark* (London: A & C Black, 1991)

Hughes, D. and M. Bennett, *God of the Poor: A Biblical Vision of God's Present Rule* (Carlisle: OM Publishing, 1998)

Hummel, C.E., *The Prosperity Gospel* (Downers Grove: InterVarsity Press, 1991)

Hunt, D. and T.A. McMahon, The *Seduction Of Christianity: Spiritual Discernment in the Last Days* (Eugene: Harvest House Publishers, 1993)

Hunt, S., 'Magical Moments: An Intellectualist Approach to the Neo-Pentecostal Faith Ministries', *Religion* 28 (1998), 271-280

Jackson, R., 'Prosperity theology and the faith movement', *Themelios* 15.1 (Oct. 1989), 16-24

Joyner, R., *Overcoming the Spirit of Poverty* (Charlotte: MorningStar Publications, 1996)

Justice, N., 'Bakker Apologizes for Prosperity Gospel', *Charisma* (Dec. 1992), 49

Kaiser, W.C., Jr., 'The Old Testament Promise of Material Blessings and the Contemporary Believer', *TrinJ* 9.2 (1988), 151-170

Kay, W.K., *Pentecostals in Britain* (Carlisle: Paternoster, 2000)

Kee Hwang, C., 'A Response', *EvRevTh* 20 (1996), 47-48

Kenyon, E.W., *Identification* (Lynnwood, Washington: Kenyon's Gospel Publishing Society, 1995 (original date not given))

—, *New Creation Realities* (Lynnwood, Washington: Kenyon's Gospel Publishing Society, 1996 (original date not given))

—, *What Happened from the Cross to the Throne* (Lynnwood, Washington: Kenyon's Gospel Publishing Society, 1998 (original date not given))

Kim, Sang-Bok D., 'A Bed of Roses or a Bed of Thorns', *EvRevTh* 20 (1996), 14-25

Knight, G.W., *The Pastoral Epistles: A commentary on the Greek text* (Grand Rapids: Eerdmans, Carlisle: Paternoster, 1992)

Kole, A., 'Illusion and Reality', *Now* (Jan. 1998), 12

L. Morris, *The Gospel According to John* (London: Marshall, Morgan & Scott, 1972)

Lane, W.L., *The Gospel of Mark* (Grand Rapids: Eerdmans, 1974)

Lie, G., 'E.W. Kenyon: Cult Founder or Evangelical Minister?' (unpublished English translation of master's thesis submitted to the Faculty of the Norwegian Lutheran School of Theology, October 1994, available at http://home.no.net/geilie/Kenyon_eng.htm)

—, 'E.W. Kenyon: Cult Founder or Evangelical Minister?' (*European Pentecostal Theological Association Bulletin* 16, 1996), 71-86

—, 'The Charismatic/Pentecostal Movement in Norway: The Last 30 Years' (*Cyberjournal for Pentecostal Charismatic Research*, 7, Feb. 2000) (http://www.pctii.org/cyberj/cyber7.html)

—, 'The Theology of E.W. Kenyon: Plain Heresy or Within the Boundaries of Pentecostal-Charismatic "Orthodoxy"?', (*Pneuma* 22.1, 2000), 85-114

Lincoln, A.T., *Ephesians* (Dallas: Word Books, 1990)

Longenecker, R.N., *Galatians* (Dallas: Word Books, 1990)

Ma, Wonsuk, 'Biblical Studies in the Pentecostal Tradition: Yesterday, Today, and Tomorrow', in M.W Dempster, B.D. Klaus and D. Petersen (eds.), *The Globalization of Pentecostalism* (Oxford: Regnum, 1999), 52-69

MacArthur, J., *Whose Money Is It Anyway?* (Nashville: Word Publishing, 2000)

Macchia, F.D., 'The Struggle for Global Witness', in M.W. Dempster, B.D. Klaus and D. Petersen, (eds.), *The Globalization of Pentecostalism* (Oxford: Regnum, 1999), 8-29

Marshall, I.H., *Acts* (Leicester: IVP, Grand Rapids: Eerdmans, 1980)

Martin, R.P., 2 *Corinthians* (Waco: Word Books, 1986)

—, *Carmen Christi: Philippians ii. 5-11 in Recent Interpretation and in the Setting of Early Christian Worship* (Cambridge: Cambridge University Press, 1967)

—, *James* (Waco: Word Books, 1988)

McConnell, D.R., *A Different Gospel* (Peabody: Hendrickson Publishers, 1988, 1995), published in the UK as *The Promise Of Health And Wealth* (London: Hodder and Stoughton, 1990)

McGrath, A.E., *Christian Theology: An Introduction* (Oxford: Blackwell Publishers, 1994)

McIntyre, J., *E.W. Kenyon and His Message of Faith* (Orlando: Creation House, 1997)

Meilaender, G., 'To Throw Oneself into the Wave: The Problem of Possessions', in R.J. Neuhaus (ed.), *The Preferential Option for the Poor* (Grand Rapids: Eerdmans, 1988)

Mills, P., 'Christians and Financial Security', in Schluter, M. (ed.), *Christianity in a Changing World* (London: Marshall Pickering, 2000), 191-203

Moo, D., 'Divine Healing In The Health And Wealth Gospel', *TrinJ* 9.2 (1988), 191-209

—, *The Epistle to the Romans* (Grand Rapids and Cambridge: Eerdmans, 1996)

Mounce, W.D., *Pastoral Epistles* (Nashville: Thomas Nelson Publishers, 2000)

Murray, S., *Beyond Tithing* (Carlisle: Paternoster Press, 2000)

Nash, R.H., *Poverty and Wealth: The Christian Debate over Capitalism* (Westchester, Illinois: Crossway Books, 1986)

Newlands, G., 'Christology', in A. Richardson and J. Bowden (eds.), *A New Dictionary of Christian Theology* (London: SCM Press, 1983), 100-108

Newport, T. *Your Provision and Prosperity* (Chichester: New Wine Press, 1998)

Nolland, J., *Luke* (3 vols.) (Dallas: Word Books, Publisher, 1993)

O'Brien, P.T., *Colossians, Philemon* (Waco: Word Books, Publisher, 1982)

Ojo, M.A., 'Charismatic Movements in Africa', in C. Fyfe, and A. Walls (eds.), *Christianity in Africa in the 1990s* (Edinburgh: Centre of African Studies, University of Edinburgh, 1996)

Onken, B., 'The Atonement of Christ and the "Faith" Message', CRI statement DP060, accessed online June 2002 at http://www.equip.org/free/DP060.htm

Osborn, T.L., *The Message that Works* (Tulsa: OSFO Publishers, 1997)

Osgood, H., 'Prosperity Teaching and "Contractual" Exegesis' (unpublished paper for the ACUTE working group on the Prosperity Gospel, 1998)

—, 'Prosperity Teaching and Evangelical Unity' (unpublished paper for the ACUTE working group on the Prosperity Gospel, 1998)

Price, F.K.C., *Prosperity on God's Terms* (Tulsa: Harrison House, 1990)

Riss, R.M., 'Hagin, Kenneth E.', in S.M. Burgess and G.B. McGee (eds.), *Dictionary of Pentecostal and Charismatic Movements* (Grand Rapids: Zondervan, 1988), 345

—, 'Kenyon, Essek William', in S.M. Burgess and G.B. McGee (eds.), *Dictionary of Pentecostal and Charismatic Movements* (Grand Rapids: Zondervan, 1988), 517-518

Roberts, D., 'A Different Gospel', *Today* (April 1990), 31-33

—, 'Discerning the Truth', *Today* (May 1990), 15-17

Sarles, K.L., 'A Theological Evaluation of the Prosperity Gospel', *BibSac* 143 #572 (Oct.-Dec., 1986), 329-352

Schmidt, T.E., 'Burden, Barrier, Blasphemy: Wealth In Matt 6:33, Luke 14:33, And Luke 16:15', *TrinJ* 9.2 (1988), 171-189

—, *Hostility to Wealth in the Synoptic Gospels* (Sheffield: Sheffield Academic Press, 1987)

Sider, R., *Rich Christians in an Age of Hunger* (4th Edn., London: Hodder and Stoughton, 1997)

Sizer, S., 'A Sub-Christian Movement', in Hilborn, D. (ed.), *'Toronto' in Perspective* (Carlisle: ACUTE/Paternoster, 2001), 45-63

Smail, T., A. Walker, and N. Wright, '"Revelation Knowledge" and Knowledge of Revelation: The Faith Movement and the Question of Heresy', *JPT* 5 (1994), 57-77

Stackhouse, M.L., 'Protestantism and Poverty', in R.J. Neuhaus (ed.), *The Preferential Option for the Poor* (Grand Rapids: Eerdmans, 1988)

Stott, J., *New Issues Facing Christians Today* (London: Marshall Pickering, 1984, 1990, 1999)

Strang, S., 'Benny Hinn Speaks Out', *Charisma* (Aug. 1993), 22-29

Thomas, J.C., *The Devil, Disease and Deliverance* (Sheffield: Sheffield Academic Press, 1998)

Tillin, T., 'Wells Without Water: The Errors of the Word-of-Faith Movement' (Banner Ministries, 1999), accessed online at http://www.banner.org.uk/wof/wells1.html

Tucker, R., *Strange Gospels* (London: Marshall Pickering, 1989, 1991)

Turner, N., *A Grammar of New Testament Greek* (Edinburgh: T & T Clark, 1963)

Warner, R., 'Postscript: Reflections following the EA Consultation' (unpublished paper for the ACUTE working group on the Prosperity Gospel, 1998)

Watts, J.D.W., *Isaiah 34-66* (Waco: Word Books, 1987)

Wenham, G.J., *Genesis 1-15* (Waco: Word Books, 1987)

Whitacre, R.A., *John* (Downers Grove and Leicester: InterVarsity Press, 1999)

Wilkinson, B., *The Prayer of Jabez* (Sisters, Oregon: Multnomah Publishers, 2000)

Williams, D.T., 'Prosperity Teaching and Positive Thinking', *EvRevTh* 11.3 (1987), 197-208

Wilson, D.J., 'Cho, Paul Yonggi', in S.M. Burgess and G.B. McGee (eds.), *Dictionary of Pentecostal and Charismatic Movements* (Grand Rapids: Zondervan, 1988), 161-162

Winner, L.F., 'T.D. Jakes Feels Your Pain', *Christianity Today* 44.2 (Feb. 7, 2000), 46

Young Hoon Lee, 'The Case for Prosperity Theology', *EvRevTh* 20 (1996), 26-39

Index of names and major subjects

Index of texts

New Testament